Additional Praise for Roadmap:
The Law Student's Guide to Meaningful Employment

"In these challenging markets, each student needs to synthesize his or her life experience with his or her law school experience into a biographical coherence or story about how his or her unique strengths and skills can serve others well in meaningful employment. The *Roadmap* guides each student through this process."
—Deanell Tacha, Former Pepperdine University School of Law Dean

"Faculty, staff, and alumni need to work together to help each student internalize a career-long commitment to professional development toward excellence in the competencies needed to serve others well. The *Roadmap* is a creative co-educator approach to help each student 'connect the dots' between this commitment to professional development and the student's goal of meaningful employment. The *Roadmap* is really terrific and a huge contribution to professional formation for law students."
—Mitchell Bailin, Georgetown University Law Center
Dean of Students and Associate Vice President

"I wish I had something like the *Roadmap* in law school to help me understand all the competencies needed to be successful in the practice of law and how to use the curriculum and other experiences of law school to develop the needed competencies. I think the one-on-one coaching to help each student think through his or her plan to develop toward meaningful employment to serve others well is exceptionally valuable."
—Marschall Smith, retired General Counsel, 3M Corp.,
former General Counsel of Archer, Daniels,
Midland Company (ADM) and Brunswick Corp.

"Professor Hamilton's important research and new book raise awareness of a common misperception. We often believe that smart, driven students are also automatically self-directed learners when it comes to selecting a career path and preparing to be successful professionals. While the majority is interested in examining possible career paths, most lack the tools to act on that interest. For their part, legal employers have not been transparent on the full range of competencies needed for professional success, thus creating a "secret memo" challenge for applicants and new lawyers to try to figure out on their own what is needed to achieve success. Hamilton's *Roadmap* gives students that secret memo, so to speak, and involves them in active career planning toward all the needed competencies at an early stage. Combined with support from professors, professional development administrators, and career counselors working in concert, the *Roadmap* has proved to lead to more self-directed learning for law students. This is good for students, law schools, legal employers, and the profession at large."
—Susan Manch, Founding Partner, SJL Shannon,
Legal Talent Management and Advisor on Talent
Management to the Majority of Am Law 100 Firms

"The *Roadmap* is an incredible compilation, packed full with both the pragmatic, real-world needed skills for a student to develop toward meaningful employment and the needed skills to serve all those whom we as lawyers take an oath to serve. A law student should be presented with this resource on the first day of his or her law school education, and it should be read and reread frequently not just until the end of law school but throughout a lawyer's career. Everybody comes out the winner by reading this excellent work: lawyer-to-be, the employer, the practicing lawyer, the clients we serve, and anyone who cares or needs to know more about what it means to be a competent, ethical, and professional lawyer."

—John Berry, Director of the Florida Bar Legal Division supervising lawyer regulation and professionalism, former Chair of the ABA Professionalism Committee, and past winner of the ABA's highest award, the Michael Franck Award for Professionalism

ROADMAP

The Law Student's Guide to Meaningful Employment

SECOND EDITION

NEIL W. HAMILTON

Cover design by Elmarie Jara/ABA Design.

The materials contained herein represent the opinions of the authors and/or the editors and should not be construed to be the views or opinions of the law firms or companies with whom such persons are in partnership with, associated with, or employed by, nor of the American Bar Association unless adopted pursuant to the bylaws of the Association.

Nothing contained in this book is to be considered as the rendering of legal advice for specific cases, and readers are responsible for obtaining such advice from their own legal counsel. This book is intended for educational and informational purposes only.

Printed in the United States of America.

22 21 20 19   5 4

Library of Congress Cataloging-in-Publication Data

Names: Hamilton, Neil W., author.
Title: Roadmap : the law student's guide to meaningful employment / Neil W.
   Hamilton.
Other titles: Law student's guide to meaningful employment
Description: Chicago : American Bar Association, 2017.
Identifiers: LCCN 2017052424 | ISBN 9781641050227
Subjects: LCSH: Law students--Employment--United States. | Law
   students--Vocational guidance--United States. | Law--Vocational
   guidance--United States.
Classification: LCC KF287 .H36 2017 | DDC 340.023/73--dc23 LC record available at https://
lccn.loc.gov/2017052424

Discounts are available for books ordered in bulk. Special consideration is given to state bars, CLE programs, and other bar-related organizations. Inquire at Book Publishing, ABA Publishing, American Bar Association, 321 N. Clark Street, Chicago, Illinois 60654-7598.

www.ShopABA.org

To my wife, Uve, whose love and support inspire me each day to be as kind and selfless as she is.

CONTENTS

ACKNOWLEDGMENTS

During my service as an interim dean at the University of St. Thomas School of Law in 2012, I grew increasingly aware of the new market realities that challenge students, lawyers, and law schools. While law students and lawyers still must develop to become highly competent legal technicians, they must equally develop all the other competencies that today's clients need and want. To reach the goal of meaningful employment, each law student and lawyer needs to realize that he or she is essentially the owner/entrepreneur for a service business, providing the broad range of competencies needed to serve clients well.

To support students in meeting these market challenges, I decided to spend the summers of 2013, 2014, and 2017 with a team of research assistants to create materials and teaching engagements to help each law student create and implement a plan for meaningful employment that the student could use throughout all three years of law school. This book is the result of that collaboration. I want to express deep appreciation to the teams of research assistants who worked with me. The team in the summer of 2013 included Madeleine Coulter, Katherine Jirik, Peter G. Leslie, Patrick Lucke, Carl J. L. Numrich, Sarah Schaefer, Colin Seaborg, and Bryan M. Wachter. In the summer of 2014, the team included Christopher Damian, John Fandrey, Robert Maloney, Kaylin Ness, Catherine Underwood, Bradley Yenter, and Bryan M. Wachter as team leader. In the summer of 2016, I worked with Christopher Clark on a first revision of some of the chapters in the first edition. In the summer of 2017, the team included Emily Palmer, Emilee Walters, Shana Tomenes, and Matthew Wilson, with Emily and Emilee as the team leaders. All contributed suggestions at weekly meetings. I want to give particular thanks both to the student and lawyer coauthors of many of the chapters who are listed at the beginning of each chapter and to the team leaders Carl J. L. Numrich, Bryan M. Wachter, and Katherine Jirik. I greatly appreciate also chapter authors Benjamin Carpenter and Greg Stephens, and especially Thomas E. Holloran, who has been faithfully supportive throughout the whole project. I am grateful for the support of the University of St. Thomas School of Law in this project, for Jerry Organ, Robert Vischer, Joel Nichols, and Greg Sisk, my colleague who teaches the other section of professional responsibility, for his willingness to require his section also to participate in this Roadmap initiative.

Helpful comments from many students doing the Roadmap have resulted in a much-improved version. Finally, I want to express my deepest gratitude to my wife, Uve, who helped by reading and commenting on many drafts and who was tirelessly supportive of three summers spent helping the students connect the dots to be successful in their search for meaningful employment.

ABOUT THE AUTHOR

Neil W. Hamilton is Thomas Patricia Holloran Professor of Law and Codirector of the Holloran Center for Ethical Leadership in the Professions at the University of St. Thomas School of Law (MN) since 2001. He served as Interim Dean in 2012 and Associate Dean for Academic Affairs twice at St. Thomas. He served from 1980–2001 as Trustees Professor of Regulatory Policy at William Mitchell College of Law. He has taught both the required course in Professional Responsibility and an ethics seminar for more than thirty years. He is the author of four books, more than eighty longer law journal articles, and more than one hundred shorter articles as a bimonthly columnist on professionalism and ethics for the *Minnesota Lawyer* from 1999 to 2012.

Hamilton's research focus is on the professional formation of new entrants into the ethics of the peer-review professions, including the legal profession. In 2002 the *Minnesota Lawyer* selected him as one of the recipients of its Lawyer of the Year awards, and in 2003 he received the Hennepin County (Minneapolis) Professionalism Award. In 2004, the Minnesota State Bar Association presented him its highest award, the Professional Excellence Award, given to recognize and encourage professionalism among lawyers. He received the University of St. Thomas Presidential Award for Excellence as a Teacher and Scholar in 2009. In 2012, *Minnesota Lawyer* honored him again for outstanding service to the profession and placed him in its Circle of Merit for those who have been honored more than once. Most recently, he published *Roadmap: The Law Student's Guide to Preparing and Implementing a Successful Plan for Meaningful Employment* (ABA Books 2015), which received the American Bar Association's Gambrell Award for excellence in professionalism.

FOREWORD

I have studied *Roadmap*. It is unique, prescient, and needed. I urge you to master the particulars of the document, reflect on its importance to your future, and use it to "get on the road." Follow it and start your journey toward employment now.

Until this effort, it is remarkable that so little has been studied on the values, virtues, and capacities law firms seek in hiring associates and in promoting those associates to partner. The profession owes gratitude to Neil Hamilton and his supporting team for their leadership in assembling the data that are the basis of *Roadmap*.

You are working hard to understand and master "the law." Clearly, your sight is on establishing sufficient grounding to pass the bar examination—your minimum essential. This is a major focus of your law school. But remember, the learning of the law and the practice of law are distinct and different. Your future employer will readily assume that you have a sufficient understanding of the law and will focus on your human relationship capacities. Your interviewer will scan your supporting résumé and will probe your work ethic, your common sense, your compatibility with others, and, most of all, your fit with the organization. The interviewer will endeavor to translate the experience you display in your short time together and make a judgment, up or down.

Roadmap is a guide to sharpen your awareness of the characteristics most valued in the workplace—whether it is in a law firm, a company, or a government entity. The map encourages you to use your time in law school to develop the competencies important to your future. It is in your interest to form a conscious plan as to how you can demonstrate these self-development experiences. Only then will you be prepared to enter your search for employment.

It has been sixty years since I was admitted to the Minnesota Bar. Over those years, I have been a senior partner and the hiring partner in a major law firm, a general counsel, the CEO of two publicly held corporations, a member of numerous corporate and not-for-profit boards, and a public officeholder. My training and experience as a lawyer have given me very transferable skills, as will your experience. Over the course of your career, there will be many ways for you to contribute to the common good.

Rarely have I seen one lose a job because of a lack of technical expertise. Much more often, I have seen departure because of failure to display the characteristics described in *Roadmap*. Those characteristics are necessary for one to be hired and to be retained.

Know that while *Roadmap* is designed as a straight route, there will be detours in your journey. The course of life does not proceed in a straight line, and neither will your career. Dealing positively with detours is critical to your well-being. There will be times in your professional life when you will make a mistake. We all have. My experience teaches me that one should own up when one screws up. It will be appreciated by those with whom you work (they too will make mistakes), and the experience will make you a better lawyer. It will sharpen your ability to counsel others.

So often in my life and the lives of my contemporaries, bad news has led to good news, and often in an unexpected way. Let me illustrate. When I was in law school at the University of Minnesota, I was within nine months of graduation. North Korea invaded South Korea, and the United States became engaged in the conflict. I had a reserve commission in the Navy and was called to active duty. My plan to finish school, enter the profession, and marry Patty was put on hold. After two years of sea duty, I returned with heightened leadership skills, married Patty, finished law school, and joined the Fredrikson & Byron law firm in Minneapolis. Later, I incorporated a then-small company operating out of a garage—Medtronic—and became its general counsel. Later I left the law firm and became the president of Medtronic. I served on its board of directors for forty years.

None of that would have happened if I had graduated two years earlier and then found employment. My life experience, I'm convinced, would have been different but every bit as fulfilling. The experience of disappointment followed by exhilarating success is not unique to me. It will happen to you too—bad news will often turn into good news. Don't lose courage when the detour hits you. Rather, follow Willie Nelson's admonition to "get on the road again . . . insisting that the world keep turning your way."[1]

Sincerely,

Thomas E. Holloran

Thomas E. Holloran

---

[1] WILLIE NELSON, *On the Road Again*, on HONEYSUCKLE ROSE (Columbia Records 1980).

SECTION I

BUYING INTO THE ROADMAP

A. Introduction[1]

What do you say when a potential employer says to you, "Tell me about a project that you have managed and what you learned from that experience; tell me specifically about how you handled a difficult team member in implementing the project?"[2] If you are like most law students, the slightest mention of "project management" or "difficult team member" makes you cringe, evoking painful memories of free-riding classmates. Once your discomfort passes, you either struggle to come up with a meaningful answer or fail to think of an experience demonstrating your project management and teamwork competencies. Would it surprise you to know that was supposed to be an easy question? What happens when you get a tricky question, such as, "What value do you bring beyond just technical legal skills to help our clients be successful?"[3]

The Roadmap process transforms this type of challenging question into an opportunity to differentiate yourself from other students. You will not need to wait for a specific question about the value you bring beyond technical legal skills to help legal employers and clients. Instead, you will understand what skills legal employers and clients need and will be able to explain how your strongest skills can help them succeed. You will be prepared with your best stories to demonstrate persuasive evidence of your strongest skills.

---

[1] Authored by Neil W. Hamilton and Carl J. L. Numrich.

[2] E-mail from Thomas E. Holloran, Senior Distinguished Fellow, The Holloran Center for Ethical Leadership in the Professions, former General Counsel and President, Medtronic Corp., to author (Dec. 17, 2014, 14:45 CST) (on file with author).

[3] E-mail from Dennis Monroe, Founder of Monroe, Moxness, Berg PA and former CEO of Parasole Restaurants, to author (Dec. 17, 2014, 11:58 CST) (on file with author).

Every law student desires meaningful employment to serve others well upon graduation from law school. The challenging legal job market does not necessarily mean legal employers are not hiring; in fact, the proportion of gross domestic product (GDP) for legal services is holding steady, but legal employers (and clients) are emphasizing additional experience and skills to add value for the clients.

In this new legal economy, law students will secure meaningful employment by differentiating themselves from other law students. The problem is "virtually all [law students] lack the skills to differentiate themselves."[4] Therefore to become employable and to develop professionally, most law students need help determining how they can develop and present a unique package of capabilities and skills that appeal to legal employers and clients.

The most effective way for you as a law student to gain meaningful, long-term, JD-required or JD-preferred employment is to: (1) understand your own strengths and motivating interests; (2) understand the competencies desired by clients and legal employers; (3) discern how your strengths and motivating interests best meet the competencies that clients and employers want; (4) design your time in law school (and early years in practice) with the goal of developing those competencies; and (5) effectively communicate and demonstrate evidence of those competencies to potential employers.

To better enable law students to do this, some law schools are becoming more deliberate about helping each student develop and implement a plan for meaningful employment to serve others well. With the help of a comprehensive, curriculum-based employment-planning program, you can be more prepared, more persuasive, and more competitive when entering the legal employment market.

Although there are a number of available resources, including your law school's career services office, you can successfully attain meaningful employment by committing yourself to the Roadmap steps, approaching them with purpose and total honesty, completing the self-assessments, and actively seeking feedback from others throughout the process. The following sections explain why *you* should buy into the Roadmap process.

During your three years in law school and throughout your entire career, the Roadmap process can empower you to take charge in telling the story of how you add value beyond just technical legal skills to help employers and clients.

B. How to Use the Roadmap

The Roadmap will take you through the following steps to develop the skill you will need to obtain meaningful employment so that you can serve others well:

---

[4] William D. Henderson, *Blueprint for Change*, 40 Pepp. L. Rev. 461, 494 (2013), *available at* http://ssrn.com/abstract=2202823.

Assessment of Yourself

1. What are your strengths?
2. What are the characteristics of past work/service experience where you have found the most meaning and positive energy? Is there a particular group of people you have served from whom you have drawn the most positive energy in helping? What specific strengths and competencies were you using in this work or service?
3. To what degree have you taken ownership over your own continuous proactive professional development? Have you made the step from a student's passive mindset where you do what professors ask to proactive ownership to develop the competencies legal employers want?
4. Looking at the competencies that clients and legal employers want, how do you self-assess what your strongest competencies are? How do others who know your past work/service assess your strongest competencies?
5. How do your strengths from question 1, your motivating interests from question 2, and your strongest competencies from question 4 match up with the competencies that legal employers and clients want?

Assessment of Your Most Promising Options for Employment

6. Can you create a tentative list of the most promising options for employment where you see the best match among your strengths, the characteristics of past work that have given you the most positive energy, and the competencies that legal employers want?
7. What is your value proposition to demonstrate to those employers that you can add value beyond the standard technical legal skills to help the employers' clients and the employers themselves to be more successful?
8. Step back and think creatively about the changing legal market and possible entrepreneurial responses to those changes. Could you demonstrate a particular strength that you have (or even a specific innovative idea) to help potential employers and clients be more successful in this changing legal market?

Your Professional Development Plan

9. How do you plan to use your remaining time in law school to gain good experiences that will assist you in attaining your most promising options for meaningful employment so that you can confirm, eliminate, or add to the list of your most promising employment options? What metrics will you create to assess whether you are implementing your plan?
10. How do you plan to use your remaining time in law school, including the curriculum and all the other out-of-the-classroom experiences, most effectively to develop competencies supporting your value proposition?

11. What evidence are you collecting to demonstrate to potential employers your growth to the next stage of development at your strongest competencies? What evidence do you want to develop going forward?

12. How do you plan to develop long-term relationships based on trust with other lawyers, particularly senior lawyers and judges, who can give feedback on your employment plan and help you with experiences to implement it? Are you assessing your progress in implementing this plan?

13. What is the biggest fear or roadblock holding you back from any of the previous steps?

Persuasive Communication

14. How will you most effectively communicate your value to potential employers on your list of most promising employment options?

Your work experience is an important factor to consider in the Roadmap process. There are three main categories that you may fall into: (1) students with modest work experience who do not yet have postgraduation employment, (2) students with substantial work experience who do not yet have postgraduation employment, and (3) students who already have postgraduation employment.

1. Students with Modest Work Experience Who Do Not Yet Have Postgraduation Employment

Many "traditional" law school students attend law school immediately after completing college and thereby have modest employment experience. Similarly, other students who have an extended period of time out of the workforce from common life occurrences, such as raising children or taking care of family members, may also identify most with this category. You will want to use the time you have left in law school most effectively to develop your skills toward meaningful employment to serve others well, but you do not have enough experience to know what type of employment will best fit your strengths and interests. The key is to start now. Use the Roadmap to make your best judgment regarding your motivating interests, your strongest competencies, and the types of legal employment that might be the best "fit" for you and offer the most promising employment options. From there you should seek experiences that will help you develop your strongest competencies and confirm, eliminate, or add employment options. Veteran lawyers can most effectively help you if your message is, "I have a plan for employment with these top-priority strengths and options that I am exploring, and I am looking for experience to build these strengths and explore these options. If you are willing, I would love your input on my plan." Notice that you are focusing your message on wanting experience with certain transferable skills and competencies as discussed in parts C and D of this section rather than just on wanting experience in identified practice areas like litigation. With this strategy, you are also sending the message to senior lawyers that you are at a later stage of development of the key competencies employers want, including initiative, drive, and commitment to professional development.

2. Students with Substantial Work Experience Who Do Not Yet Have Postgraduation Employment

While you may initially be resistant to a project that seems less applicable to your situation because you have done some earlier self-assessment, you should note that the Roadmap benefits you by (1) sharpening your focus in your employment search, (2) demonstrating professional career planning and giving you concrete evidence of later-stage development of the competencies of initiative and commitment to professional development, (3) helping you craft a clear value proposition and an "elevator speech," (4) packaging your experience for a specific legal market, and (5) getting input from veteran lawyers.

1. *Sharpening your focus*: You probably came to law school with a well-thought calculus of the job you want upon graduation. Even if you know what area of law you want to practice, the Roadmap helps to focus your research on that area and identify specific competencies useful to legal employers in your field. This research—and your creation of a powerful narrative around your strengths and experiences that add value to your targeted employer—is vital for effective messaging.

2. *Demonstrating professional career planning*: You know you have competencies and skills that have value in the marketplace. You also recognize that because you are more experienced than many other students, you may not have the extra ten years to learn from mistakes after graduation. You want to leverage your experience with your new legal education to land the most meaningful employment. You need to identify the competencies that you already possess, develop those competencies and bolster them with legal experiences, create concrete evidence of the later-stage development of your competencies, and identify specific steps that you can take right now to achieve your career goals.

3. *Helping you craft a value proposition and an elevator speech*: While less experienced students may be working to build more career experience to develop a sixty-second elevator speech, students with substantial work experience must learn to skillfully condense past experiences, future career goals, and competencies while crafting their elevator speech. You must also answer the "elephant in the room" question: why law school/a legal career now? Why didn't you stay in your previous career?

4. *Packaging your experience for the legal market*: You may know generally about your skills, experiences, and accomplishments, but the Roadmap

can help you to better articulate that information in language that will resonate most with legal employers.

5. *Getting input from veteran lawyers*: While you may have experience, it is important to understand what the veteran members of the legal profession are looking for and how they react to your experience, your goals, and your plan for employment.

3. Students Who Already Have Postgraduation Employment

The Roadmap is not simply about finding employment; it is a career-advancement tool to further develop the specific competencies that your employer, mentors, and coaches want you to develop. Seek feedback on your Roadmap from your employer.

You should use the Roadmap to demonstrate to your employer your initiative and commitment to professional development toward excellence. You should take the opportunity to give your Roadmap to mentors and coaches at your future employment, ask for feedback from them, and then discuss the feedback with them. In section II.D, you will find instructions to access a Roadmap template specifically tailored for students who already have postgraduation employment.

C. Foundational Realities for Every Law Student to Understand

1. Changing Markets for Legal Services

Do you believe that you are entering a changing market for legal services? Your answer to this question, as explained further in this section, must be an unequivocal "Yes." This foundational reality can contribute to anxiety and loss of confidence if you focus on, "How in the world will I learn both the basic knowledge and skills needed to pass the bar and satisfy employers and also acquire the knowledge and skills required in changing markets?"

To respond to the challenge of changing markets for legal services, a better and more productive question for a law student is, "How do I signal to potential employers and clients that I am trying to transform market changes into opportunities by committing myself to continuous professional development over a career?" Researchers, policy makers, and managers overwhelmingly agree about the need for each worker in a rapidly changing market to take ownership over continuous development of new knowledge and skills that meet employers' (and clients') needs.

A law student should signal that he or she is embracing change through proactive ownership of professional development that meets both employers' and clients' needs in changing markets. Creating, implementing, and continuously revisiting and revising your Roadmap plan as you gain experience will send a signal of ownership over your continuous professional development.

With respect to changing markets for legal services specifically, you can communicate during your time in law school to potential employers that you understand the basic contours of these changing markets and how best to meet employer needs in these markets. Influential futurist Richard Susskind emphasizes three main drivers of change for the legal services market in *Tomorrow's Lawyers: An Introduction to Your Future*: (1) the principal driver is the "more for less" challenge in which clients, especially organizational clients with in-house lawyers, want legal services delivered at lower cost; (2) the increasing capabilities of information technology that computerize and streamline current processes in the legal services market will transform the way lawyers and courts operate; and (3) the liberalization of licensing to permit nonlawyers to participate more fully in providing legal services to clients.[5] Susskind predicts that "[t]hese market changes open up the possibility of important new forms of legal service, of exciting new jobs for those students who are sufficiently flexible, open-minded, and entrepreneurial to adapt to changing market conditions."[6] Furthermore, "[l]awyers in training should be proactive . . . always on the lookout for experiences that prepare them for tomorrow."[7]

Indiana University Maurer School of Law professor William D. Henderson and second a influential futurist, Jordan Furlong, also emphasize client demands for better, faster, and cheaper legal services are causing a structural change in the legal services market. To thrive in the years ahead, lawyers will need to become more entrepreneurial, more efficient, and less expensive through collaboration and technology. They also stresses the need for both project management skills and collaboration skills in teams of lawyers, nonlawyers, and clients as a major contributor to greater efficiency and lower costs.[8]

Harvard University's Clayton Christensen Institute for Disruptive Innovation similarly emphasizes that "advances in technology alongside business model innovations are altering the traditional legal services values network" that includes all entities involved in the provision of legal services, from law firms to in-house corporate, government law departments to social justice lawyers.[9] These technology and business model innovations are bringing about three

---

[5] RICHARD SUSSKIND, TOMORROW'S LAWYERS: AN INTRODUCTION TO YOUR FUTURE 4–14 (Oxford Univ. Press 2013); Jordan Furlong, LAW IS A BUYER'S MARKET: BUILDING A CLIENT-FIRST LAW FIRM 29, 73–81, 145–52 (2017).

[6] *Id.* at 109.

[7] *Id.* at 29.

[8] William D. Henderson, *Efficiency Engines: How Managed Services Are Building Systems for Corporate Legal Work,* ABA JOURNAL, June 1, 2017, at 38–45.

[9] Michele R. Pistone & Michael B. Horn, *Disrupting Law School: How Disruptive Innovation Will Revolutionize the Legal World,* CLAYTON CHRISTENSEN INST. FOR DISRUPTIVE INNOVATION 5 (2016), *available at* http://www.christenseninstitute.org/publications/disrupting-law-school/.

significant changes in the market for legal services similar to those that Susskind emphasized:

1. Bringing more standardized, systematized, and, in some cases, commoditized offerings to the market;[10]
2. Allowing lawyers with traditional offices to boost productivity and reduce costs; and
3. Creating new nonlawyer service providers aided by software that can provide similar services to lawyers.

Columbia University's Center for Public Research and Leadership sees professional service markets, in general, responding to "situations . . . in which clients themselves have considerable access to information, expertise, and techniques that once were the sole domain of the professional . . . [In these situations], the professional's value lies not in defining the problem and crafting a solution separate from and for the clients.[11] Instead the professional's value lies in helping the clients discover what they already know, clarifying what they need, and in the process co-producing a solution with them . . . Rather than knowing what others want, the modern professional is defined by her ability to: (1) continuously learn more herself; (2) co-produce knowledge with colleagues and clients; and in the process (3) empower colleagues and clients to learn rapidly on their own."[12] In this changing market, the skills of continuous learning and professional growth over a career will be critically important.[13]

The concept of coproduction is a powerful response to changing markets for legal services. Dr. Maren Batalden and others explain that, at the most basic level, good service coproduction requires effective communication, deeper trust and understanding of one another's expertise and values, more cultivation of shared goals, and more mutuality in responsibility and accountability for performance.[14]

To summarize, you can signal to potential employers that you understand the basic contours of four related changes in legal services markets:

1. The "more for less" challenge of becoming more efficient and less expensive in serving client needs;
2. The importance of technology and machine intelligence in increasing efficiency and reducing costs;

---

[10] "Standardized" would include services such as form documents; "systemized" would encompass document assembly systems; "packaged" would include services like turnkey regulatory compliance programs; and "commoditized" would be any information technology–based legal product that is undifferentiated in a market with many competitors.

[11] Kimberly Austin et al., RE-ENVISIONING PROFESSIONAL EDUCATION (2017).

[12] *Id.* at 3.

[13] *Id* at 1, 3.

[14] Maren Batalden et al., *Coproduction of Healthcare Service*, 25 BMJ QUAL. S.F. 509, 511 (2016).

3. The importance of project management and collaboration in teams with clients and nonlawyer, lower-cost providers to increase efficiency and reduce costs; and

4. The usefulness of coproduction of legal services with the client to better understand and define client needs and meet them at lower cost.

What specific steps should you consider including in your Roadmap professional development plan (and in communicating it to employers)?

1. If your law school offers a course on market changes affecting legal services, especially the interface of machine intelligence and human intelligence, take it. Strongly consider attending continuing legal education (CLE) courses on this topic. This effort becomes part of your story.

2. Read "Project Management Skills: How Law Students Can Learn and Implement the Skills Employers Value" and "The Basics of Teamwork" in section III. In your Roadmap professional development plan, seek experiences that help you to grow toward later stages of these key competencies. Seek experiences where senior lawyers evaluate these competencies and you receive feedback.

3. Be intentional in your interactions (see "Building Relationships Based on Trust through Networking" in section III) with experienced lawyers to inquire about how the business model of the employer works. How does the employer (whether private firm, government, nonprofit, etc.) cover the costs of delivering the legal services? What are the challenges they face? What solutions are they adopting?

4. Remember that your creation, implementation, and regular reconsideration and revision of your Roadmap professional development plan demonstrates your ongoing commitment to professional development toward the competencies that employers and clients say are needed in changing legal services markets.

2. Entrepreneurial Mindset

A major theme in changing markets for legal services is the need for lawyers to think more like an entrepreneur. To reach your goal of meaningful postgraduation employment, you need to realize that you are essentially the owner or entrepreneur of a service business providing competencies that legal employers and clients need.

The following discussion of the entrepreneurial process includes an additional lens through which to view the Roadmap process specifically and the legal services market generally. Take the time to study the small-business plan outline presented here and consider how it relates to your task of finding meaningful employment. Having an entrepreneurial-like Roadmap plan sends a unique and powerful message to potential employers. It is evidence of ongoing initiative and commitment to professional development to meet employer and client needs.

a. Introduction

What does it mean to be an entrepreneur? One definition of the word characterizes an *entrepreneur* as "one who organizes, manages, and assumes the risks of a business or enterprise."[15] A person who sells his or her professional services to help others is essentially an entrepreneur of a service business. As a law student, you are preparing for a career in which you sell professional services. You are, in essence, starting a service business.

When deciding to go to law school, you probably researched different law schools, different areas of the law, and maybe even explored various law firms or departments. After some reflection about the benefits, costs, and risks, you decided to attend law school. You decided to organize, manage, and assume the risks of entering a service business over a career. When you decided to come to law school, you acted on a belief that your small service business could fill a need in the market. You took a substantial financial risk in the hope of one day making a living and making a difference—you were enterprising. Enrolling in law school was entrepreneurial.

b. Embracing an Entrepreneurial Mindset

You might be asking "So what?" When you ask a potential employer for employment, you are asking for more than a job; you are asking the employer to invest in you. While your ultimate goal as a law student is to develop a "small business" providing services for which others will pay over the course of an entire career, for a first job, you simply need to secure an employer's investment. This investment requires the employer to allocate significant resources to your training and development as an aspiring attorney. For the potential employer to invest in you, the employer must believe that its investment will yield a positive return. This is true of all employers, not just law firms. In many ways, seeking employment from a potential employer parallels an entrepreneur's pitch of a start-up business to investors.

To prove that a business venture is viable, the entrepreneur must develop a plan for the creation, growth, differentiation, direction, and management of that business. Without a well-thought-out plan, it is unlikely that potential investors will believe their investment will yield a positive return. Similarly, legal employers seek individuals in whom they can make a viable investment—they seek individuals who will add value and help them to be successful with their vision.

The most successful entrepreneurs are those who recognize some need in the market and seek to fill that need. It is the desire to actively fulfill others' needs, rather than stand by and wait for others to take the initiative, that defines entrepreneurship. The law students with the most success in searching for legal employment are those who understand the needs of potential employers and clients and how the student can meet those needs. "Help Wanted: Legal Employers Seek New Lawyers

---

[15] *Entrepreneur*, MERRIAM-WEBSTER, *available at* http://www.merriam-webster.com/dictionary/entrepreneur (last visited July 10, 2017).

with Professional Competencies" of page 17 analyzes competencies that different legal employers are seeking and expecting. Employers in the new legal economy are looking for graduates who understand how to add value beyond just technical skills in helping a client. There is an unmet need in the legal employment market: legal employers are hungry for law students who are more than legal technicians. But most law students are unable to communicate to potential employers anything more than their comprehension of the law and aptitude at legal analysis, research, and basic written and oral communication skills. These students are unable to differentiate themselves from all other law students. So how are you going to meet employers' and clients' needs and help them to be successful?

c. The Entrepreneurial Process

In order to differentiate yourself, you must develop tangible skills like "[i]nitiat[ing] and maintain[ing] strong work and team relationships."[16] Unfortunately, legal education often fails to provide law students the opportunity to develop these tangible professional competencies. By purposefully planning your time in law school with the goal of gaining demonstrable experience in these other professional competencies, you are more likely to be able to persuasively communicate how you might add value to an employer's operation. You are becoming an entrepreneur who organizes and manages the development of your professional services business.

i. The First Step: Create a Unique Service

The first thing a successful entrepreneur does is "create a product or service that makes the world a better place."[17] In your case, the world that you need to better is that of legal employers and clients, and the service is you. The most prominent problem in the employment prospects of law students is that "virtually all [law students] lack the skills to differentiate themselves."[18] They provide the same service—the basic technical legal skills of a first-year lawyer. In order to differentiate yourself from the masses, it is essential to consider how you can package the strongest skills you have into a unique product for potential employers. You need a persuasive story to convince employers that you will make them more successful and make their lives easier.

ii. The Second Step: Define Your Mission

In recent years, the business world has been plagued by deceit, fraud, and corruption. To guard against contagious corruption, entrepreneurs should

---

[16] *See* Neil W. Hamilton, Most Common Values, Virtues, Capacities and Skills from Analysis of the Associate Evaluation Forms of the 14 Largest Minnesota Law Firms (Apr. 15, 2013) (unpublished manuscript) (on file with author).

[17] Guy Kawasaki, The Art of the Start: The Time-Tested, Battle-Hardened Guide for Anyone Starting Anything 3–4 (2004).

[18] Henderson, *Blueprint, supra* note 4, at 494.

consider their role in the market, the values expected of players in that market, and their personal value system. Entrepreneurs must then define a mission or "mantra" of excellence and care for the stakeholders on which to base all aspects of their businesses in order to ensure the integrity of all of the competing value systems.[19] This will create trustworthiness in the services, which is one of the most important competencies legal employers want and is explored in "Trustworthiness: Building Lasting Professional Relationships" in section III.

iii. The Third Step: Seek Experiences to Differentiate Yourself

Every business starts with an idea, but an idea alone does not constitute a business. In order to move from an idea to a business, the first step is to "[s]tart creating and delivering your product or service."[20] Right now you think you want to be a lawyer and have taken the necessary steps to get the ball rolling. You will study the competencies presented in section III of this book and will have a pretty good sense of what employers want from you. In the first entrepreneurial step, you thought about what your unique service is. Now it is time to begin gathering experiences that will help you develop the services to differentiate yourself from your peers. The best way to do this is to make a list of your strongest skills and a list of the competencies desired by the employers you hope to work for someday. Where do they match up best? Then develop a corresponding list of experiences you have had and that you might complete in order to properly demonstrate your development of those several strongest competencies. For example, if teamwork is one of your strongest competencies, look for employers who want teamwork skills. What are your experiences prior to law school that involve teamwork? What did you learn about teamwork from those experiences? How can you build on those experiences in law school to learn more about teamwork and move toward a later developmental stage? Can you provide evidence demonstrating a later stage of teamwork skills?

iv. The Fourth Step: Develop a Written Plan

For the entrepreneur, the fourth step is to create a sustainable business model and plan that tells the entrepreneur's story.[21] Much like an entrepreneur needing to create a plan to prove to investors that a venture is viable, you should create a written plan to prove your viability to employers. Ultimately, you need to create and communicate a comprehensive story of who you are and what you can do for an employer. Developing professional competency is the first step, but competency is useless if you are unable to effectively communicate it in your search for employment. You must tell your "story." Essentially, you are using

---

[19] John M. Darley, *The Cognitive and Social Psychology of Contagious Organizational Corruption*, 70 Brook. L. Rev. 1177 (2004).

[20] Kawasaki, *supra* note 17, at 3–4.

[21] *Id.*

your developing skills of persuasion for yourself. This is the Roadmap plan you will create in section II that tells your story of value to employers of interest to you. As you gain experience, test your top employment options and develop your strongest competencies; keep an entrepreneurial mindset as you revisit and revise your Roadmap plan to better meet employer and client needs.

3. Uncertainty about Career Direction, the Reality of Substantial Early Career Mobility, and the Importance of Transferable Skills

You are an entrepreneur seeking meaningful postgraduation employment in changing markets. You may have substantial uncertainty about: (1) the type of people/organizations you want to serve; (2) the type of legal or other work that you want to do and are best able to do for these people/organizations (where do your strengths best fit their needs?); and (3) the type of employers with whom you want a job. In addition, you are generally aware that over a career, markets and employers may change, and you may experience some job mobility.

This is where the Roadmap professional development planning process is critical. It is a tool to help you use your time in both law school and the early years of your career to effectively gain experience that will bring you increasing confidence in your answers to the topics above, especially where you have uncertainty. The key first step is to realize that at various points in law school—based on your best judgment at that time—you need to have a list of the most promising employment options you want to explore and your best strengths or skills for those employers. You then should seek experiences to help confirm, eliminate, or add an option and to develop your strongest skills. This step is not meant to limit your options but instead to teach you to focus on being strategic and efficient in exploring promising employment options at any given time in law school. For example, veteran lawyers can be helpful in answering your three questions if you give them the employment options you are most interested in exploring. But if you say, "I don't know what I want to do with my degree" or "I really don't know anything that distinguishes me," a veteran lawyer will struggle to help you. You need to move from option maximization and toward option prioritization. Then seek experiences to test your employment options and to develop your strengths to a later stage of competence.

Reaching option prioritization and testing your top employment options can be accomplished through an iterative loop of gaining experience at your most promising options and then through further reflection and discernment based on those experiences. "Iterative" means that you keep repeating the following steps to sort through and test your most promising employment options and your strengths to help a legal employer. These are the Roadmap steps in section II:

1. Identify your strengths.
2. Identify work/service characteristics that give you meaning and positive energy.

3. Assess your degree of ownership of your own professional development and your degree of responsibility to others.
4. Identify your strongest competencies and skills.
5. Discern how your strengths and strongest competencies match up with the competencies legal employers and clients want.
6. Tentatively list the most promising options for employment that best match your strengths and motivating interests.
7. Discern the most important strengths/competencies you possess that these employers need.
8. Create and implement a plan both to use the remaining years of law school most effectively to develop the competencies these employers need and to gain experience with this type of employment to test whether this is a good option for you.
9. Actually gain experiences in your most promising employment options and revisit steps 1–8.

It is invaluable to seek input from others when discerning your career path. However, it is equally important to ensure the people from whom you are seeking feedback have your best interest in mind and will give you honest, constructive feedback. To engage in discernment with others, first turn to a constellation of trusted advisors and mentors to get input on your Roadmap. This can include professors, mentors in or out of the profession, parents, siblings, partners, spouses, coaches, close friends, and colleagues.

In addition, you should move beyond the constellation of trusted advisors and mentors to seek input from others. You can accomplish this in a number of ways. First, read "Building Relationships Based on Trust through Networking" in section III. Focus particularly on the explanation of informational interviews. Second, contact your school's career development office to seek regular opportunities for consultation that could broaden your horizons and help you understand different career options more fully. Third, to test whether particular employment options are a good fit, seek experiences through all the curricular and extracurricular activities of law school, including internships, externships, simulation courses, clinics, and paid and unpaid clerkships.

a. Selecting Several Options

At the end of the Roadmap template in section II, you should have a workable understanding of your preferences, strengths and talents, the value you bring to an employer, and what different careers actually entail. Armed with this self-knowledge and field research, you can move to later parts of the template: selecting several of these career options to pursue using the Roadmap.

During your 2L and 3L years, by using the Roadmap strategy, you will experience an extensive process of discernment for your career path. You will weigh options, receive substantial and trusted input, do extensive field research, seek actual experience to test those options, and take time for deep self-reflection. The last step is pulling the trigger and choosing a career option. Moving from option-maximization mode toward option-selection mode is important, especially in the context of law school—a brief, three-year stint that you want to end in meaningful employment.

Option selection can be scary. You might feel like you don't know enough about what you are doing. Section III's "Building Confidence through Creative Problem Solving When 'I Don't Know What I Am Doing.'" Lawyers must learn how to make best-judgment calls under conditions of substantial uncertainty. You are doing that here for yourself. Then test your best judgment with experience. You also might feel like you are closing too many doors by focusing on only a few career choices. But, in reality, remaining in a constant holding pattern of option maximization is not getting you anywhere. Refusing to choose any career path or refusing to develop a plan around that potential path has the same effect as not having any options at all. None of the opportunities you have identified will be of any use without action.

Making a decision can be frightening, but forge ahead knowing that you have weighed the options with care and you have a network of mentors, advisors, family, and friends for support. While it may be true that there is anxiety amid the confusion of choosing between different routes, it is never good to say you are without a plan. No matter how you choose to navigate through your time in law school, you must have evidence of initiative and commitment to professional development.[22] This requires an understanding that the job market is evolving.[23] Therefore, you must respond by testing your options and by being mindful in seeking experiences or course work that will highlight competencies and transferable skills. You should be strategic in forming relationships with mentors and coaches. By doing so, you display evidence of initiative and commitment to professional development regardless of your employment focus.

b. Focusing on Transferable Skills

Transferable skills or competencies can be described in a variety of ways: "a portable skillset";[24] "functional skills—the common thread among all jobs and careers . . . [that] are an important building block for all of your occupational endeavors";[25] or the "bridge to your career mobility."[26]

---

[22] See "Initiative, Drive, Work Ethic, and Commitment to Professional Development" in section III.

[23] See "Changing Markets for Legal Services" found earlier in this section.

[24] *Transferable Skills*, U.S. Cal. Student Aff. (last visited July 10, 2017), http://careers.usc.edu/students/find-a-job/tips/transferable-skills/.

[25] Maribeth Gunner Pulliam, *Your Transferable Skills: What Are They? And What Can You Do with Them?*, *in* Career Corner, Series No. 4, 1 (Excelsior Coll. 2001).

[26] *Id.*

It is vital to focus on transferable skills in changing legal services markets. The research presented here points students in this direction and for good reasons. Not only do students need to differentiate themselves by presenting more than technical skill to employers, but job mobility is equally important once in the marketplace.

After the JD II,[27] a longitudinal study of law school graduates admitted to the bar in 2000, revealed that "attorneys change jobs more often today than they did in years past."[28] An entire section of the study is dedicated to the mobility of the recent law school graduates, and they found "[b]etween 2003 and 2007, [*After the JD II*] lawyers had held an average of two different jobs. Sixty-two percent (62 %) of attorneys had changed jobs at least once between 2003 and 2007."[29] Not only had many job changes already occurred in the surveyed population, but "[a]bout one third of surveyed attorneys were intending to change jobs."[30]

The data from the third phase of research, *After the JD III*, indicates continuing mobility, with 20 percent of respondents working in the business sector in 2012, compared with only 8.4 percent in 2003 (and 3.5 percent in 2012 working in "other settings" compared with 0.3 percent in 2003).[31] At the same time, the percentage of respondents in private law firm practice moved from 68.5 percent in 2003 to 48.5 percent in 2012.[32]

These data indicate the frequency of job changes that many new lawyers experience. Given this reality, law students should think strategically about their years in law school and their early years of practice as a time to develop transferable skills or competencies—the functional skills that are essential building blocks for all jobs and careers, even those jobs that do not involve practicing law. Many of the competencies in table 6 on hiring models in "Help Wanted: Legal Employers Seek New Lawyers with Professional Competencies" are transferable skills.

Furthermore, many students may want to pursue other employment paths outside of the law firm environment. All of the research presents a clear picture for law students: transferable skills are essential for future employment and for job mobility. By focusing on transferable skills during law school, students will be better situated in the marketplace created by the emerging new legal economy regardless of where they seek and find employment.

No matter which career avenue you decide to pursue, focus on academic courses that highlight transferable skills and competencies. There remains

---

[27] Surveys were done of 4,160 sample members after seven years of practice.

[28] Robert L. Nelson, Ronit Dinovitzer & Gabriele Plickert, *After the JD II: Second Results from a National Study of Legal Careers,* Am. Bar Found. & NALP Found. for Law Career Research & Educ 54 (2009).

[29] *Id.*

[30] *Id.* at 57.

[31] Ronit Dinovitzer, *In After the JD III: Third Results from a National Study of Legal Careers,* Am. Bar Found. & NALP Found. for Law Career Research & Educ., Practice Settings (2012), at p. 29.

[32] *Id.*

a misconception that concentration in an area of substantive law is the recommended route to success in the job market. Transferable skills and competencies are critical in this evolving marketplace. A substantive law concentration is useful as much for the message that you have initiative and commitment to professional development as for the message of doctrinal knowledge. Regardless of the substantive focus of your education, choosing a road that highlights competencies and transferable skills remains the most important way to differentiate yourself to potential employers.

Both quantitative and qualitative research support these conclusions. In the last few years, a variety of studies have revealed that it is not substantive knowledge or specific academic concentrations that legal employers perceive as most important. The competencies legal employers are looking for when making a hiring decision are discussed in "Help Wanted: Legal Employers Seek New Lawyers with Professional Competencies."

No matter where your career path takes you—even if it is away from the career options you selected initially in the Roadmap iterative process of discernment—the experiences you gain in pursuing these career options will never be wasted. Instead, you will carry forward the competencies you gain from those experiences. Eliminating a possible career option does not erase all of the benefits of pursuing it in the first place and actually gives you valuable experience and competencies for moving forward.

4. Importance of a Plan Showing Ownership over Your Own Professional Development

By now, it should be absolutely clear that you must stop being a passive student by "doing what the faculty tells you to do" and instead take ownership over your continuous development of the competencies required to meet employers' and clients' needs. The Roadmap plan you create, implement, revisit, and revise as you gain experience will demonstrate this ownership to legal employers and clients. Part D, which follows, outlines the competencies that legal employers want. Section II then takes you through the Roadmap process.

D. Help Wanted: Legal Employers Seek New Lawyers with Professional Competencies[33]

When a new lawyer joins an employer (or when a law student on day one of law school joins the legal profession), he or she asks, "What are all the competencies and skills I need to be successful in this work?" Historically, law schools send a message that success is only about grades and ranking; they do not clearly

---

[33] This section borrows substantially from Neil W. Hamilton, *Law-Firm Competency Models and Student Professional Success: Building on a Foundation of Professional Formation/Professionalism*, 11 U. St. Thomas L.J. 6–38 (2013), *available at* http://ssrn.com/abstract=2271410.

explain all of the competencies that legal employers and clients want and will assess. Legal employers also often do not explain to the new lawyer all the competencies needed for success. They leave it to the new lawyer to figure out the "secret memo" for success and then only promote the ones who do. We call this the "secret memo challenge" for the new lawyer. The competency model data presented in "Competencies a New Law Graduate Needs to Practice Law" and the assessment and hiring model data in "Assessment Competency Models" and "Competency Models for Hiring Decisions" will help you with the "secret memo challenge."

To help you figure out the "secret memo challenge" and discern how your strengths and motivating interests match up with legal employer and client needs, part D.1 answers the question, "What do we know empirically about the competencies that a new law graduate needs to practice law?" Parts D.2 and D.3 then look at empirical studies about the competencies legal employers are assessing and considering in the hiring decision. These models will help you understand the entire range of competencies needed and help you see where your strengths fit into that range so that you can differentiate yourself from others.

Finally, to see other recent empirical studies exploring the competencies that new lawyers need in their first years of practice, turn to appendix A at the end of the book.

1. Competencies a New Law Graduate Needs to Practice Law

Educating Tomorrow's Lawyers (ETL) published a substantial empirical study in 2016 where ETL asked lawyers to identify the competencies, skills, characteristics, and qualities that new lawyers need to be ready for practice. ETL worked with focus groups in various practice areas to identify a list of 147 possible significant items to include in the survey and distributed the survey through bar organizations in 37 states to over 780,000 lawyers, ultimately receiving 24,137 survey responses.

For each item, the survey asked respondents to identify whether the item was: (1) necessary in the short term; (2) must be acquired over time; (3) advantageous but not necessary; and (4) not relevant. The items rated "necessary in the short term" would be the group that respondents believed the new law school graduate needs immediately upon beginning practice.

The data in table 1 indicate the percentage of the 24,137 responses from across all practice areas and geographies that answered an item was "necessary in the short term." To make the data more understandable in relation to an ethical professional identity, the various "necessary in the short term" competencies are grouped into umbrella categories of Trustworthiness; Relationship Skills, Including Respect for Others and Responsiveness; Strong Work Ethic/Diligence; and Common Sense/Good Judgment. The number to the left of the competency indicates the relative ranking of that competency as "necessary in the short term" out of the 147 possible competencies. The number to the right of each competency is the percentage of respondents who indicated it is "necessary in the short term."

Table 1 Educating Tomorrow's Lawyers' Data on Competencies "Necessary in the Short Term" for Law Graduates[34]

Trustworthiness		
1	Keep confidentiality	**96%**
3	Honor commitments	**94%**
4	Trustworthiness/integrity	**92%**
15	Take individual responsibility	**82%**
18	Strong moral compass	**79%**
Relationship Skills, Including Respect for Others and Responsiveness		
2	Arrive on time	**95%**
5	Treat others with respect	**92%**
6	Listen attentively and with respect	**92%**
7	Respond promptly	**91%**
17	Emotional regulation and self-control	**80%**
20	Exhibit tact and diplomacy	**78%**
Strong Work Ethic/Diligence		
8	Strong work ethic	**88%**
9	Diligence	**88%**
10	Attention to detail	**88%**
11	Conscientiousness	**86%**
Common Sense/Good Judgment (85%, this was twelfth)		

Note: Research the Law was thirteenth (84 percent), Intelligence was fourteenth (84 percent), Speak Professionally was sixteenth (80 percent), and Write Professionally was nineteenth (78 percent).

A number of the most important competencies "necessary in the short term" are what we call the *professional-formation competencies* (ETL calls these competencies "the character quotient"). These are values, virtues, and habits that can be developed over a career and include the competencies related to trustworthiness (keep confidentiality, honor commitments, trustworthiness/integrity, take individual responsibility, and strong moral compass), the competencies

---

[34] Alli Gerkman & Logan Cornett, Educating Tomorrow's Lawyers, FOUNDATIONS FOR PRACTICE: THE WHOLE LAWYER AND THE CHARACTER QUOTIENT (2016).

related to respect for others and relationship skills (arrive on time, treat others with respect, listen attentively, respond promptly, emotional regulation and self-control, and exhibit tact and diplomacy), the competencies related to strong work ethic/diligence (strong work ethic, diligence, attention to detail, and conscientiousness), and common sense/good judgment.

Although there are few empirical studies on how clients define the values, virtues, capacities, and skills of an effective lawyer, there is one rigorous empirical study of what competencies lawyers as clients would want if they were hiring a lawyer. In 2003, Professors Marjorie M. Shultz and Sheldon Zedeck at the University of California at Berkeley identified twenty-six factors important for lawyer effectiveness by interviewing people from five stakeholder groups associated with Berkeley Law: alumni, students, faculty, clients, and judges.[35] They asked questions such as, "If you were looking for a lawyer for an important matter for yourself, whom would you identify, and why?" and "What qualities and behavior would cause you to choose that attorney?"[36] The twenty-six factors important to lawyer effectiveness that emerged from the interviews are shown in table 2.

The Shultz–Zedeck study did not list the twenty-six lawyer effectiveness factors in order of importance, so for comparative purposes, table 2 lists the twenty-six lawyer effectiveness factors using the same umbrella categories as table 1 on the ETL competencies "necessary in the short term."

Table 2 Shultz–Zedeck List of Twenty-six Lawyer Effectiveness Factors

Trustworthiness

- Integrity/honesty
- Self-development

Relationship Skills

- Building relationships with clients and providing advice and counsel
- Developing relationships within the legal profession
- Networking and business development
- Listening
- Able to see the world through the eyes of others
- Community involvement and service
- Organizing and managing others
- Evaluation, development, and mentoring of others

(continues)

---

[35] Marjorie M. Shultz & Sheldon Zedeck, *Predicting Lawyer Effectiveness: Broadening the Basis for Law School Admission Decisions*, 36 Law & Soc. Inquiry 620, 629 (2011).
[36] *Id.*

Table 2 Continued

Strong Work Ethic/Diligence

- Passion/engagement
- Diligence
- Stress management

Common Sense/Good Judgment

- Problem solving
- Practical judgment
- Creativity and innovation

Technical Competencies

- Analysis and reasoning
- Researching the law
- Fact finding
- Questioning and interviewing
- Influencing and advocating
- Writing
- Speaking
- Strategic planning
- Organizing and managing one's own work
- Negotiation

Nearly all of the remaining studies regarding client assessments of lawyer effectiveness are studies of how in-house counsel for corporate clients evaluate the effectiveness of outside counsel.[37] These studies reveal that in-house counsel and corporate clients seek outside counsel who provide the greatest value to the client through (1) relationship skills[38] ("commitment to achieving needed client results in a timely way, respect for others, good judgment on when to challenge a client decision, and prompt communication both when asked for assistance and when appropriate regarding the status of a project"[39]) and, most frequently, (2) client responsiveness[40] ("including learning the client's business, discounting

---

[37] Hamilton, *supra* note 33, at 13 (citing Shultz & Zedeck, *supra* note 47, at 629) ("It seems reasonable that 'Organizing and Managing One's Own Work' and 'Organizing and Managing Others' from [the effectiveness factors] are included in 'Project Management' from [the large law firm competencies]. Similarly 'Passion and Engagement' in [the effectiveness factors] is implicit in 'Initiative/Drive/Strong Work Ethic' in [the large law firm competencies], and 'Diligence' in [the effectiveness factors] is implicit in 'Dedication to the Client' in [the large law firm competencies].").

[38] Ass'n of Corporate Counsel, How to Evaluate the Performance of Litigation Law Firms 1–2 (2008); *see also* Nabarro LLP, General Counsel: Vague about Value? 1 (2011).

[39] Hamilton, *supra* note 33, at 13.

[40] Altman Weil Inc., Chief Legal Officer Survey (2008); *see also* Nabarro LLP, *supra* note 37, at 1.

fees in light of the market realities, and staffing to address the client's unique needs"[41]), while (3) strong technical legal skills are considered to be a given because of the global availability of high-quality legal work.[42]

The BTI Consulting Group's 2017 survey asked more than 300 corporate clients to identify outside counsel who stood out for delivering "superior client service."[43] The dominant factor (55.4 percent) distinguishing "the absolute best client service" is "client focus." Client focus includes understanding the client's business and legal objectives and recognizing and demonstrating a mutual interest in achieving client goals.[44] Client focus overlaps with the second-most-important factor (22.8 percent) distinguishing "the highest levels of client service"—understanding the client's business.[45] This has become increasingly more important and has gone up 11.4 percent since the 2016 study alone. This increase is thought to be due to the "dramatic increase in Bet-the-Company work."[46]

Similarly, the Altman Weil 2016 Chief Legal Officer Survey found the most important efforts outside counsel could make to improve relations with the client were all related to improved responsiveness to the client's needs, including greater cost reduction, improved budget forecasting so that the client will know what the service will cost, more efficient project management, nonhourly-based pricing structures, modification of work to match legal risk, more efficient project management, improved communication and responsiveness, and greater effort to understand the client's business.[47] The Association of Corporate Counsel (ACC) created the ACC's Value Index in 2009, which defined six key criteria of high-value service: (1) understanding client objectives and expectations; (2) legal expertise; (3) efficiency/process management; (4) responsiveness/communication; (5) predictable cost/budgeting skills; and (6) results delivered.[48]

These studies converge on this critical point: corporate clients are seeking outside counsel possessing excellent client relationship skills, demonstrating "(1) a strong understanding of the client's business and needs, (2) good judgment

---

[41] Hamilton, *supra* note 33, at 13–14.

[42] E-mail from Susan Hackett, Gen. Counsel, Ass'n of Corporate Counsel, to author & Verna Monson (Aug. 13, 2010) (on file with author); *see also* Nabarro LLP, *supra* note 37, at 1.

[43] BTI Consulting Grp., *Executive Summary*, *in* The BTI Client Service All-Stars for Law Firms 1–2 (2017).

[44] *Id.*

[45] *Id.* at 3–4.

[46] *Id.* at 3.

[47] Altman Weil, 2016 Chief Legal Officers Survey 26 (2016), *available at* http://www.altmanweil.com/CLO2016.

[48] Larry Bodine, *ACC Launches Controversial "Value Index" Ranking of Law Firms*, Law Marketing Blog (Oct. 20, 2009), http://blog.larrybodine.com/2009/10/articles/current-affairs/acc-launches-controversial-value-index-ranking-of-law-firms/.

and problem solving in light of that understanding of the client, (3) strong responsiveness to the client, and (4) a focus on cost-effective solutions that provide value to the client."[49]

The few empirical studies of how individual clients assess lawyer effectiveness reveal that clients highly value client responsiveness and client relationship skills. In a major 1993 American Bar Association (ABA) study, both individual and corporate clients believed that lawyers are technically skilled, although clients generally did not believe that lawyers are committed or responsive to their needs (and were excessively focused on money).[50] A 1997–1998 study in England and Wales revealed similar client perceptions of lawyer effectiveness, and clients indicated effective communication (including attentive listening, clear explanations, empathy, and respect) was important to them.[51] In 2001, the ABA Section of Litigation commissioned a survey of 450 U.S. households plus focus groups in five cities to explore public perceptions of lawyers. On the positive side, respondents generally thought lawyers were knowledgeable about the law, and the majority of respondents who had hired a lawyer were satisfied,[52] but on the negative side, 69 percent of the respondents thought many lawyers are "more interested in making money than serving their clients," "manipulative," and "do a poor job of policing themselves."[53] Two empirical surveys from the early 2000s revealed that criminal defendants value some client relationship skills (such as caring about the client, keeping the client informed, and listening skills) as much as, or more than, technical legal skills.[54]

Technical legal skills are considered to be a given by clients, and, to stand out, an attorney must demonstrate strong client relationship skills and client responsiveness. Whether serving individual or corporate clients, attorneys need to understand the client context and develop the ability to relate to their clients. For corporate clients, this can be demonstrated through a solid understanding of the client's business and legal objectives so that attorneys can provide the greatest value in their service. For individual clients, this client focus can be demonstrated through strong communication skills in which attorneys listen

---

[49] Hamilton, *supra* note 33, at 21.

[50] Stuart A. Forsyth, *Good Client Relations: The Key to Succe$$*, 34 Ariz. Att'y 20, 21 (1998).

[51] *See* Clark D. Cunningham, *What Clients Want from Their Lawyers* 2–3 (Aug. 3, 2006) (essay prepared for Society of Writers to Her Majesty's Signet), *available at* http://clarkcunningham.org/PR/WhatClientsWant.pdf.

[52] ABA Section of Litig., Public Perceptions of Lawyers Consumer Research Findings 17, 19 (April 2002).

[53] *Id.* at 7–10.

[54] Marcus T. Boccaccini, Jennifer L. Boothby & Stanley L. Brodsky, *Client Relations Skills in Effective Lawyering: Attitudes of Criminal Defense Attorneys and Experienced Clients*, 26 Law & Psychol. Rev. 97, 100, 111, 118–19 (2002); Marcus T. Boccaccini & Stanley L. Brodsky, *Characteristics of the Ideal Criminal Defense Attorney from the Client's Perspective: Empirical Findings and Implications for Legal Practice*, 25 Law & Psychol. Rev. 81, 97 (2001).

attentively and provide clear explanations and information to their clients. Students who develop these skills will make themselves more attractive to legal employers and clients.

2. Assessment Competency Models

Many legal employers, including law firms, are developing "competency models." A competency model begins with identification of characteristics of an organization's most effective and successful lawyers.[55] The organization then develops a framework of core competencies for new attorneys to master, providing associates with a roadmap for success.[56] These models are used to assess the professional development of junior lawyers, and some legal employers are beginning to use these models to inform "behavioral interviewing" in the hiring process. As Harvard Law School explains, "Employers use behavioral interview questions to assess your past and future performance. An interviewer will ask you to provide an example of a time you demonstrated a particular skill required of the position. Likewise, an employer may ask how you handled or faced a specific situation or assignment. For example, an employer might ask an applicant to describe a time he or she had to work with a difficult client. Interviewers use behavioral interview questions to determine whether you will be a good fit for the position. Your past performance serves as a strong indicator of future performance. By asking you to elaborate upon your prior professional experiences, employers can assess whether you possess the requisite skills for the position."[57]

Law students who understand legal employer competency models can differentiate themselves from other graduates by using the three years of law school to develop—and to create supporting evidence to demonstrate—specific competencies. A law school implementing a "competency-based curriculum"[58] can provide graduates who have more of the competencies that legal employers need.[59]

A 2011 survey of professional development directors and chief talent officers indicated 66 percent of the sixty responding firms had, or were in the process of developing, competency models for associates.[60] A July 2009 survey of

---

[55] Susan Manch & Terri Mottershead, *Introduction: Talent Management in Law Firms—Evolution, Revelation, Revolution or Business as Usual?, in* THE ART AND SCIENCE OF STRATEGIC TALENT MANAGEMENT IN LAW FIRMS 1, 9 (Terri Mottershead ed., 2010).

[56] Neil W. Hamilton, Verna Monson & Jerome M. Organ, *Encouraging Each Student's Personal Responsibility for Core Competencies Including Professionalism*, 21 PROF. LAWYER 5 (No. 3, 2012).

[57] Susan Manch, *Competencies and Competency Models: An Overview, in* THE ART AND SCIENCE OF STRATEGIC TALENT MANAGEMENT IN LAW FIRMS, at 77, 85 (Terri Mottershead ed., 2010).

[58] Henderson, *Blueprint, supra* note 4, at 492.

[59] *Id.* at 464–65, 491–92, 503–04.

[60] IDA ABBOTT, LAWYERS' PROFESSIONAL DEVELOPMENT: THE LEGAL EMPLOYER'S COMPREHENSIVE GUIDE 140 (2d ed. 2012).

U.S. law firms revealed that almost 75 percent of the firms had, or were planning to develop, a competency-model approach to talent management.[61]

There is strong evidence this trend of developing competency models is widespread. For example, table 3 shows data from ten state attorney general offices that assess certain competencies evidenced by junior attorneys. The data shows that in 2012 all the largest Minnesota law firms (65–740 lawyers) had adopted assessment competency models.

a. What Attorneys General Are Assessing

Table 3 Synthesis of Competency Models for Junior Attorneys from Ten States' Attorney General Offices (AGs)[62]

Competencies	Number of AGs Assessing the Competency
Initiates and maintains strong work and team relationships	10
Good judgment/common sense/problem solving	8
Effective written/oral communication skills	9
Project management, including high quantity and quality, efficiency, and timeliness	10
Business development/marketing/client retention	0
Dedication to client service/responsive to client	3
Analytical skills: identify legal issues from facts, apply the law, and draw conclusions	5
Initiative/ambition/drive/strong work ethic	3
Legal competency/expertise/knowledge	9
Commitment to professional development toward excellence	9
Research skills	6
Commitment to firm/department, its goals, and its values	4
Integrity/honesty/trustworthiness	4
Delegation, supervision, mentoring	4

(continues)

---

[61] Manch, *Competencies, supra* note 57, at 77, 85.

[62] In April–December 2013, the offices of ten state attorneys general (California, Colorado, Georgia, Iowa, Missouri, New Hampshire, New Mexico, Rhode Island, Washington, and Wisconsin) provided Neil Hamilton with their attorney evaluation forms. The competencies that the state attorneys general are evaluating were synthesized and tabulated to create this table.

Table 3 Continued

Competencies	Number of AGs Assessing the Competency
Pro bono, community, bar association involvement	0
Seeks feedback/responsive to feedback	4
Stress/crisis management	1
Inspires confidence	5
Ability to work independently	3
Negotiation skills	1
Strategic/creative thinking	6
Leadership	2
Demonstrates interest in business and financial arrangements with clients	0

b. What Large Firms Are Assessing

In May and June 2012, the fourteen largest law firms in Minnesota (ranging in size from 67 to 740 lawyers)[63] made their associate evaluation forms available. All fourteen had developed competency models and were using them to gauge the effectiveness of associate attorneys.

Four other separate studies analyze the competency models of individual firms: a 2012 study of a firm larger than 250 lawyers,[64] a 2008 study of a firm of approximately 750 lawyers,[65] a 2007 study of a firm of more than 300 lawyers,[66] and a 2006 study of a firm of approximately 600 lawyers.[67]

Table 4 provides a synthesis of the 2012 survey of the largest law firms in Minnesota and the four separate studies, from 2006 to 2012, analyzing the competency models of individual firms.

---

[63] Hamilton, *supra* note 33 (including lawyers outside of Minnesota, the firms ranged in size from 67 to 740 total lawyers).

[64] Lori Berman & Heather Bock, *Developing Attorneys for the Future: What Can We Learn from the Fast Trackers?*, 52 SANTA CLARA L. REV. 875 (2012).

[65] SCOTT A. WESTFAHL, YOU GET WHAT YOU MEASURE: LAWYER DEVELOPMENT FRAMEWORKS AND EFFECTIVE PERFORMANCE EVALUATIONS (2008).

[66] PETER B. SLOAN, FROM CLASSES TO COMPETENCIES, LOCKSTEP TO LEVELS: HOW ONE LAW FIRM DISCARDED LOCKSTEP ASSOCIATE ADVANCEMENT AND REPLACED IT WITH AN ASSOCIATE LEVEL SYSTEM (Blackwell Sanders Peper Martin LLP 2002).

[67] HEATHER BOCK & ROBERT RUYAK, CONSTRUCTING CORE COMPETENCIES: USING COMPETENCY MODELS TO MANAGE FIRM TALENT (Am. Bar Ass'n 2006).

Table 4 Most Common Values, Virtues, Capacities, and Skills from Analysis of Studies' Research on the Competency Models of Eighteen Individual Firms

Number of Firms Included in Competency-Model Studies That Considered Each Value/Virtue/Capacity/Skill in Their Evaluation of Associates	
Initiates and maintains strong work and team relationships	18
Good judgment/common sense/problem solving	18
Effective written/oral communication skills	17
Project management, including high quantity, quality, efficiency, and timeliness	17
Business development/marketing/client retention	16
Dedication to client service/responsiveness to client	16
Analytical skills: identify legal issues from facts, apply the law, and draw conclusions	15
Initiative/ambition/drive/strong work ethic	15
Legal competency/expertise/knowledge	14
Commitment to professional development toward excellence	12
Research skills	12
Commitment to firm, its goals, and its values	10
Integrity/honesty/trustworthiness	9
Delegation, supervision, mentoring	9
Pro bono, community, bar association involvement	8
Seeks feedback/responsive to feedback	5
Stress/crisis management	5
Inspires confidence	4
Ability to work independently	4
Negotiation skills	4
Strategic/creative thinking	4
Leadership	2
Demonstrates interest in business and financial arrangements with clients	2

There is a high degree of convergence on the competencies the firms are assessing, with twelve or more of the firms (66 percent) assessing eleven of the competencies and nine or more of the firms (50 percent) assessing fourteen of the competencies.

As competency models become the norm, some firms are going beyond a simple model by developing a stage-specific model. See diagram 1, which shows a general model of levels of mastery of a competency.

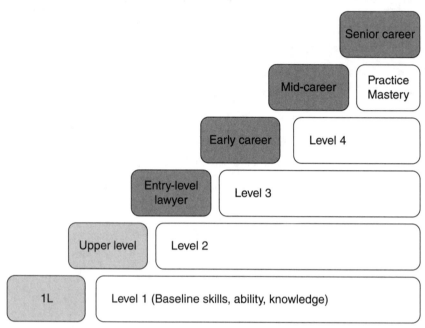

Diagram 1 Levels of Practice Mastery of a Competency

Table 5 shows stage development competency models for teamwork in the Minnesota law firm study. These more complex competency models break down general competencies into the specific subcompetencies expected at each stage of a new lawyer's career.

A comparison of the competency models for junior attorneys from ten state attorney general offices with the eighteen law firm competency models leads to three main observations:

1. The large law firm and the attorneys' general competency models all emphasize teamwork, good judgment, effective written and oral communication, and project management skills.
2. The attorneys' general competency models placed significantly more emphasis on commitment to professional development toward excellence and research skills.
3. The large law firms placed significantly more emphasis on dedication to client service/responsive to client and business development/marketing/client retention.

Table 5 Developmental Stages to Assess Associate–Attorney Teamwork Capacities (in a Minnesota Law Firm Study)[68]

	Firm A	Firm B	Firm C	Firm D
Junior associate	• Works effectively with others to address client and firm needs • Interacts well with staff and other lawyers	• Communicates and collaborates with others as part of a team • Communicates effectively with staff	• Finds common ground and works effectively with other attorneys and staff to address issues and complete assignments • Is viewed as a contributing member—one who encourages cooperation, collaboration, and respectful candor • Learns to work effectively and respectfully with all members of the staff • Is timely for meetings and conference calls	• Interacts well with other attorneys and staff • Manages upward well by regularly communicating with assigning attorneys around work progress against deadlines • Requests help as needed
Mid-level associate	• Accepts leadership responsibilities • Works effectively with others to address client and firm needs • Interacts well with staff and other lawyers	• Functions well as a member of a team • Effectively supervises staff • Functions as a positive role model and is beginning to develop leadership responsibility over staff and colleagues	In addition: • Delegates assignments appropriately to junior associates	• Is a strong team player who interacts well professionally and respectfully with other attorneys/staff • Is sensitive to interpersonal dynamics with the team, the firm, and clients • Effectively delegates • Is becoming an effective coach and mentor to junior associates

(continues)

[68] Neil W. Hamilton, *Changing Markets Create Opportunities: Emphasizing the Competencies Legal Employers Use in Hiring New Lawyers (Including Professional Formation/Professionalism)*, SOUTH CAROLINA L. REV. 65 (2014), *available at* http://papers.ssrn.com/sol3/papers.cfm?abstract_id=2412324.

Table 5 Continued

	Firm A	Firm B	Firm C	Firm D
Senior associate	• Demonstrates strong leadership capabilities • Works effectively with others to address client and firm needs • Interacts well with staff and other lawyers	• Delegates tasks to and effectively supervises junior lawyers • Demonstrates leadership responsibilities over teams of lawyers and staff	In addition: • Can deal effectively and maturely with interpersonal conflict with team members	• Effectively delegates and treats team members with respect, even under stress • Is sought out by junior associates and staff because of reputation for managing teams smoothly and providing helpful coaching and feedback • Is open to receiving feedback and improving leadership style

3. Competency Models for Hiring Decisions

William D. Henderson, a law professor at the Indiana University Maurer School of Law, noted, "[t]here is a paucity of high quality empirical research on the factors that contribute to lawyer effectiveness."[69] This section adds four new studies to define the competencies that legal employers in Minnesota (legal aid, county government, small firms, and large firms) value most in their decisions to hire new lawyers.[70]

Table 6 sums up the four studies to capture the competencies considered most important by all four types of legal employers. Appendix B reports the data from each of the individual studies.

Table 6 The Relative Importance of Different Competencies in the Decision to Hire a New Lawyer—Average Ratings across All Four Studies (of Legal Aid, County Attorney, Small-Firm, and Large-Firm Employers)

The following competencies show an average ranking between 1 and 5, where 5 is very important to critically important, 4 is important to very important, 3 is significant to important, 2 is modest to significant, and 1 is not important.

Competencies Considered Very Important to Critically Important	
1. Integrity/honesty/trustworthiness	4.76
2. Good judgment/common sense/problem solving	4.63
3. Analytical skills: identify legal issues from facts, apply the law, and draw conclusions	4.37
4. Initiative/ambition/drive/strong work ethic	4.33
5. Effective written/oral communication skills	4.33
6. Dedication to client service/responsiveness to client (first for legal aid)	4.29
7. Commitment to firm/department/office, its goals, and its values	4.25
8. Initiates and maintains strong work and team relationships (fourth for county attorneys)	4.14
Competencies Considered Important to Very Important	
9. Project management, including high quality, efficiency, and timeliness	3.91
10. Legal competency/expertise/knowledge	3.87
11. Ability to work independently (sixth for small firms and seventh for county attorneys)	3.83
12. Commitment to professional development toward excellence	3.68

(continues)

---

[69] Henderson, *Blueprint, supra* note 4, at 498.
[70] Neil Hamilton, *Changing Markets Create Opportunities: Emphasizing the Competencies Legal Employers Use in Hiring New Lawyers,* 65 S.C.L.REV. 547 (2014).

Table 6 Continued

Competencies Considered Important to Very Important	
13. Strategic/creative thinking	3.66
14. Research skills (ninth for large firms)	3.62
Note that for large firms, business development/marketing/client retention was ranked the fifteenth-most-important competency, and for small firms, this was ranked the fourteenth most important, but this competency was not included in the legal aid and county attorney surveys.	
Competencies Considered Important to Very Important	
15. Inspires confidence (eighth for large firms)	3.60
16. Seeks feedback/responsive to feedback (twelfth for small firms and eleventh for county attorneys)	3.53
17. Stress/crisis management	3.45
18. Leadership	3.10
19. Negotiation skills	3.10
Competencies Considered Somewhat Important to Important	
20. Pro bono, community, bar association involvement (thirteenth for legal aid)	2.48
21. Delegation, supervision, mentoring	2.37

The data support several significant conclusions. Overall, there is wide agreement among these types of legal employers on the competencies that are important in the decision to hire:

- All four types of legal employers agree that the following five competencies are very important to critically important in the decision to hire: (1) integrity/honesty/trustworthiness; (2) good judgment; (3) analytical skills; (4) initiative/drive/strong work ethic; and (7) commitment to the firm or department and its goals and values.
- Three out of the four types of legal employers agree the following three competencies are very important to critically important in the decision to hire: (5) effective communication skills; (6) dedication to client service/responsiveness to client; and (8) initiates and maintains strong work and team relationships. The fourth type of employer considers these competencies important to very important.
- All four types of legal employers believe that the competencies from number 9 (legal competency/expertise/knowledge) up to number 16 (seeks feedback/responsive to feedback) are at least important to very important in the decision to hire, with one or two types of legal employers including numbers 9–15 as very important to critically important in hiring.

- All four types of employers ranked knowledge of doctrinal law from ninth to fourteenth in importance in the decision to hire. Many law professors and law students believe that a doctrinal law specialty in law school— through a concentration of some sort—is a more important factor than these legal employers are reporting. Students should not overemphasize the use of a concentration to differentiate themselves but instead should emphasize some of the other competencies.[71]

Note that with respect to social justice employers like legal aid, these employers made clear that the candidate must have a demonstrated record of passion for and service to the disadvantaged. With respect to large-firm employers, these employers made clear that they initially limit the applicant pool to the top 10–20 percent of the 1L class by rank but then looked at these competencies to differentiate candidates within that group.

4. Convergence in the Various Data Sets

We can see substantial convergence among the ETL data on what competencies are "necessary in the short term" for law graduates, the data on the competencies that legal employers value, and the Shultz–Zedeck data on lawyer effectiveness factors (from a survey of lawyers as clients). Table 7 sets forth this convergence.

Table 7 Convergence of the Empirical Studies on the Nontechnical, Professional-Formation Competencies That Legal Employers and Clients Want

Ownership of Continuous Proactive Professional Development over a Career
• Commitment to professional development toward excellence, including habit of actively seeking feedback and reflection • Initiative/strong work ethic/diligence plus project management that demonstrates these
Internalization of Deep Responsibilities to Others **(the client, the team, the employing organization, the legal system)**
• Trustworthiness and integrity • Relationship skills, including respect for others, understanding of and responsiveness to client, and listening • Good judgment/common sense • Teamwork and collaboration

Note that the first two competencies in table 7, commitment to professional development toward excellence and initiative/strong work ethic, are part of a larger umbrella category in section III titled "Ownership of Continuous

---

[71] *Id.*

Proactive Professional Development over a Career." This group of competencies is closely related to self-directed learning, a common term in higher education. Malcolm Knowles defines self-directed learning as "a process by which individuals take the initiative, with or without the assistance of others, in diagnosing their learning needs, formulating learning goals, identifying the human and material resources for learning, choosing and implementing appropriate learning strategies, and evaluating learning outcomes."[72] Earlier discussion emphasized the foundational importance of continuous professional development over a career to respond to changing legal markets. Growing toward later stages of self-directed learning is a foundational transferable skill. Your written Roadmap professional development plan that you create, implement, and revisit and revise as you gain experience is good evidence of your growth toward later stages of self-directed learning

The remaining four competencies in table 7 (trustworthiness; relationship skills, including understanding and responsiveness to the client; good judgment; and teamwork and collaboration) are part of a larger umbrella category in section III titled "The Internalization of Deep Responsibilities to Others, Especially the Client, the Team, the Employing Organization, and the Legal System." Your written Roadmap professional development plan can also signal that you understand these competencies and are working on growing toward their later stages.

Section III of the Roadmap has parts on how you can develop and create evidence for each of the major competencies listed in tables 6 and 7. Please read the relevant parts on the differentiating competencies you want to emphasize. Refer to appendix A for more data on competencies that new lawyers report they need most.

5. What Can We Learn from Competencies Needed for Business?

The foundational competencies identified previously overlap with what have historically been considered the competencies desired in business managers. A number of empirical studies of the competencies desired in business managers are discussed in appendix C.

When examining these studies and appendix C together, it is clear the competencies emphasized in the various studies overlap. This is especially true for foundational competencies, such as teamwork, initiative, communication skills, critical thinking/problem solving, and organizational skills, which are those that higher-level competencies are built upon.

These results show the competencies sought in the legal services industry are also desired in nonlegal industries. Assuming law students develop these

---

[72] MALCOLM KNOWLES, SELF-DIRECTED LEARNING: A GUIDE FOR LEARNERS AND TEACHERS 18 (1975).

competencies during law school, graduates who pursue nonlegal employment will be equipped with competencies that are transferable to a career outside the legal industry.

Employers also struggle to find applicants with the skills and competencies they desire. While "hard" (technical) skills were once the key to employment, the ManpowerGroup found that employers increasingly seek applicants with "soft" (employability) skills.[73] Rather than just technical knowledge, employers need applicants with interpersonal skills, enthusiasm and motivation, collaboration and teamwork skills, professionalism, flexibility, adaptability, the ability to deal with ambiguity and complexity, attention to detail, and problem-solving and decision-making skills.[74] The Society for Human Resource Management and AARP also found an applied-skills gap exists between young workers and experienced workers in the categories of professionalism, critical thinking and problem solving, written communication, leadership, information and technological application, teamwork, and creativity.[75] Legal education helps students develop these skills.

As lawyers in the new legal economy increasingly serve an interdisciplinary role, they will need to integrate necessary business competencies into their legal skill sets. Transferable skills will remain useful and attractive to potential employers no matter how the legal services market continues to change. Because new lawyers face substantial market changes, they must be equipped with skills applicable to new and constantly evolving situations.

---

[73] MANPOWERGROUP, 2012 TALENT SHORTAGE SURVEY RESEARCH RESULTS (2012), *available at* https://candidate.manpower.com/wps/wcm/connect/93de5b004b6f33c0ab3cfb4952b5bce9/2012 +Talent+Shortage+Survey+Results_A4_FINAL.pdf?MOD=AJPERES.

[74] *Id.*

[75] *SHRM Survey Findings: SHRM-AARP Strategic Workforce Planning* (Apr. 9, 2012), https://www .shrm.org/hr-today/trends-and-forecasting/research-and-surveys/Pages/StrategicWorkforcePlanning .aspx.

YOUR TIMELINE FOR THE ROADMAP PROCESS AND YOUR ROADMAP TEMPLATE[1]

Now that you understand the foundational realities relating to your development of competencies that a new lawyer needs to practice law and that legal employers and clients want, you can begin the Roadmap process itself, as you move toward meaningful employment.

A. Introduction

Part B, which follows, provides a timeline for your Roadmap process so that you may effectively use your remaining semesters in law school, as well as your summers, to achieve your goals. Part C then outlines the entire Roadmap template to give you a clear idea of where you are going. Part D gives you directions on how to access both the preliminary self-assessments and the electronic Roadmap template. Part E provides ideas for integrating your Roadmap planning process to effectively use the curriculum in the 2L and 3L years. Part F discusses the importance of developing a portfolio on each of your two or three most important and strongest competencies in your value proposition.

Your Roadmap will evolve over your time in law school, as well as during the years following graduation as you discern your strengths in the context of both the competencies that legal employers and clients want and the available

---

[1] Authored by Neil W. Hamilton, Bryan M. Wachter, and Carl J. L. Numrich.

employment opportunities at any given time. The Roadmap is an ongoing tool for discernment and will change continuously as you gain more experience. An initial job experience may or may not be what you ultimately discover as the best vocational fit with your motivating interest and strengths, but you may be able to cross off one of your top options after you have tried the work and you grow through the experience toward later stages of your transferable skills.

Diagram 2 gives you a visual outline of the Roadmap process up to the point where you are planning to use your remaining time in law school most effectively to grow toward meaningful employment. Each of your experiences may land you in different areas of the diagram, but the purpose of gaining experience is to help you move toward the center: meaningful employment that you are paid for.

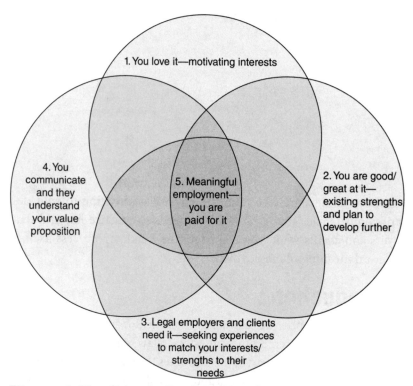

Diagram 2 Visualizing the Roadmap Template

Each Roadmap component has various steps. Each student will be developing a uniquely specific, individualized product, so the time for completing each step will vary for each student. For the various components, there is a suggested and approximate time for completion, but this exists to set the parameters for a minimum good-faith initial effort.

If your law school requires the Roadmap, then each student needs to certify that a minimum good-faith effort of five hours was devoted to the completion of this Roadmap project. This signed certification will accompany the Roadmap that you give to your assigned coach.

B. Timeline for Roadmap Steps[2]

In the Roadmap template, you will develop a value proposition, assess your strongest competencies, and identify the employment options that interest you most. Then, you need to focus on how to best use your remaining time in law school. Each semester should provide opportunities both to gain experience that test your employment options and to create evidence supporting your value proposition. In particular, you need to create evidence of particular professional competencies through your use of the law school curriculum and extracurricular experiences.

This part provides a general timeline of milestones related to your Roadmap. Use it as a checklist to help you navigate your way through your three years of law school and to create evidence of your commitment to professional development. Keep in mind, however, that professional development is an ongoing project that will continue after you have finished law school.

As you consider your professional development, also think about how this timeline can act as a bridge between your Roadmap and the mindset behind developing your strongest competencies. As you identify experiences, relationships, and courses for your own timeline, consider the competencies discussed in section III, and use the discussions in that section to fully understand each competency.

It is also critically important that you read "Ideas to Make Effective Use of the 2L and 3L Curriculum" and "Creating a Portfolio for Two or Three of Your Strongest Competencies" in section II, as this will further guide you on how to develop evidence of your differentiating competencies.

In addition to following the timeline outlined here, it is important to review and update your Roadmap during periods of transition. At each transition, revisit your top options and skills, as well as your progress on your metrics, evidence creation, and goals. Some key transitions are noted throughout the timeline. Additionally, you should revisit your Roadmap after each professional milestone and paid or unpaid work experience, as well as after completion of a clinic or externship opportunity. The timeline is available electronically at **http://ambar .org/roadmap**.

1. 1L Fall Semester

- Receive and read through this timeline for Roadmap steps.
- Understand the competencies that legal employers and clients want. Determine which competencies are the focus of required 1L curriculum and which competencies you should develop in the elective curriculum and other experiences of law school.

---

[2] Authored by Neil W. Hamilton, Carl J. L. Numrich, Bryan M. Wachter, Emilee Walters, Emily Palmerr, Shana Tomenes, and Christopher Damian.

Key Transition Point:

Early Job Fair Deadlines

Specialty legal areas, such as intellectual property, and certain diversity job fair applications close in early December. Meet with your coach or career services personnel prior to completing applications.

Key Transition Point:

Results from Fall Grades

Regardless of your feelings about your results, this is an important time to reflect on what went well and what can be adjusted in the future. Meet with your coach or career services personnel to discuss the semester and get tips moving forward.

- Explore various organizations, volunteer opportunities, and campus events with an eye toward developing the important competencies.
- Update your résumé, and schedule a meeting with your school's office dedicated to career and professional development after October 15.
- Reflect on your strengths, weaknesses, and values. Begin discerning what direction you are headed and how you will get there.
- Seek out upperclassmen and practicing attorneys for advice, recommendations, and tips as you navigate your first year.
- Begin forging a relationship with a professor who knows your work well enough to write you a letter of recommendation after your first year.
- Create and implement a networking plan. See "Building Relationships Based on Trust through Networking" in section III.
- Explore your interests and engage in the profession through joining the American Bar Association and affinity bar mentorship programs. Some application processes close before winter break.
- Become familiar with your law school's job bank site, such as Symplicity. You can begin applying for summer positions in December.

2. 1L Spring Semester

- Complete the Roadmap template, and discuss your plan for employment with a senior advisor.
- Continue exploring various organizations, volunteer opportunities, and campus events. Commit yourself to an on-campus organization, and seek out leadership, project management, and teamwork experiences.
- Continue updating your résumé.
- Research and seek out employment/volunteer/research opportunities for the summer after 1L year that will help you both explore your most promising employment options and develop the competencies on which you want to focus. Ask professors if they need summer help. Meet with your career services office to learn about upcoming application deadlines that may interest you.

- Consider your summer options early and often. Many 1L opportunities are unpaid. Begin looking for summer funding early, and consider any externship opportunities offered through your school.
- Register for classes for the following semester that will highlight the competencies you want to emphasize.
- Continue forging a relationship with a professor who could write you a letter of recommendation after your first year, and begin forging a similar relationship with another faculty member who knows your strongest competencies.

> **Key Transition Point:**
>
> **Roadmap**
>
> After finishing your Roadmap, be sure to check in, debrief, and discuss future goals with your coach or career services personnel.
>
> **Key Transition Point:**
>
> **Selecting 2L Courses**
>
> Before registration, reflect upon and update your Roadmap. Be sure to include classes supporting your value proposition.

- Continue updating and implementing your networking plan, and try other networking opportunities in fields compatible with your areas of interest.
- Run for an executive position for an on-campus organization in which you could demonstrate project management and teamwork competency skills.
- Look carefully at the bar examination subjects in the state where you intend to take the bar. *Note that an increasing number of states are moving to the Uniform Bar Examination. Make a determination about whether you want to take a course on each bar subject.*
- Before registration for the fall semester, plan out the sequence of courses in your last four semesters, including prerequisites.

3. 1L Summer

a. *June (Prior to Beginning of 2L Year)*

- Research and familiarize yourself with legal employers in the geographic region in which you wish to work.
- Reach out to attorneys in areas of law that interest you to schedule informational interviews over the summer. (See "Building Relationships Based on Trust through Networking" in section III for more information.) Implement your networking plan in general.
- Decide whether you will participate in on-campus interviewing (OCI).
- Finalize your summer plans to gain legal experience. If you have already begun your summer work, make sure you are turning in good work and building trusting relationships with your colleagues and supervisors.

You need, at minimum, one supervisor who really knows your work and strongest competencies.

- Research and familiarize yourself with summer job fairs in geographic legal markets or practice areas that interest you, and make note of upcoming summer deadlines. Many off-campus job fairs have application deadlines in early summer and conduct interviews in July and August.

b. July (Prior to Beginning of 2L Year)

- If you intend to participate in OCI:
  - Research the legal employers participating in OCI.
  - Discuss the OCI process with your school's office dedicated to career and professional development, taking note of important dates and procedures.
  - Create or update your résumé.
  - Create and carefully proofread cover letters for target employers.
  - Select writing samples, making sure to secure permission if using a sample from a work or volunteer project.
  - Prepare references.
  - Generate an unofficial transcript.
  - Convert all files to PDF format.
  - Meet someone at your school to review your application materials.
  - Schedule a mock interview.
  - Meet with attorneys to whom you reached out in June.
  - Attend networking events hosted by firms participating in OCI.
- Attend off-campus job fairs applied for in June.
- Continue researching and familiarizing yourself with legal employers in the geographic region and general field of law in which you wish to work. Consider getting lists of alumni from your undergraduate institution and alumni from your law school who are lawyers in that region and field of law.

c. August (Prior to Beginning of 2L Year)

- Meet with attorneys you reached out to in June.
- If you are participating in OCIs, take note of important deadlines. Ensure that you have gathered and reviewed all necessary documents.
- Update your résumé to reflect any legal work or course work you completed during the summer.

Key Transition Point:

Reflect on Summer Experience

Which of your top employment options have you confirmed or eliminated? Did you grow to a later developmental stage on any competency? What evidence do you have regarding growth to a later stage of your strongest competency?

- Continue researching and familiarizing yourself with legal employers in the geographic region and field of law in which you wish to work.
- Select an assignment from your 1L year that could be used as a writing sample. Take the time to review it and polish it if possible. Consider having a mentor or other senior lawyer review the document for you.
- Review your law school's job bank for fall experience opportunities.

4. 2L Fall Semester

a. Ongoing over the 2L Year

- Select an upper-level paper topic that helps you demonstrate competencies for the area of employment you want. Do the upper-level paper early enough in law school so that it is both useful as a basis for discussion with potential employers and a good example of your writing ability and overall implementation of your Roadmap. Also, completing an upper-level paper earlier during your law school career provides you with a potential source for a letter of recommendation from a professor who will know your writing skills and project management skills well. Consider a plan where you develop at least two strong references from two professors about your research, writing, and project management skills by doing an upper-level writing requirement for two credits with one professor and then another two-credit supervised research with another professor.
- If you are planning on applying for appellate-level judicial clerkships in the summer after your 2L year, expedite your plan to have two strong references from professors and your plan to have strong writing samples. Consider taking multiple classes with the same professor, taking classes with smaller class sizes, or working as a research assistant to a professor to help build relationships with professors.
- Seek out opportunities in the curriculum to develop portfolios of experiences in the competencies you wish to emphasize. Ask professors for assessments and feedback so that you create evidence that demonstrates these competencies. Keep track of these experiences so that you have a story to tell about your development of a competency. See section II.F regarding portfolios.
- Based on your Roadmap, consider what experiences in student organizations, pro bono work, paid and unpaid clerkships, externships, and so forth will best help you implement your Roadmap. Secure at least two such experiences that you will complete during your 2L year.
- Research test dates and decide when you want to take your state's ethics exam (if applicable). Many students take a Professional Responsibility course during their 2L year. Consider whether you want to take the test soon after finishing the course, and plan accordingly.

> ### Key Transition Point
>
> **Completion of OCI**
>
> If you participated in your school's on-campus interview process, after its completion, you should reflect upon and update your Roadmap. What went well? What did you learn? Consider meeting with your coach or career services personnel to discuss future plans.

b. September

- Meet with your career services professionals and a faculty member to review and get input on your application materials such as résumé, cover letter, and writing sample.
- Schedule a mock interview.
- Create a one-minute elevator speech to make your value proposition.
- Create a list of the main points you will make and how you will make them so that an employer understands your value proposition and your experience in specific competencies in a twenty-minute screening interview.

c. October

- Revisit your draft of the Roadmap, and have a debrief session with a coach.
- If possible, share the Roadmap with other trusted advisors and coaches and get feedback.
- Continue implementing your networking plan and your Roadmap.

d. November

- Look carefully at the bar examination subjects in the state where you intend to take the bar. *Note that an increasing number of states are moving to the Uniform Bar Examination. Make a determination about whether you want to take a course on each bar subject.*
- Before registration for the spring semester, plan out the sequence of courses for your last three semesters, including prerequisites. Consider if you want to take externships or clinic classes.

e. December

- Secure two references from faculty who know your work well. Ask them to focus on the strongest competencies you want to emphasize.
- In bullet-point format, draft a reference letter of the aspects that you hope the faculty member might include that support the "value proposition" you are trying to make to potential employers. Ask the faculty member if he or she would like to see this. This helps you to see how your persuasive case fits together.
- Continue implementing your networking plan and your Roadmap.
- Update your résumé to reflect first-semester grades, GPA, awards, experiences with competencies, and class rankings.
- Update your writing sample.

5. 2L Spring Semester

a. January

- Check in with your school's office dedicated to career and professional development. Update them on your professional goals, if they have changed. If you are considering an appellate judicial clerkship after graduation, check for the application due date.
- Revisit your Roadmap. With the help of your mentors and coaches, make any revisions or updates you feel are necessary.
- Seek out opportunities in the curriculum to develop portfolios of experiences of the competencies you want to emphasize. Ask professors for assessments and feedback in order to create evidence that demonstrates these competencies.
- Continue implementing your networking plan. Set benchmarks or milestones for how many new contacts you will make each semester to implement your Roadmap.
- Continue implementing your Roadmap.
- Apply for summer positions, and routinely check job search engines for new opportunities.

> **Key Transition Point:**
>
> **After Fall Grades**
>
> You are halfway through law school! This is a great time to reflect on what went well and what can be adjusted in the future. Did you have any work or other experiences in the fall that confirmed or eliminated one of your top employment options? Did you grow to a later stage on any competency? Can you provide evidence of this growth? Meet with your coach or career services personnel to discuss the semester and get tips moving forward.

> **Key Transition Point:**
>
> **Selecting 3L Courses**
>
> Before registration, reflect upon and update your Roadmap. Be sure to include classes that support your value proposition.

b. February

- Begin searching for potential summer experiences and employment.
- Update your résumé with any experiences you gained since first semester.
- Continue implementing your networking plan and your Roadmap.
- Apply for summer positions.

c. March

- Apply for summer positions.
- Continue implementing your networking plan and your Roadmap.

d. April

- Continue implementing your networking plan and your Roadmap.

Key Transition Point:

After Spring Grades

This is a great time to reflect on what went well and what can be adjusted in the future. Did you have any work or other experiences in the fall that confirmed or eliminated one of your top employment options? Did you grow to a later stage on any competency? Can you provide evidence of this growth? Meet with your coach or career services personnel to discuss the semester and get tips moving forward.

Key Transition Point:

Reflect on Summer Experience

Which of your top employment options have you confirmed or eliminated? Did you grow to a later developmental stage on any competency? What evidence do you have regarding growth to a later stage of your strongest competency?

e. May

- Update your résumé to reflect second-semester grades, GPA, awards, experiences in the competencies you are trying to emphasize, and class rankings.
- Update your writing sample.
- Continue implementing your networking plan and your Roadmap.

6. 2L Summer

- Research and seek out employment, volunteer, and research opportunities for the summer that will help you both explore your most promising employment options and develop the competencies that you want to focus on.
- Reach out to attorneys in areas of law that interest you to schedule informational interviews. Implement your networking plan in general.
- If you have begun your summer work, remember that you need, at the minimum, one supervisor who really knows your work and strongest competencies.
- Continue researching and familiarizing yourself with legal employers in the geographic region and general field in which you want to work. Consider getting lists of alumni from your undergraduate institution and alumni from your law school who are lawyers in that region and field.
- Update your résumé.
- Review your law school's job bank for fall experience opportunities.

7. 3L Year

- Revisit your Roadmap with help from mentors and coaches. Make any revisions or updates you feel are necessary.
- Continue implementing your networking plan.
- Seek out opportunities in the curriculum to develop portfolios of experiences in the competencies you wish to embrace. Ask professors for assessment and feedback so that you acquire evidence that demonstrates

these competencies. Keep track of these experiences so that you have a story to tell about your development of a specific competency.

- Apply for the bar examination in the state where you plan to practice.
- Schedule a meeting with a representative from your school's office dedicated to career and professional development to talk about your postgraduation plans.
- Research and plan your bar examination preparation.
- Check online resources for postgraduation job postings.
- Apply for postgraduation jobs that interest you.
- Consider if you want to pursue trial court judicial clerkships. Trial court judges often begin accepting applications for postgraduate clerkships during the spring semester of the 3L year.

> **Key Transition Point:**
>
> **After Fall Grades**
>
> This is a great time to reflect on what went well and what can be adjusted in the future. Did you have any work or other experiences in the fall that confirmed or eliminated one of your top employment options? Did you grow to a later stage on any competency? Can you provide evidence of this growth? Meet with your coach or career services personnel to discuss the semester and get tips moving forward.

Ongoing

- Schedule a meeting with a senior advisor or coach for review and feedback on execution of your Roadmap.
- Seek out opportunities in the curriculum to develop portfolios of experiences of the competencies you want to emphasize. Ask professors for assessments and feedback so that you create evidence that demonstrates these competencies.
- Continue implementing your networking plan. Set benchmarks or milestones for how many new contacts you will make each semester to implement your Roadmap.

C. Overview of the Preliminary Assessments and the Roadmap Template[3]

As you read the following overview of the six components of the Roadmap template, think about the questions posed. Read through the entire overview to unearth the whole Roadmap process. After you have finished reading, please visit **http://ambar.org/roadmap** to access the preliminary assessments and the

---

[3] Authored by Neil W. Hamilton, Carl J. L. Numrich, Bryan M. Wachter, Emilee Walters, Emily Palmer, and Colin Seaborg.

Roadmap Template. The electronic Roadmap template offers prompted questions (many of which you will see in this overview) and spaces to fill in your answers to each of the questions posed. The electronic Roadmap template is meant to give you all the space you need for your answers and allows you to save (or print) a copy to revisit later in your law school journey.

1. Roadmap Template Component 1: What Is My Value Proposition before Beginning the Roadmap?

The first component of the Roadmap is an initial statement of your value proposition. The value proposition is a clear statement of (1) who you are, (2) what makes you unique, and (3) what value you bring to a potential employer. This initial component should take approximately 15 minutes. It will serve as a starting point as you move throughout this Roadmap and as a primer to get you thinking in terms of what value you offer potential employers. To aid you as you begin articulating your unique value proposition, keep the following things in mind:

- What's your story? What differentiates you?
- What two or three things do you most want an employer to know that you have to offer?
- Try thinking of this in terms of a one-minute elevator speech.
- Visit your school's office dedicated to career and professional development for sample interview questions for additional direction and guidance.

Note: The Roadmap is a project about *you*, not your classmate, friend, or colleague. Do not worry about what other people are doing or how other people are answering these questions. Each Roadmap, by definition, will be different, and each value proposition should be unique to each student's individual experiences, strengths, and aspirations. Remember, you will be receiving feedback and guidance from your employment coach, so do not get hung up about whether you are doing it "right" or not.

2. Roadmap Template Component 2: Where Do I Begin? Self-Evaluation

The second component of the Roadmap template consists of three steps: (1) self-assessment, (2) assessment by others, and (3) a stage development analysis of your strongest competencies. This component is labeled "Where Do I Begin? Self-Evaluation" because it is designed for internal investigation and assessment. The estimated amount of time for this component is two hours, but—like all six components of this Roadmap template—much more time can be dedicated to completing this component if you wish to do so.

An important step in your Roadmap process is to identify your strongest competencies/skills that legal employers and clients want. A closely related step is understanding what evidence you need to gather to show you are at a later stage of development of your strongest competencies/skills. This component will help you achieve these two steps.

a. Step 1: Self-Assessment

This component of the Roadmap template begins with the Self-Directed Learning Readiness Scale (SDLRS) assessment. However, before completing this assessment, you will be asked to self-assess where you are now in terms of the four developmental stages seen in diagram 1 "Levels of Practice Mastery of a Competency" in section I, which include dependent, interested, involved, and self-directed. After you understand these stages, you will determine which developmental stage most accurately reflects you. As section I made clear, growing toward later stages of self-directed learning and ownership over your continuous, proactive development as a lawyer is a foundational competency. The SDLRS assessment, which you will complete after self-assessing your developmental stage, is designed to measure the complex of attitudes, skills, and characteristics that comprise an individual's current level of readiness to manage his or her own learning[4] and will give you good data on your present stage of development on this foundational competency. Answer it as honestly as you can. One weakness of the SDRLS assessment is that it does not provide clear instructions on how to grow toward a later stage of self-oriented learning. This Roadmap process will help you develop toward later stages of ownership over your continuous professional development. Reflecting upon your results and any discrepancies between your initial self-assessment of your stage of development and your results from the SDLRS assessment will also help you to grow toward later stages of development.

The second assessment, "Motivating Interests Assessment," is an individual assessment of your motivating interests and types of work or service that give you the most positive energy. This helps you to begin thinking about your stories and what competencies they demonstrate to the interviewer. This assessment, along with the 360-degree assessment (third assessment in this section), will help you to match your interests and passions to the competencies that employers want. Thus, after completing these assessments, you will be able to reflect upon what your strongest competencies are at this point in time. Step 1 should take approximately one hour.

In addition to the three assessments in this section, you are encouraged to take two optional assessments: the Law Fit Assessment™ and *StrengthsFinder 2.0.* Although the Law Fit Assessment™ is expensive ($95.00 as of the print date of this book), it provides an extremely detailed report on both legal and general careers that best match with your personality. The Law Fit Assessment™ is especially helpful if you are quite unsure of what exactly you want to do with your law degree. *StrengthsFinder 2.0* ($14.95 as of the print date of this book) is a very positive assessment, revealing your top five strengths; however, these

---

[4] GUGLIELMINO & ASSOCIATES, LLC, http://www.lpasdlrs.com (last visited July 13, 2017).

StrengthsFinder strengths may prove difficult to translate into competencies that legal employers look for.

b. Step 2: Self-Assessment of Your Strongest Competencies in Comparison with Assessment by Others (360-Degree Assessment)

The third required assessment tool is a 360-degree assessment tool, which provides you with an external evaluation. It consists of determining who will assess you, getting into contact with them, gathering their completed assessments, and compiling the results and comparing them with your self-assessment. This assessment is divided into two steps, making up steps 2 and 3 of component 2 of the Roadmap template. Together, these two steps should take approximately one hour.

First, you will review the competencies/skills in the list that follows. You will then rank your top **ten** competencies, with 1 being your strongest or most developed competency. You will then proceed to distribute a blank copy of the form to *at least two* people who know your work as a student or employee well enough to give you constructive, honest, and thorough feedback (coaches, mentors, professors, peers, coworkers, employers, supervisors). Finally, you will reflect on the comparison of others' responses and your own evaluation.

You should note that this assessment is only valuable when you receive candid and honest feedback. It is not necessarily helpful to simply distribute this assessment to two close friends who are either biased toward trusting you or are too nice to answer the questions truthfully. It would be extremely helpful for you to distribute this to current or former employers (whether the work was paid or unpaid).

Competencies/Skills

1. Is trustworthy
2. Demonstrates good judgment and problem-solving skills
3. Has good analytical skills
4. Has a great deal of initiative/drive
5. Has a strong work ethic
6. Is effective in written/oral communication
7. Has internalized a responsibility to help others
8. Demonstrates strong relationship skills in helping and serving others
9. Has effective teamwork skills
10. Demonstrates commitment to organization and its values in paid/unpaid work
11. Is well organized in his or her work
12. Is able to manage projects with efficiency, timeliness, and high quality
13. Can be relied upon to get things done
14. Does what he or she says he or she is going to do
15. Has basic doctrinal knowledge needed for practice
16. Is committed to professional development
17. Seeks feedback
18. Reflects on feedback

19. Admits when he or she is wrong
20. Has strong research skills

c. Step 3: Strongest Competencies Stage Development Analysis

After completing step 2, you will choose the two or three competencies that you think are your strongest. Here, you will self-assess those competencies to determine what stage of development you are at. You will evaluate those competencies in both a legal and a nonlegal context and write one or two stories for each context that you could share with an employer to demonstrate evidence of your developmental stage. Once you have determined your two or three strongest competencies, you can use this knowledge to seek experiences that test "fit." This process consists of participating in different types of employment, externships, clinics, and volunteer work to determine where you best fit. These experiences can help to strengthen your top competencies, and even if you do not find the fit to be compatible, you will still develop transferable skills.

3. Roadmap Template Component 3: Getting to Know Areas of Employment That Might Fit Me

The third component focuses on identifying areas of employment that might be of interest to you based on your identified strengths and motivating interests.

The first step asks you to consider the strengths and motivating interests that you identified in the previous components and attempt to align them with potential employers. Then, after conducting further research, you will determine what competencies and transferable skills you think are important to those potential employers. Your list of potential employers might change as you gain experience and information to test your options, but it is critical that you have a list of options that you are testing.

The second step asks you to step back and think creatively about the emerging legal market for the types of employers you are most interested in. It may help to reread "Changing Markets for Legal Services" and "Entrepreneurial Mindset" in section I.C. Component 3 should take approximately one hour and fifteen minutes.

While this component may be time-consuming and challenging for nearly all students, it is crucial for you to identify areas of employment you might be interested in and then, in component 5, focus on how to gain experience to test these interests. In this component, you will answer the following questions:

- Where do you want to live and work?
- What types of people or organizations do you want to serve? (e.g., individuals and families, the disadvantaged, the elderly, organizations such as local or state governments, nonprofits, for-profits, etc.)
- What general field of law most interests you at this time? (e.g., litigation—civil or criminal, commercial, transactional, compliance, government relations, nonlegal work, etc.)

- What type of employers might be the best fit for you? (e.g., legal aid, government, large firm, small firm, business, nonprofit, judicial clerk, etc.)
- Do you have enough experience so that you already have specific practice areas within a field that is of most interest? (e.g., wills and trusts, family law, personal injury, intellectual property, various niches in corporate law, tax, regulated industries, employment law, etc.)
- Do you have any innovative ideas to help employers in these areas be more successful?

  Keep in mind that developing an innovative idea is an exceptional achievement at this time in your development. It should not be considered a defeat if you are unable to do so during this early stage of your career discernment.

4. Roadmap Template Component 4: Defining My Value Proposition for the Employment Options of Greatest Interest to Me

The fourth component requires you to assess all you have completed so far in the Roadmap in order to define a clear value proposition for your most promising employers. It should take approximately thirty minutes. You will describe the value that you bring to potential employers in the employment areas of interest to you by considering the following questions:

- What competencies do you have that bring value to the employer and its clients?
- What is the story you are going to tell about yourself regarding your two or three strongest competencies that adds value to a potential employer?
- What do you offer that will make your potential employer and its clients more successful?
- Keep in mind what evidence you have to support your value proposition that could be shared when a potential employer asks follow-up questions. Focus particularly on the top two or three points you want the employer to remember about you after you leave an interview.

5. Roadmap Template Component 5: Planning My Remaining Time in Law School

The fifth component asks you to conduct prospective thinking about how to best utilize your remaining time in law school to gain experiences that will permit you to confirm, eliminate, or add to your possible employment options; to use the curriculum and other experiences of law school to develop your strongest competencies; and also to develop good evidence that you have these competencies. The simple act of developing a plan for your remaining time in law school is evidence of the competencies of initiative and commitment to professional development. Reading section II.E before completing this section will aid you in developing your curriculum plan. Additionally, this component is best completed with senior input (academic advisor, coach, representative from career or professional development office, mentor, professor, supervisor for research or upper-level writing, etc.). If your school does not provide you with a coach, it is strongly recommended that you reach out and get into contact with someone who could be your coach. This step should take approximately one hour.

- What specific curricular steps will help you grow to later stages of development on your strongest competencies?
- What specific extracurricular steps will help you with this challenge?
- What experiences do you have to help you "make the case" for your strongest competencies?

6. Roadmap Template Component 6: Effectively Communicating My Value Proposition

The sixth component simply asks you to reach out to the career and professional development office at your law school and discuss how to best communicate the value proposition that you have developed through this project. How will you communicate your value proposition through the employment-search process? How can you incorporate your message into your résumé, cover letters, interviews, and reference letters? Section II.F can assist you in answering these questions.

a. Value Proposition

Articulating your value proposition is not part of any *one* specific component because your value proposition will—and should—evolve throughout the Roadmap process. It will continue to evolve as you gain experience. Articulating a strong, personal value proposition is your goal; therefore, it represents the conclusion to the Roadmap. You should attempt to answer the question: "What is the strongest value I bring to an employer (what is my story)?" Different students will be at different levels of self-awareness and market awareness. However, every student is capable of producing an initial value proposition and then seeking feedback on it and testing it.

b. Keep in Mind

While completing the Roadmap, you should keep in mind that best judgment is essential while completing each component. The Roadmap is the product of that best judgment at this present time and is a constantly evolving process. The strengths and motivators identified through self-assessment may not find a great employment fit immediately given the job market at the time. Also, it may take several completions of the Roadmap (as you gain more experience) throughout a career to discern the best fit for employment at any particular stage of your career. While in law school, however, you should seek "windows" of experience through which to look and improve discernment while building your Roadmap.

D. Accessing the Preliminary Assessments and the Roadmap Template

For the template for student who do not yet have post-graduation employment, click on **http://ambar.org/roadmap** to electronically access the instructions on how to complete the necessary assessments as you move through your Roadmap template. Additional assessments that are recommended, but not required, as well as the instructions for those assessments, may also be found by following the link for the template for student who already have post-graduation employment, click on. Finally, the Roadmap template is available to you electronically so that you may have all of the space you need to craft and write your plan.

E. Ideas on How to Make Effective Use of the 2L and 3L Curriculum

In your Roadmap template, you have identified your motivating interests and top strengths and, based on your current experience, made a best judgment on how your interests and strengths match the competencies that employers and clients want. You have made a tentative best judgment on your top three employment options at this time and your value proposition for those employers.

The main goals in planning your 2L and 3L academic years and the summers after the 1L and 2L years are as follows:

1. Ensure that you meet your school's graduation requirements and maximize the probability that you pass the bar examination;
2. Grow toward later stages of development with respect to your strongest competencies;
3. Obtain persuasive evidence that your target employers will accept regarding your growth in (2) above and your value proposition to them; and
4. Gain experience that will test whether your top employment options are a good fit for you.

1. Goal 1: Graduation Requirements and Passing the Bar Examination

With respect to the goal of ensuring you meet graduation requirements and maximizing the probability that you pass the bar examination, first go through all the graduation requirements and map out in writing the next four semesters and two summers of law school. In what specific semesters and summers will you complete the graduation requirements? Consider also the prerequisites for the upper-level elective courses you want to take and how often these electives are offered so that you have the proper sequence of courses during your 2L and 3L years.

Note that many law schools have an upper-level writing requirement. Seriously consider doing the upper-level paper (or a long paper in a seminar) in the third or fourth semester of law school so that you have a strong example (and evidence from your supervising professor) of your research, writing, and analytical competencies to show potential employers. If you meet all deadlines with good-quality work product, this is also an example of good project management. If you are applying for appellate clerkships, then by March of your 2L year, you should have one or two longer written projects as evidence of your research, writing, and analytical competencies.

Next, write down all the subjects that are tested in the state where you intend to take the bar examination. Decide whether you will take a course on all of the bar examination subjects or nearly all of them (and leave a few bar examination subjects to be covered by the bar review course and your independent study). Seek counsel on these choices from your law school's academic support staff person or a knowledgeable student services professional. The staff person will have the best judgment on whether you should take a course in all of the bar examination subjects and, if you decide not to do so, which bar examination subjects are less difficult to study on your own.

Note, if you are ranked in the lower 30–40 percent of your class, you have a higher probability of failing the bar examination. You need the counsel of an academic support person to draft a written plan of how to use your remaining time in law school most effectively to maximize your probability of passing the bar. Seriously consider taking a course on each of the bar examination subjects.

You should add to your written map of the next four semesters and two summers when you will take courses on the bar examination subjects.

2. Goal 2: Growth toward Later Stages of Development with Respect to Your Strongest Competencies

Write down the two or three strongest competencies you identified in your Roadmap template. Read the relevant part in section III on each of these competencies, and then make a best judgment on the stage of development in each competency, in a legal context, that you are in now. Ask an experienced professor/lawyer/judge who knows your work well if they agree with your self-assessment of your current stage of development on each competency.

Note, in choosing your two or three strongest competencies, you should consider whether to include your ownership of continuous, proactive professional development (including initiative and the habits of actively seeking feedback and reflection) as one of your strongest competencies. If you actively follow the timeline in section II.B and implement the Roadmap, including a written networking plan, over your remaining time in law school, you will demonstrate later-stage development of professional development.

The challenge is to use your remaining time in law school, including the summers, to gain experience that helps you to grow to the next level of development in your strongest competencies. Consider the formal curriculum first. Historically, law school curriculum in the 2L and 3L years is structured to emphasize doctrinal subjects and concentrations, with upper-level courses fostering more complex legal and policy analysis, legal research, and written and oral communication. It may take some work to analyze the upper-level curriculum to find courses that offer experience and assessment of the competencies that you want to emphasize, such as teamwork or project management. Look especially at experiential courses like externships, simulation courses (including moot court), and clinics. Some doctrinal courses may be hybrids that require competencies like teamwork. Include supervised research with longer papers as a project management challenge. Remember, if your law school offers a course on market changes affecting legal services, take it; you can then apply the principles you learn to your target employers.

Be strategic with extracurricular experiences in your remaining time in law school. How will those experiences help you grow to the next stage of development in the competencies you are emphasizing? What evidence will those experiences provide to show that you are at a later stage of development for a particular competency? Extracurricular experiences include, but are not limited to clerkships (paid or unpaid), pro bono and service work, student organizations, and work with the organized Bar. Rather than create a laundry list of such activities, think strategically about activities that will be the most effective evidence of growth in one of your strongest competencies. For example, if one of your strongest competencies is project management in teams, seek a leadership position in a student organization, and define a specific new project that the team can accomplish in a specific time period. Is it possible for an experienced lawyer/judge/professor/staff member to vouch for your achievement? Creating and implementing a written networking plan to develop long-term relationships with experienced professors, staff, lawyers, and judges who observe your strongest competencies is very important.

Finally, think strategically about which two professors you will ask for references, and be certain to take enough classes or gain enough other experiences with each of them so that they both have substantial evidence of your strongest competencies. Also, think strategically about relationships and references from two experienced lawyers/judges outside of the law school who will have substantial evidence of your strongest competencies. Ideally, you will have two excellent inside references and two excellent outside references who have good evidence of your strongest competencies by the end of your fourth semester of law school.

3. Goal 3: Collection of Persuasive Evidence That Your Target Employers Will Accept about Your Growth to Later Stages of Development in Your Strongest Competencies

Section II.F discusses the creation of portfolios for two or three of your strongest competencies.

4. Goal 4: Experience That Will Test Whether Your Top Employment Options Are a Good Fit for You

Write down the top three employment options you identified in your Roadmap template. You want to be as strategic as possible to use your remaining time in law school to gain experiences that could test any one of the subquestions that informed your choice of your top three employment options:

1. Geographic location
2. What type of people/organizations do you want to serve?
3. What general field of work most interests you?
4. What type of employer most interests you?
5. What type of specific practice area within a general field most interests you? (If you have no legal experience, this question can be answered after you get experience.)

The process of testing answers to any of these five subquestions as they inform your top three employment options necessitates seeking a variety of experiences where you use your strongest competencies both in the formal curriculum and in paid or unpaid experiences outside of the law school. Note that even if an experience proves not to be a good fit, you still may be able to cross out one of the employment options you were considering, and the experience can still help you to grow toward a later stage of development of your strongest competencies (transferable skills). Note also that your written networking plan to develop long-term relationships can help with experiences that provide answers to the questions above and test one or more of your top employment options.

5. Goal 5: A Written Map for Your Remaining Time in Law School

Make a tentative map for *each* period of time you have remaining in law school, including each semester and summers. List the courses you will take and the extracurricular experiences you will have in each time period to achieve goals 1–4 listed at the beginning of this part. At each key transition point in the timeline, revisit your top three employment options and your strongest competencies, reflect on what you have learned, see your coach, and make needed changes to your employment options and top strengths. Make necessary updates to this map for each period of time remaining.

F. Creating Portfolios for Two or Three of Your Strongest Competencies

In your Roadmap template, you identified two or three of your strongest competencies and your best stories that provide evidence of your later-stage development of those competencies. These are your principal "transferable skills" that legal employers want, as discussed in section I.

You need to think strategically about developing evidence of your strongest competencies that legal employers will value as you navigate your remaining time in law school. As you gain experiences both in law school and outside of law school, developing a portfolio on your two or three strongest competencies is both an important and smart choice. The portfolio will serve as an easily accessible collection of stories that you can use to provide evidence of competencies you have intentionally developed. By organizing a portfolio, you are giving yourself an advantage when it comes time for an interview; also, the simple act of creating and maintaining a portfolio signals a potential employer of your intentionality about professional development.

The concept of building a portfolio is initially a daunting task—it seems abstract and difficult to imagine, and it seems to imply an overwhelming amount of work ahead of you. This is a misconception of what building a portfolio really means. An easy way to think about a portfolio is as "a 'collection of evidence' of student learning"[5] or "purposeful collections of evidence used by students to document and reflect on learning outcomes."[6] Portfolios are a simple way of organizing evidence of your hard work over the three years of law school and the years preceding law school. Essentially, portfolios are stories that you can tell when someone asks, "Can you tell me when and how you have developed this competency?"

There is no single way to build a portfolio. For our purposes, the portfolio is not a formally reviewed document but rather a tool designed to help students as they create their Roadmap plan and seek out employment. Therefore, the most helpful style of portfolio for law students is the "Shopping Trolley" style currently used in the medical community.

This model is an informal collection of "a body of evidence about [your] learning."[7] Students can compose their portfolios on their strongest competencies from anything that has been used or produced throughout their learning, which might include any of the following:

- Course work, including papers
- Other education/training activities
- Experiential learning, including externships, clinics, and simulations
- Work activities (with care about confidential client information)
- Achievements

---

[5] Sharon Buckly, Jamie Coleman & Khalid Khan, *Best Evidence on the Educational Effects of Undergraduate Portfolios*, 7 CLINICAL TCHR. 188 (2010).

[6] Elaine F. Dannefer, *The Portfolio Approach to Competency-Based Assessment at the Cleveland Clinic Lerner College of Medicine*, 82 ACAD. MED. 495–96 (2007).

[7] *E&T Network Event 28 June 2010*, LONDON PHARMACY EDUC. & TRAINING, http://www.lpet.nhs.uk/Portals/0/Documents/Professional%20Development/Learning%20Events/ET%20network/Portfolios%20as%20Competence%20assessment%20tools%20Handout.pdf (last visited Nov. 17, 2014).

- Reflections
- Records of meetings with mentors, coaches, and so forth

It is important to include the best evidence of your strongest competencies that legal employers will find most helpful on a hiring decision. The 2016 Educating Tomorrow's Lawyers (ETL) study (with responses from 24,000 lawyers), discussed in section I, asked respondents what criteria were most helpful in the decision to hire an attorney. Table 8 has the thirteen most helpful criteria.[8]

While the ETL survey found that all the criteria were helpful in making a hiring decision, the six most helpful criteria were all related to practical experience. It is very important your portfolio includes evidence of your practical experiences that have been evaluated by experienced lawyers, judges, and professors who have seen your work in experiential situations. Their recommendations will be the best evidence that you are at a later stage of development on your strongest competencies. You should tell your mentors, coaches, and supervisors what

Table 8   The Thirteen Most Helpful Hiring Criteria for Employers Hiring Students for Postgraduation Employment

Hiring Criteria	% of Respondents Answering "Somewhat Helpful" or "Very Helpful"
Legal employment	88.3%
Recommendations from practitioners or judges	81.9%
Legal externship	81.6%
Other experiential education	79.4%
Life experience between college and law school	78.3%
Participation in law school clinic	77.3%
Law school courses in a particular specialty	70.3%
Recommendations from professors	63.3%
Class rank	62.5%
Law school attended	61.1%
Extracurricular activities	58.7%
Ties to a particular geographic location	54.3%
Law review experience	51.2%

---

[8] Alli Gerkman & Logan Cornett, *Educating Tomorrow's Lawyers*, FOUNDATIONS FOR PRACTICE: HIRING THE WHOLE LAWYER: EXPERIENCE MATTERS 7–8 (2016).

competencies you are emphasizing and ask for help in developing them to the next level.

Note that the Roadmap process itself—where you are asking for and receiving regular feedback from experienced lawyers, judges, and professors on your progress regarding your strongest competencies—is excellent evidence of your initiative/drive and commitment to professional development in an experiential situation.

The portfolio is different from a checklist-style document, such as the timeline previously visited in section II.B. This is in agreement with the medical community's choice not to consider "tick-list" style documents as portfolios because "they [do] not require the student to engage with the material."[9] Reflection is required as you build this document, and you should consciously select your most persuasive and specific examples of your strongest competencies. Experiences with competencies where you sought feedback, an expert assessed your performance, and, after reflection, you improved on a competency are particularly valuable. In your portfolio, be sure to include your plan to grow toward the next stage of development for each of your strongest competencies.

Each portfolio is unique to the student creating it because the portfolio exists for the sole purpose of personal reflection and as a record of experiences gained throughout law school and the years preceding law school. Students should understand portfolios as opportunities to organize their experiences and evidence of their strongest competencies in one easily accessible document, not as a daunting and endlessly time-consuming chore.

DEVELOPING YOUR STRONGEST COMPETENCIES

A. Introduction[1]

Let's take the combination of meeting a law school's graduation requirements and passing the bar examination as two important indicators of minimum competency to practice law (and also factor in the reality that nearly all bar examination failures come from the bottom third of the class, and most of those initial failures will pass on the second try). Law school graduation and bar passage signal that the vast majority of law students are demonstrating capability of the basic competencies taught in the required curriculum: doctrinal knowledge in the foundational areas of law, legal analysis, legal research, and some experience with effective written and oral communication.

Section III has chapters on the other competencies that legal employers want beyond the basic competencies taught in the required curriculum. The challenge you face is that few students can tell a persuasive story about how their strengths with competencies other than those taught in the required curriculum meet the needs of the legal employers whom the student has targeted. Refer back to section I's discussion of the empirical studies of the competency models for legal employers for a list of these other competencies. Section III organizes these other competencies into two groups, following table 7 in section I. Group 1 has chapters on the competencies relating to "Ownership of Continuous Proactive Professional Development over a Career." Group 2 has chapters on the

---

[1] Authored by Neil W. Hamilton.

competencies relating to "Internalization of Deep Responsibilities to Others" (the client, the team, the employing organization, and the legal system). A list of the chapters within each of the two groups is as follows:

Group 1 Chapters: Ownership of Continuous Proactive Profesional Development

- B. Initiative, Drive, Work Ethic, and Commitment to Professional Development
- C. Building Self-Confidence through Creative Problem Solving When "I Don't Know What I'm Doing"
- D. Project Management Skills: How Law Students Can Learn and Implement the Skills Employers Value

Group 2 Chapters: Internalization of Deep Responsibilities to Others

- E. Commitment to Others
- F. Trustworthiness: Building Lasting Professional Relationships
- G. Dedication and Responsiveness to Clients
- H. The Basics of Good Judgment to Help Clients
- I. The Basics of Teamwork
- J. Commitment to the Employing Organization
- K. Building Relationships Based on Trust through Networking
- L. Cross-Cultural Competency: Developing Cultural Competencies for the Changing Workplace
- M. Listen to Persuade: How Attentiveness Leads to Value

The chapters in section III will help you understand how to gain experience and develop evidence of these other competencies that will emphasize your strengths and differentiate yourself. These chapters will also give you a vocabulary that legal employers use to describe the competencies they want so that you can tell your story of adding value in the language that legal employers will understand.

Many of the chapters also include a self-assessment and a 360-degree assessment to provide you with feedback and reflection that will help you develop a competency. Read about developing good evidence of a competency by using portfolios in section II.F, "Creating Portfolios for Two or Three of Your Strongest Competencies." The key to remember in behavioral interviews is that you must have stories, not about what you will do, but what you have done regarding specific competencies. For each of your strongest competencies, know your best story, your second-best story, and so forth., that will resonate with the particular employer. At the conclusion of each chapter in this section, you will be prompted to access a Reflection Dashboard at **http://ambar.org/roadmap**. You should complete this exercise to develop a better understanding of what developmental stage you are at for that specific competency and what steps you will take to grow to the next stage.

Group 1: Competencies Related to "Ownership of Continuous Proactive Professional Development over a Career"

B. Initiative, Drive, Work Ethic, and Commitment to Professional Development
C. Building Self-Confidence through Creative Problem Solving When "I Don't Know What I Am Doing"
D. Project Management Skills: How Law Students Can Learn and Implement the Skills Employers Value

Indiana Law professor Will D. Henderson emphasizes that the "A" players in law firms' talent management systems "typically earn that designation because of their self-directed ability to continuously learn and adapt."[2] In conversations about associates in large firms, senior lawyers focus on the degree to which an associate goes "above and beyond" in taking ownership over the associate's projects and his or her role on the team and in the firm itself.

A recent empirical study of lawyers who made partner in a firm in contrast to those who did not found the lawyers who made partner "were masters of their fate; they tend to strategically plan both their day-to-day work and their careers. As a group, they tend to make and stick to plans more than lawyers who did not make partner."[3] Fast-tracking partners "are more likely to 'tune' their plans as they encounter new information. They seek out constructive feedback and use it to improve their work."[4] The same study concludes that "[f]lourishing is also enabled by something we call 'focused ownership'—taking initiative and ownership to solve problems and accomplish goals."[5]

The next three chapters look at the competencies that legal employers value with respect to your ownership of your professional development.

B. Initiative, Drive, Work Ethic, and Commitment to Professional Development[6]

Initiative is one of the competencies that legal employers most highly value in a prospective employee. Initiative itself, however, is part of a larger family of overlapping competencies that include drive, work ethic, and professional development. These four competencies, in turn, relate back to others, such as entrepreneurial mindset and trustworthiness, making this family of competencies a key component of professional success.

---

[2] William D. Henderson, *Talent Systems for Law Firms* Prof. Devel. Quarterly 1, 7 (Feb. 2017).
[3] Lori Berman, Heather Bock & Juliet Aiken, Accelerating Lawyer Success: How to Make Partner, Stay Healthy, and Flourish in a Law Firm 7–8 (2016).
[4] *Id.* at 26.
[5] *Id.* at 29.
[6] Authored by Neil W. Hamilton and Catherine Underwood.

Initiative is a proactive approach to improving or enhancing the situation at hand.[7] It requires an ability to see a problem, an area for improvement, or an opportunity to add value and then to act on it—without being told and sometimes without seeking permission. Today, employers are looking for people with potential who will search for new experiences, knowledge, and candid feedback.[8] All of these are indicators of initiative. Students who are proactive about their professional development or otherwise demonstrate an entrepreneurial spirit are also exhibiting initiative.[9] *Drive* gives a person the determination, grit, and resilience to follow through on his or her initiative, as it entails a systematic effort toward a goal or idea. Once a student uses initiative to identify a gap and how to fill it, it is the persistence and determination associated with drive that allow her or him to see the project through to completion. Like drive, **work ethic** connotes a strong sense of responsibility not just to get work done as needed but also to "go the extra mile."[10] Reliability is at the heart of work ethic; a person with a good work ethic is consistently reliable as well as hardworking, always prepared, and willing to follow through. As "Trustworthiness: Building Lasting Professional Relationships" points out, reliability over time is a key element of trustworthiness. Finally, **professional development** is a commitment to growing in excellence in the competencies needed in one's field. This includes an increase in both technical skills of the field as well as all of the necessary interpersonal competencies. Thus, professional development requires students to develop not just the technical legal competencies but also the other key competencies that legal employers need. One tool that young professionals have available to them for this development is the input of more experienced veterans; ideally, aspiring attorneys should be constantly seeking feedback from those who have more knowledge of the field and then adjusting their strategy accordingly.

In both hiring and ongoing assessment, legal employers emphasize an internalized commitment to professional development toward excellence at all the competencies needed for effective and successful lawyering. This drive toward excellence is also one of the key differentiating competencies that separate a "high-performing" associate from others.

An internalized drive toward excellence flows from a student's and lawyer's internalized moral core characterized by deep responsibilities to others, particularly the client. William Sullivan, the codirector of all five Carnegie Foundation studies of higher education for the professions, recognizes the importance of this bedrock foundation of an internalized moral core of deep responsibility for others. Sullivan believes that the "chief formative challenge" is to help students entering

---

[7] Lawyer Metrics, University of St. Thomas Structured Panel Interview 2 (2014) (on file with the author).

[8] Claudio Fernández-Aráoz, *The Big Idea: 21st-Century Talent Spotting*, HARV. BUS. REV. (June 2014), *available at* http://hbr.org/2014/06/21st-century-talent-spotting/ar/1.

[9] *See* "Entrepreneurial Mindset" in section I.

[10] Lawyer Metrics, *supra* note 7, at 2.

a profession to change from thinking like students, in which they learn and apply routine techniques to solve well-structured problems, toward the acceptance and internalization of responsibility for others (particularly the person served) and for the students' own development toward excellence as a practitioner at all of the competencies of the profession.[11] As a patient or client, we need to trust that our physician or lawyer is dedicated above all else to caring for us with all of his or her ability.[12] This is essentially a fiduciary disposition, using *fiduciary* in the general meaning of "founded on trustworthiness." Each student must internalize a fiduciary disposition for others, particularly the client.[13]

Note that Sullivan includes internalization of responsibility for the student's own development toward excellence in all of the competencies of the profession, along with the internalization of responsibility to others, particularly the client. The two responsibilities go hand in glove since a fiduciary disposition toward others requires the fiduciary to develop excellence at all the capacities required to fulfill his or her responsibility for others. To paraphrase Samuel Johnson, a fiduciary's service to others without excellence in the competencies required is weak and useless, and excellence in the competencies required without a fiduciary disposition to serve others is dangerous.[14]

Tables 9 and 10 show how a potential employer evaluates qualities like initiative and commitment to professional development from an applicant's résumé. Such knowledge is supplemented in interviews by statements such as, "Describe a time when you thought you needed to learn a new skill or task and you did" or "Talk about a time when you had a vision of how to improve something and carried it out." These questions are aimed at assessing initiative. Other questions, such as, "Tell me about a time when you went above and beyond the call of duty" or "Talk about a time when you handled multiple commitments," are aimed at uncovering evidence of drive or work ethic. Competencies like professional development are highlighted by having evidence of plans such as this Roadmap—a written plan for professional success that you are in the process of implementing.

It is important that you take time to develop evidence of initiative, drive, work ethic, and professional development during law school. This Roadmap is an excellent beginning: recent surveys have found that it is a helpful tool in moving students forward in their plans for employment.[15] The Roadmap demonstrates

---

11 WILLIAM M. SULLIVAN, *Foreword* to TEACHING MEDICAL PROFESSIONALISM, at xi, xv (Richard Creuss et al. eds., 2009).

12 *See Id.* at ix.

13 For practical ideas on how to implement this, *see* "Dedication and Responsiveness to Clients" in section III.

14 SAMUEL JOHNSON, RASSELAS ch. 41 (1759).

15 Neil W. Hamilton, *Law-Firm Competency Models and Student Professional Success: Building on a Foundation of Professional Formation/Professionalism*, 11 U. ST. THOMAS L.J. 597 (2013), *available at* http://ssrn.com/abstract=2271410.

your initiative in planning for the future, your drive to complete the Roadmap and carry it out, your work ethic by doing the job well and reliably, and your commitment to professional development as you deliberately set metrics to monitor progress and seek—and reflect on—feedback on the Roadmap from veterans. A networking plan would provide even more evidence of these competencies.[16]

Take time to go through each of these four competencies and reflect on how they have been a part of your own experience thus far and how you can use them to your best professional advantage in the future. You could likely begin with examples from high school of times when you took initiative on a project or in starting a club. Then, as you trace your steps through college, work experience you may have had, and now law school, you will hopefully see patterns of initiative, drive, work ethic, and professional development that you will be able to draw upon when presenting yourself to potential employers.

In general, students do not often present positive evidence of these competencies; thus, employers infer them from the résumé, cover letter, and references a student provides. Employers can infer initiative from the following pieces of a résumé or portfolio:

- Growing up on the family farm
- Achieving Eagle Scout status
- Serving in the military
- Demonstrating a record of initiative in previous employment
- Waitressing or holding a sales job
- Starting a business
- Excelling at sports
- Excelling at art or music
- Training for and completing a marathon
- Assuming increasing responsibility at work
- Having and implementing a written plan
- Seeking counsel and feedback from other, more experienced people and implementing their suggestions
- Overcoming hardships/adversity
- Having references that can speak to specific examples of initiative
- Demonstrating multiple commitments and successful involvement in each commitment

A useful window into how some employers are evaluating initiative is shown in table 9, which is a compilation of data from Vinson & Elkins and two of the largest law firms in Minnesota.

---

[16] For more direction on a networking plan, *see* "Building Relationships Based on Trust through Networking" in section III.

Table 9 Firm Models Evaluating Initiative and Drive in Associates[17]

Junior associate (1–3 years)	• Performs assigned work in a manner that meets expectations • Makes commitments and sacrifices necessary to complete assignments within the required time and to acquire skills to develop as an attorney • Seeks out work when not busy • Seeks assignments that will enhance the associate's professional development • Demonstrates initiative and personal responsibility necessary to develop successfully • Displays ability and efforts to develop professional and personal relationships within the firm necessary for successful development
Mid-level associate (4–6 years)	In addition: • Seeks ways to contribute to the achievement of significant project/client/firm outcomes, not just to complete specific tasks • Accepts responsibility for identifying and meeting client needs and objectives • Demonstrates ability and willingness to rally others to meeting the tasks at hand • Shows initiative in anticipating needs and solving problems
Senior associate (7 or more years)	In addition: • Acts as a steward of the firm while actively seeking ways to add significant value by identifying and capitalizing on new opportunities for growth or improvement • Makes sacrifices and commitments necessary to satisfy client demands • Seeks out opportunities to lead projects and take part in firm/department administrative and marketing activities • Provides leadership and example to other attorneys to assist in meeting the firm's mission

Focusing on professional development, table 10 provides information on how the three firm models discussed in table 9 assess this particular competency in their associates.

Our hope in giving students this information is twofold: first, that you will be more aware of the importance of initiative, drive, work ethic, and professional development in the workplace and can identify more readily what employers are looking for; and second, that you will self-assess where you are developmentally

---

[17] Synthesis of data from two of the largest Minnesota law firms and Vinson & Elkins.

Table 10 How Firms Assess Professional Development in Associates[18]

Junior associate (1–3 years)	• Attends mandatory training programs appropriate to practice area • Uses continuing legal education (CLE) or other sources to supplement knowledge of intended practice areas as necessary • Shows willingness to undertake firm committee tasks/assignments • Willing to assist in speaking and/or writing engagements for professional associations • Willing to work hard and demonstrate a learning mindset
Mid-level associate (4–6 years)	In addition: • Exhibits engagement in the practice of law • Claims assignments as own and is accountable for those engagements • Instills consistent and sustainable levels of confidence and trust in other attorneys and clients as a result of quality of work product and interpersonal interactions • Seeks areas of expertise within practice area and develops knowledge and experience in such area
Senior associate (7 or more years)	In addition: • Exhibits enthusiastic dedication to client service and professional involvement • Demonstrates a willingness to learn the business of the practice of law and law-firm management • Demonstrates a commitment to developing the human resources of the firm, including training, development, and mentoring of less senior associates and paralegals • Makes a significant individual contribution in time and attention to the practice of law, including a willingness to devote extra effort when needed and to effectively deal with difficult legal and client situations and problems • Actively participates in firm committee activities and/or other professional development activities, such as giving in-house or outside CLE programs or writing articles or providing legal updates

with regard to initiative, drive, and commitment to professional development. What are your best stories of initiative, drive, and commitment to professional development? After completing this chapter, you will be able to take a closer look at yourself and where you fall along the spectrum. Seeking feedback from trusted mentors should further help in this self-assessment. Such introspection offers an excellent opportunity for you to set goals and plan how you will move forward. It also allows you to reflect on areas you have already mastered and

---

[18] Synthesis of data from two of the largest Minnesota law firms and Vinson & Elkins.

should highlight to potential employers. Note that a student who creates and implements a Roadmap process using the timeline in section II.B is demonstrating several of these important competencies.

Now that you have read "Initiative, Drive, Work Ethic, and Commitment to Professional Development," complete the Reflection Dashboard at **http://ambar .org/roadmap** to develop a better understanding of what developmental stage you are at and what steps you will take to grow to the next stage.

C. Building Confidence through Creative Problem Solving When "I Don't Know What I Am Doing"[19]

Having confidence that you can do work competently is not a competency specifically listed by legal employers, but it is very important as a foundation for the work you do. If you have ever begun a legal research project for a professor or supervisor and felt unsure of your skills, you are not alone. Feeling and communicating confidence in your own work product is an exceedingly important attitude and skill that must be formed over time. Confidence is crucial to your growth as an effective lawyer. A 2016 empirical study of lawyers who made partner emphasized:

> Flourishing lawyers—like lawyers who make partner—feel in control of their lives. They are not passive beings in the world; rather they know that they can take control of situations . . . for example in our story, 75% of flourishing lawyers said they prefer challenging tasks over tasks they know they can accomplish. Only 44% of the non-flourishing lawyers said that.[20]

Law students and beginning lawyers, however, tend to feel a lack of confidence in their skills and work product. For example, a 2L reflected upon her experience in a placement at a large corporation in the Twin Cities in the following way:

> Each time I received a new research project, my supervisor requested my answer by the next day. I was determined to meet my deadline, so I would research and research, write a short memo, and give her my best guess. But that is exactly what it felt like—a total guess at the answer. I was always thinking that if I just had 3 more days, I would give her an amazing answer. But I only had 5 or 6 hours. So I just gave my best guess. And it always felt like I was cobbling together answers that may be entirely wrong!

Note that essentially all new lawyers must answer a difficult question, "How do I build confidence when I don't know what I am doing?" Even veteran lawyers face totally new situations with substantial complexity where the veteran

---

[19] Authored by Neil Hamilton and Chris Clark.
[20] BERMAN ET AL., *supra* note 3.

may feel "I don't know what I am doing," but the veteran has confidence in her basic problem-solving skills and knows that, if needed, with the help of others, "I will figure this out." A veteran in-house counsel was asked to remark on the confidence issue inherent in judgment calls while practicing. He responds:

> The more experienced you get, the more comfortable you become in telling yourself that you are really just cobbling together this whole thing. Your facts are changing, the clock is ticking, and you have to give an answer. It's your best call in that situation. And sometimes, you feel that you have no idea. But you do. You have an idea and you have to offer your best one. The main issue is that you feel insecure about the call you make, but everyone else around you thinks you have all the right answers already at hand, by nature of your title.[21]

Law professor Neil Hamilton's response to the story above was the following: "It's always best judgment, given the time and resources available. And it doesn't change for a senior lawyer. We have the experience of professionally masking our uncertainty and nervousness, but we are still just giving our best judgment in complex problems where there is some significant degree of uncertainty."[22]

One more example of the commonality of lawyers' uncertainties in the context of their practice shows that this phenomenon is global. A 2012 study of new Australian lawyers revealed that developing professional judgment means that a lawyer must learn to deal with the uncertainties of practice. The study stated: "Professional work is often complex and uncertain. The everyday practice of law is frequently characterized by risk management, novel problems, the cautious and strategic use of words, and constantly changing facts and issues. In this environment, uncertainty is often one of few constants."[23]

It should be clear by now that all professionals—not just lawyers—face this dilemma of feeling confident in their problem-solving skills. Doctors Sean Hilton and Henry Slotnick comment that all professionals must develop the skill of creative problem solving in the face of ill-structured new problems. These problems are "complex and ambiguous, described with incomplete information, requiring multiple perspectives, and resulting in multiple possible solutions all demanding to be evaluated."[24] Law students, beginning lawyers, and veterans alike must build confidence in their skill of "best judgment under the circumstances, and going forward with uncertainties."[25]

---

[21] E-mail from Andrew Pugh, Associate General Counsel, Children's Hospital & Clinics of MN, to author (July 7, 2015, 14:00 CST) (on file with author).

[22] Interview with Neil Hamilton, Professor of Law, Director of the Holloran Center for Ethical Leadership in the Professions, University of St. Thomas School of Law, in Minneapolis, Minn. (June 15, 2015).

[23] Vivien Holmes et al., *Practising Professionalism: Observations from an Empirical Study of New Australian Lawyers*, 15 LEGAL ETHICS 29, 46 (2012).

[24] Sean Hilton & Henry Slotnick, *Proto-professionalism: How Professionalism Occurs across the Continuum of Medical Education*, 39 MED. EDUC. 58, 62 (No. 1 2005).

[25] *Id.*

Hopefully, you are noticing that developing this confidence and good judgment is a process and a journey, not simply a checkmark on your skills portfolio.[26] You are learning to "fake it till you make it," so to speak. But "making it" is different from what you may have thought earlier. It is not certainty; it is growing a sense of confidence that under conditions of substantial uncertainty when working with others, including the client, "I can figure out reasonable solutions." As such, this is a process of acculturation into a confidence that comes primarily through experiences with problem solving. Through experiences and reflection, you will learn that you have the skills to solve problems competently, and you will in effect gain the requisite confidence.

This process has begun for you in a myriad of ways for many years, and it will only continue to grow and increase during your remaining time in law school. You are becoming a competent lawyer, of course. You have effective written communication skills—you finished law school applications, you were accepted, and you are now completing the arduous law school curriculum. You know how to solve problems—you chose a particular career path and a particular law school. You then began school, learned a specialized legal language, and crafted meaningful new friendships. You have some knowledge of substantive and procedural law—you can investigate facts, spot issues, and generally apply law to the problem at hand. You can certainly research the law and have at hand the most up-to-date methods of legal research. You are forming meaningful strategic relationships with experienced lawyers, and these people will buttress your confidence by answering your questions and helping you work through challenging situations.

You have already accomplished a great deal, all of which evinces your competence to not only complete the job but to do it exceedingly well. So, how can you gain the confidence to trust your competence and take pride in your work product? In other words, how can you develop inside of yourself the attitude of sufficient expertise?

We will, therefore, set out for you the ways in which you can gain experiences during your time in law school to cultivate the confidence you will need in your practice of law.

1. The Challenge

So why exactly do law students and beginning lawyers feel this lack of confidence in their skills and work product? There may be any number of reasons a person lacks confidence in his or her skills, but three common themes emerge: (1) not understanding your existing narrative of strengths, especially problem solving in new situations; (2) misunderstanding the expectations laid upon you; and (3) not realizing that all lawyers have faced the challenge that "I don't know what I am doing," and the solution is to be patient, to stay focused, and to seek counsel from experienced professionals.

---

[26] *See* "The Basics of Good Judgment" in section III.

a. Not Understanding Your Existing Narrative of Strengths

At this point in your career, you have likely attended at least 16 years of school. You have had countless learning experiences with new material and new challenges, and you have solved those challenges. You have learned to identify issues, research, and find answers. You are learning to solve problems when presented with a new situation or challenge. For example, you managed to figure out how to navigate college in the early months of your freshman year and law school in your first semester. Whether with employers, teachers, or friends, you have succeeded, failed, and learned from each experience during high school, college, and now law school. Furthermore, you bring to law school an existing narrative of certain skills. For example, you can read critically, you can analyze, you can write and speak effectively, and you can handle projects from your class work. All of these are just from your experience in the formal curriculum. From your life experience, you may have also learned how to fix things, manage projects, speak a foreign language, build strategic relationships, and intuit other persons very well. Have you ever had an experience in life where you did not think initially that you could do something, but you did it anyway?

This is to say, you gained a number of skills throughout your experiences. It simply takes renarrating your story in order to bear witness to those skills. For example, while in college, perhaps you gathered a group of friends to take a road trip to Colorado and climb mountains. You researched the specific mountains to climb, learned the permitting process, designated drivers and the specific roads to use, and determined pricing for everyone. If you did all of this, you effectively managed a large (and exciting) project! This list could go on, but you should sense that your story is full of skills, especially problem-solving skills, that you have developed over time. It only takes your creative storytelling to reflect those skills to employers and clients. You will find a checklist of these skills following the conclusion.

b. Misunderstanding the Expectations Laid upon You

Another challenge to gaining confidence in your skills is your discernment of your supervisor's expectations. It is clear that supervising lawyers have expectations. If your employer is a larger law firm or organization, it probably has a competency model with benchmarks defining the expectations of your employer at the different levels of experience each employee may have. Ask to see this model.

With respect to the specific supervisor that you have now, you have to learn how to have a frank conversation about the supervisor's expectations. It is good to ask for clarification if an assignment is not clear. You can mirror back to the supervisor what you understood him or her to be asking you to do to see if you understand the project well. If it is possible, submit some work product early on in the project to get feedback on whether you are on the right track.

It is something of an art to learn how each supervisor manages his or her team and projects. Ask other associates for guidance if you are getting a project from a new supervisor. The goal is to make sure the supervisor knows that you are trying your best to make his or her life easier and successful.

c. Not Realizing That All Lawyers Have Faced the Challenge That "I Don't Know What I Am Doing," and the Solution Is to Be Patient, to Stay Focused, and to Seek Counsel from Experienced Professionals

Regardless of the anxiety or the lack of comfort, know that every lawyer before you has had the same experience and that you are equipped to practice law. You will find as you enter practice that your ability to solve problems is strong, relative to other people. At the very least, you will be able to quickly identify important facts, frame an issue, and bring possible solutions to the table in a way that others will not. Furthermore, you are developing the capability of asking good questions, researching the law and potential solutions, and offering an answer according to your best judgment in the context of uncertainty. You have developed, therefore, numerous skills that may be subtle, yet are formidable.

You are now an experienced problem solver, and you are getting better. If the problem is complex, you simply must take your best initial shot at identifying the issues and possible solutions. Then find creative ways to ask for advice from experienced lawyers (see "Building Long-Term Relationships Based on Trust" later in section III) to see if there are issues you may have missed.

2. Gaining Experience to Build Your Confidence

a. Renarrate Your Skills

A simple way of building confidence in your skills—and one that costs very little of your time or energy—is to reframe or renarrate your existing skills set. As mentioned previously, you already carry with you a multitude of skills and competencies from your past experiences. Recall the 360-degree assessment of your competencies from the Roadmap template where you were assessing your competencies in both a nonlegal and legal context. From your nonlegal experiences, you bring a variety of valuable capacities to the table, including problem-solving techniques, research skills, close reading, analysis, project management experience, common sense, and a mastery of language.

Once you reflect upon and reframe your current skills set, you need to articulate ways in which you have brought your skills to bear in the past and ways in which you will use them in the future. For example, a 2L reflected upon his time as the volunteer-organizing chair in his fraternity during his undergraduate years. He recognized the extent that his project management and teamwork skills developed during that time, as he coordinated with local nonprofits and other social organizations on his campus to gather a group large enough to make it worth everyone's time. He set the dates of the volunteer projects, managed the various times and organizations, set the volunteers in motion, and accomplished a great deal of good work in his college town. He would not have recognized this as project management until his recent reflection; yet, it was precisely this type of work in his college years that prepared him for his work as an attorney.

Now, having developed those skills, it is likely that you use them in a number of ways. Where else have you used them? More importantly, though, how will those skills be useful for future legal employers? Reframing your skills and creatively thinking of ways in which to bring these skills to the table will indeed build confidence in your skills and work product, without the need to learn any new ones. You will find a checklist of these skills following the conclusion.

b. Cultivating Strategic Networking Relationships with Experienced Lawyers and Staff

When you have a network of senior lawyers and experienced staff who will return your phone call, you have a great strength in dealing with a new challenge. Even further, when these veteran lawyers will give feedback on your best judgment in a complex problem, you have an exceedingly good gift. This alone should give you a sense of confidence in your work product. As a beginning lawyer, these veterans will make all the difference in your practice by offering feedback on your writing, your analysis, your problem solving, and your solutions. In effect, they will mentor and coach you in your development toward becoming a superb lawyer.

Graduate medical education has already taken note of the importance of experienced physicians offering help to residents. Thus, medical students are given a competency table regarding their capacity to seek help from veteran physicians.

A University of St. Thomas School of Law alumnus has a helpful story. He graduated with a not-very-high rank in his class. He is now practicing in a two-lawyer firm in Outstate Minnesota with an estate-planning emphasis. He said that after approximately six months in the practice, about 50 percent of the matters became routine, straightforward problems where he could just do them on his own. At that point, 30 percent of the matters involved issues where he needed to do research but could ultimately solve the problem. Finally, there was the 20 percent of the matters that were really complex, and he knew they were complex. With these, he did his research and problem solving, but he knew he needed to run things by a more seasoned lawyer, or several, to get input. He never asked for "advice from scratch," though; he always said: "Here is where I have come out, and I am hoping you might give me a reaction." He has developed trust relationships with senior lawyers and paralegals from whom he can receive this help. At two years into practice, he felt that 75 percent of the matters were routine issues that he could handle without research, 20 percent involved some research to solve the problem, and 5 percent involved complex issues where he needed a more experienced lawyer's help.

You can use table 11 to assess your own stage of development on the capacity to seek help. At which developmental stage are you now? How will you grow to the next stage? Be specific.

Table 11   American Council for Graduate Medical Education Milestones, the Capacity to Seek Help[27]

Stage of Development	Characteristics
Novice	• Lacks insight into limitations, so need for help goes unrecognized
Advanced Beginner	• May recognize limitations, but motivation to seek help is externally prompted • Continues to demonstrate concern that limitations will be seen as weakness
Competent	• Recognizes limitations but occasionally does not engage in appropriate help-seeking behavior due to overriding sense of professional autonomy
Proficient	• Recognizes limitations and appropriately seeks assistance • Personal value of optimizing outcomes in patients supersedes all other impulses in this domain
Expert	• Demonstrates personal drive to continually improve through help-seeking behaviors
Master	• Role models and encourages others to develop and demonstrate appropriate help-seeking behaviors

c. Seek Stretch Experiences

A recent study of new lawyers in Australia asked about their development of self-confidence. Those most happy with their development of trust and competence reported two factors as critical to their formation—namely, "exposure to challenging learning experiences in which they felt they were being stretched beyond their comfort zone; and a tailored mentoring/supervisory program which acted as a 'safety net' to ensure that experiences were a catalyst for improvement."[28]

During your remaining time in law school, seek "stretch" experiences in both your curricular and your extracurricular work. For example, externship and clinic opportunities at your school are a wonderful place for you to seek stretch experiences and gain hands-on experience. Your supervised research and writing requirements are another place to seek stretch experiences. You can make mistakes that will be covered by your supervisor's oversight without the

---

[27] Neil W. Hamilton, Verna Monson & Jerome M. Organ, *Encouraging Each Student's Personal Responsibility for Core Competencies Including Professionalism*, 21 PROF. LAWYER 1, 13 (No. 3, 2012).
[28] Holmes et al., *supra* note 23, at 42.

worry of losing your job. Your career is not on the line in these opportunities. Everyone hates making mistakes and falling flat on their face. But during law school, you get the chance to return to your class, discuss your failings, and have teachers and peers offer insight about what could have been more effective in that situation.

Finally, the externship, clinical, and clerkship opportunities offer you the space to have evidence of your competency from experienced lawyers. You will be working largely with veteran attorneys in these situations. You will also be finishing work product for them. You will leave these experiences with two important things: real work product and evidence of your competence by those senior lawyers for whom you work. Their evidence of your work is the invaluable product of your time in these opportunities.

Whether your stretch experiences are curricular or extracurricular, learning experiences and completing projects are insufficient without feedback. Indeed, "[r]eflective practice, engaging in reflective conversations with oneself and a supervisor," is also necessary.[29] Whether in the form of constructive criticism (which is very important), a star on your work product, or simply clarifying how the issue was resolved, you need to hear something back from your supervisor. Furthermore, you need to have evidence that you are always improving your skills—that you took advice from supervisors and reflected on it to develop your competence. So, ask for feedback.

This process is described in "The Basics of Good Judgment to Help Clients," later in section III, as the FDR habit—actively seeking feedback, dialogue on the tough calls, and reflection. That is, proactively seek and gather feedback from your supervisor regarding your work product. Dialogue with your supervisor and colleagues further in the context of that feedback. Reflect on the multiple conversations in order to put into practice what you have learned.

An altogether different response is that which you may receive from your supervisors to your work product, namely, silence. Likely, your work product is received unhesitatingly, read, and placed in the file, and you are left with little, if any, feedback. If there are problems, moreover, you are unlikely to know about them. Rather, they are fixed. Meanwhile, you have offered your very important work product and are left wondering whether it was any good at all. In fact, you might be feeling that you spent two whole hours cobbling together something entirely wrongheaded and fearing that you are on your way to losing your job for such poor work. Never do you realize, though, that your supervisor or your client is actually pleased with your work.

You have to develop the habit of proactively seeking feedback on your work. It is something of an art to learn how to approach each supervisor to ask for feedback. Ask other junior lawyers about what works best with respect to specific supervising lawyers.

---

[29] *Id.*

Again, clinics are a key place to develop this because they are not simply "A's" on the top of your transcript. In clinics, you will probably have more interaction with your supervisor because you will likely be in a very small class and have more face time with your professor. You should ask about your work product by seeking dialogue with your professor and reflecting on the specifics of the feedback.

Feedback on externships may be more difficult if you are under the supervision of an adjunct faculty member. Nevertheless, you should still be searching for feedback and for evidence of your competencies and the skills you want emphasized. You simply must be more proactive in inquiring about your work product in that setting. Often, your supervisor may not have the time to sit with you in his or her office and go through your work. So perhaps you can invite your supervisor to lunch or for coffee to discuss it. You can also tell your supervisor that you want to achieve evidence of your competence, which may make him or her more aware of your desire for feedback.

Remember, find the opportunities to seek feedback. More importantly, don't be afraid to request it. Put yourself on the line. It is worth the confidence and trust gained in your skills and work product.

3. Conclusion

Law students and beginning lawyers tend to feel a lack of confidence in their skills, judgment, and work product. This is common among your colleagues and even senior lawyers. There are ways to build trust and confidence in your skills, though. Reframe the many skills you already bring to the table, and put those skills to practice. Recognize how developed you already are at solving problems. Seek out and receive the feedback you need to develop those skills more properly. And then practice with confidence because you are truly becoming a competent and remarkable attorney.

Checklist of Skills Already at Hand

- Problem-solving techniques in new situations and challenges
- Written communication
- Oral communication
- Techniques to identify important facts and frame issues
- Relationship skills
- Legal-research skills
- Reasoning skills
- Analysis skills
- Close-reading skills

Now that you have read "Building Confidence through Creative Problem Solving When 'I Don't Know What I am Doing,'" complete the Reflection Dashboard at **http://ambar.org/roadmap** to develop a better understanding of what developmental stage you are at and what steps you will take to grow to the next stage.

D. Project Management Skills: How Law Students Can Learn and Implement the Skills Employers Value[30]

"For attorneys at the beginning of their career, knowing the law and providing great client service only gets them to the starting line. New lawyers who can understand project management and thus can manage their clients' work efficiently and within established budgets will move to the head of the pack."[31] The most valuable employee is the one who always delivers on what the employee said he or she would do. When that employee takes on something, the manager can take that project off the managers list. That employee is worth gold.[32]

Suppose you have been hired on as a first-year associate at a medium-size law firm upon graduation. On your first day on the job, Jane Smith, a partner at the firm, assigns you a negligent child endangerment case. She asks you to interview the client, research the relevant case law, contact the prosecutor's office, and obtain a copy of the police report. Before she leaves your office, she pauses and asks you to send her an e-mail by the end of the day telling her how many hours you plan on billing so that she can calculate a set fee for the client. On your first day, you have already been asked to employ project management techniques.

Being an effective project manager requires you to deliver a high-quality product or service effectively and on time. While project management skills are essential in any place of business, both clients and law firms evaluate associates on project management skills.[33] Traditionally, law schools have not focused on teaching these skills.[34] This creates an opportunity for law students to distinguish themselves from the competition by learning project management skills during law school.[35] A large-firm project manager emphasizes, "project management and the practice of law in today's market have become permanently intertwined. New lawyers with proficiencies in project management will quickly differentiate themselves as assets to both legal teams and their clients."[36]

One goal of a competency-based education is to give you the evidence needed to make a case to potential employers that you understand and can apply project management skills. Fortunately, there are many events, projects, assignments,

---

[30] Authored by Neil W. Hamilton and Patrick Lucke.

[31] E-mail from Lauren Mueller, Legal Project Manager at Dorsey Law Firm, to author (June 14, 2017, 12:50 CST) (on file with author).

[32] E-mail from Thomas E. Holloran, Senior Distinguished Fellow, The Holloran Center for Ethical Leadership in the Professions, forever General Counsel and President, Medtronic Corp., to author (Dec. 17, 2014, 14:45 CST) (on file with author).

[33] Hamilton, Monson & Organ, *supra* note 27.

[34] *Id.* While many law school tasks actually involve projects, law schools historically have not helped students understand and utilize the developing knowledge about effective project management. Students also receive no help on how to "market" project management strengths.

[35] *Id.*

[36] E-mail from Lauren Mueller, *supra* note 31.

and tasks in which you can apply project management skills in law school, such as organizing speaker events for student organizations, researching and writing briefs for lawyering-skills courses and upper-level writing courses, and planning and executing social events, to name just a few. "If a student can show specific examples of how he or she used project management skills effectively in law school, I would know that student would be ready to apply those skills on day one."[37]

Learning to implement the project management methodology is an invaluable "arrow in the quiver" of values and competencies that make up a student's value proposition. A 2013 survey of several large Minnesota firms yielded the competencies of new lawyers in regard to project management skills, as shown in table 12.

Table 12 Developmental Stages to Assess Associate–Attorney Project Management Competency[38]

Junior Associates	Mid-level Associates	Senior Associates
• Effectively completing assignments using time efficiently • Being well organized • Completing projects by the deadline • Working well under pressure • Managing workload to provide excellent customer service	• Keeping team members and senior attorneys apprised of deadlines • Taking responsibility for the overall project • Understanding how to develop a budget for a given matter	• Mentoring new associates in effective organization • Effectively managing others in a complex project • Consistently delivering a high-quality and timely end product

1. The Project Management Methodology

"Trying to manage a project without project management is like trying to play a football game without a game plan."[39]

So what are the warning signs that you could benefit from learning the basics of legal project management? Consider what indicators lawyers use to determine whether they can benefit from a project management course: missed internal deadlines, overresearched tasks or issues, spending hours in excess of preset quotas, miscommunication, missing time entries, and poor attendance at

---

[37] Holloran, *supra* note 32.

[38] *See* Neil W. Hamilton, *Help Wanted: Legal Employers Seek New Lawyers with Professional Competencies That Undergraduate Students Can Develop*, Planc Points, Spring 2014, at tbl.4A (Newsletter of the Pre-Law Advisors Nat'l Council).

[39] Quote attributed to Karen Tate, President and Founder of the Griffin Tate Group, Inc., (July 16, 2017), https://gcimmarrusti.wordpress.com/pm-quotes/.

scheduled meetings and calls, to name just a few.[40] Unfortunately, too many of these problems are identified after the fact and only in retrospect are determined to be a cause of inefficiency or, even worse, a lack of profitability.[41] William D. Henderson feels that the legal services industry is in the midst of a paradigm shift, and the next generation of lawyers will operate in what he calls "The Project Manager" era.[42] Lawyers working for corporate clients will increasingly need to layer the skills of a project manager on top of their specialized legal knowledge to ensure that these problems do not result. To the extent that they resist this new skill set, they will lose their seat at the economic table.[43]

The essence of project management is working through the four phases: (1) planning, (2) build-up, (3) implementation, and (4) closeout.[44] Like the traditional phases of strategic planning, project management phases can be context specific and tend to overlap. For example, your planning may begin with a ballpark budget figure and an estimated completion date. As the project progresses, new information and/or unforeseen circumstances arise, forcing a revision of your budget and end date—in other words, more planning—according to your clearer understanding of the big picture.[45] This is particularly true when dealing with projects that are new to you, have a high level of uncertainty, or have a wide range of potential outcomes. With these types of projects it may be difficult to pinpoint exactly what needs to be done beforehand.[46] Human beings, no matter how brilliant, cannot foresee all the issues that might arise in a complex project.[47] In these cases you may have to consider a more adaptive, iterative approach.[48] Table 13 outlines some activities of each of the four phases. Since many projects are team efforts and involve multiple people, some aspects of these phases interface with the teamwork competency. This provides a brief overview of the life cycle most projects go through.

Keeping table 13 in mind throughout the project management process will be of value, but every stage of your project may not fit neatly into one of the four phases. This is a natural aspect of project management, so do not be bogged down by attempts to neatly fit every stage of your project into the four phases. Effective project management will rarely work that smoothly and does not require such rigidity.

---

[40] Jim Hassett et al., The Legal Project Management Quick Reference Guide: Tools and Templates to Increase Efficiency 7–8 (2d ed. 2011).

[41] Id.

[42] William D. Henderson, *Three Generations of U.S. Lawyers: Generalists, Specialists, Project Managers*, 70 Md. L. Rev. 373, 381 (2011).

[43] Id. at 389.

[44] *The Four Phases of Project Management*, in HBR Guide to Project Management 4 (2011) [hereinafter Harvard Bus. Rev.].

[45] Id.

[46] Id. at 43.

[47] Id. at 36.

[48] Id. at 43–44.

Table 13 The Four Phases of Project Management

Planning	Build-Up	Implementation	Closeout
Activities to be completed in each phase:			
• Identify the real problem to solve and define objectives • Identify the stakeholders • Estimate time and budget needs and constraints • Identify what an acceptable end product looks like	• If a team is needed, determine whom your team members will be • Hold a kickoff meeting and inform team of project goals • Schedule a list of activities that need to be completed to successfully complete the project	• Monitor and control progress throughout the project • Regularly update stakeholders of progress and potential problems • If you have a team, check in with team members at regular intervals	• Close the project once all goals have been accomplished • Evaluate project performance: what went well and what needs improvement • If you have a team, hold a team meeting to celebrate success and evaluate performance

a. The Planning Phase

"By failing to prepare, you are preparing to fail."[49]

Project management is a conscientious strategy for accomplishing a goal with finite resources. "Project management focuses on the set of tasks that will create a unique and specific product or service within a specified timeframe."[50] The first step is to understand clearly what the goal of the project is. Take time to understand the client's context or business and the underlying issues or problems the client is trying to address. Then clarify project goals with the client. Defining the problem before diving into implementation gives the project manager a greater degree of freedom to solve it.[51] Ultimately, this is the goal of the planning phase: determining what problem needs solving, who will be involved, and what work will be done.[52]

In defining the problem, you may find it useful to work backward: imagine what the "ideal end state" would look like, and then work backward to put in as much energy as you can, given the time, budget, and political realities.[53] For most

---

[49] Benjamin Franklin.

[50] Laura Dallasord Burford, Project Management for Flat Organizations: Cost Effective Steps to Achieving Successful Results 9 (J. Ross Publ'g 2012).

[51] Harvard Bus. Rev., *supra* note 44, at 5.

[52] *Id.* at 7.

[53] *Id.* at 18.

lawyers, the "ideal end state" is defined by the client's expectations.[54] For example, what outcomes are acceptable to the client? Are there budget constraints? Deadlines? Are there any tensions in achieving those goals satisfactorily? If so, how does the client prioritize each issue? These are the sorts of questions a good project manager needs to ask, and answer, to determine the objectives and scope of the project.[55] For junior lawyers, the client is speaking through the senior lawyer assigning the work. Competent junior lawyers take care to send their supervisors a short summary of the work to be done so that they know they are on the right track and are doing work that will further the client's goals. Law students can use the "ideal end state" method for most academic and scholarly assignments because it is almost always defined by the professor's expectations. If you can anticipate what the professor is expecting, you are exercising the same muscles necessary to anticipate what a senior partner is expecting when it comes to a legal project.

b. The Build-Up Phase

"No one can whistle a symphony. It takes a whole orchestra."[56]

For multiperson projects, the build-up phase involves bringing your team together to accomplish your objectives.[57] Assembling a team requires assessing the skills needed for the project so you can get the right people on board.[58] Whether you are working with others or working alone, the build-up phase is when time estimates turn into schedules. Because most projects come with a fixed beginning and end date, the most realistic schedules often identify drop-dead deadlines and work backward to see when deliverables must be ready.[59] Whether you are preparing a legal memorandum for a client, completing an assignment for a class, or organizing a speaking event, it is crucial to identify due dates for each task. Scheduling, however, is not an exact process and may often require revision as the project progresses.[60] Thus, the project manager needs to establish methods of control and communication systems for updating and revising the schedule while keeping all stakeholders involved in, and informed of, progress and required modifications.[61]

Budgeting is also important during build-up.[62] The basic question to ask when developing a budget is, what will it take to actually do the work?[63]

---

[54] HASSETT ET AL., *supra* note 40, at 9.

[55] *Id.*

[56] H. E. Luccock, American Minister and Professor.

[57] HARVARD BUS. REV., *supra* note 44, at 7.

[58] *Id.*

[59] *Id.*

[60] *Project Schedule Development*, MIND TOOLS, http://www.mindtools.com/pages/article/newPPM_71.htm (last visited July 15, 2017).

[61] HARVARD BUS. REV., *supra* note 44, at 8.

[62] *Id.*

[63] *Id.*

Depending on the unique nature of the project and stakeholder, there will be a number of variables that determine the cost: personnel, travel, training, supplies, space, research, capital expenditures, and overhead. Keep in mind that budgets are best guesses, and the actual numbers will often deviate from those estimates. Running your budget by a trusted advisor or colleague can help ensure you did not overlook anything.[64] Also, your budget will inherently be built on certain assumptions, and there are risks involved in any project that could cause problems in achieving your desired outcomes. Documenting the assumptions you've made and sharing them with your stakeholders helps to ensure a common understanding of the true scope of the project. Considering risks ahead of time can help you react quickly should those risks occur.[65]

The same is true for estimating a timeline. For any project, it is useful to estimate up front how much time the project is going to take. Not only will it give you a good starting place to space the activities, but it is also helpful to reflect on at the end of the project. Only by comparing the estimate to the actual amount of time it took to complete the project can you learn to make more accurate time predictions. Just like budgeting, it is always helpful to run it by a trusted advisor or colleague.

c. The Implementation Phase

"No matter how good the team or how efficient the methodology, if we are not solving the right problem, the project fails."[66]

During implementation, the plan is put into action.[67] This phase includes "tracking, analyzing, and adjusting the project's work, schedule, and budget, and then reporting on the progress of the project."[68] As a project leader, you will need to actively monitor progress to determine whether your plan is really bringing you closer to the project's objectives. Whatever your monitoring approach may be, try to maintain a big-picture perspective so that you don't become engulfed in details and petty problems.[69] A departure from your plan isn't a problem unless it's likely to compromise your objectives. It would be beneficial, however, to evaluate how and why the departure happened, in case it is an indicator of a larger problem. When monitoring and managing problems, remember that meeting your objectives trumps everything else. Don't get hung up on compliance with the original plan. Almost all plans must be revised at some point, so don't be afraid to alter your course if it will bring you within reach of your goals (just be sure to keep stakeholders, supervisors, and/or clients informed).[70]

---

[64] *Id.*

[65] E-mail from Lauren Mueller, PMP, Legal Project Manager, Dorsey & Whitney, LLP, to author (June 8, 2017, 08:05 CST) (on file with author).

[66] Woody Williams, http://projectmanagementworks.co.uk/tag/pm-quotes/.

[67] Harvard Bus. Rev., *supra* note 44, at 8.

[68] Burford, *supra* note 50, at 23.

[69] Harvard Bus. Rev., *supra* note 44, at 8.

[70] *Id.* at 48.

d. The Closeout Phase

> *"Begin at the Beginning, and go till you come to the end; then stop."*[71]

After a project has been executed, the next step is to gauge the success of the project and finalize activities. Stakeholders will care far more about realizing the project's benefits than they do about adhering to specific aspects of your original plan, so focus on those benefits as you complete the project.[72] Be sure to seek consensus from the stakeholders on whether the project is finished or not.[73] Many projects undertaken by law students and student organizations will be straightforward enough that their completion will be evident. Nonetheless, take time to evaluate and reflect on the experience. Try to identify any lessons to be learned from the project. This is an opportunity for feedback, dialogue, and reflection (FDR) with mentors and advisors,[74] and it will help you sharpen your ability to select projects and establish realistic objectives in the future.[75]

The closeout phase is a good opportunity to reflect on how close your initial plan was to the end result. Did you stick to your schedule, or did you end up deviating from it? Engaging in FDR with team members or a trusted advisor can help you identify what aspects of the unique project you were well prepared for from the onset and what parts you missed. In the business world, lawyers are constantly asked to estimate the cost of projects for clients. As with any endeavor, practice makes perfect, and becoming a better estimator is one of the fruits of practicing project management skills.

2. Effective Communication to Bring About Better Project Management

Nothing is more important to the success of a project than effective communication. Because communication is the lifeblood of a project, project managers must learn how to use their time effectively or risk having all their time eaten up by communicating. This in turn will distract from what really matters in a project: the outcome. To achieve effective communication practices, a lawyer should identify the 5 "W's" and 1 "H."[76]

- **Who** needs to be communicated to? This needs to be determined in the early stages of a project to identify the relevant stakeholders.

---

[71] Lewis Carroll, Alice in Wonderland 113 (1865).

[72] Harvard Bus. Rev., *supra* note 44, at 54.

[73] *Id.* at 10.

[74] The student is well served to have experience in FDR by the time he or she graduates law school, as both clients and senior lawyers appreciate being asked for their feedback at the conclusion of a project.

[75] Harvard Bus. Rev., *supra* note 44, at 58.

[76] *Adapted from* Sivasankari Rajkumar, "Art of Communication in Project Management." Paper presented at PMI® Research Conference: Defining the Future of Project Management, Washington, DC. Newtown Square, PA: Project Management Institute.

- *What* needs to be communicated? All information related to the project need not be communicated to everyone in the team all the time.
- *When* should it be communicated? The timeline of communication should be monitored.
- *Where* should it be communicated? If the team involves many people, then individual and team-level communications need to be resolved.
- *Why* is communication of information essential and to what level is it important?
- *How* does the communication need to be done? Should it be conducted via e-mail, phone, or a presentation to the team member?

If a lawyer successfully implements methods of effective communication into his or her projects, he or she will free up time to work on delivering the outcome, saving clients time and money and increasing chances of winning bids in the future.

3. How Lawyers Are Using Project Management Skills to Succeed

Empirical research has shown that corporate clients increasingly want lawyers to fully understand the client's business needs.[77] As section I on emerging legal markets demonstrated, clients are emphasizing a "more-for-less" mentality. In addition to traditional law skills, firms and clients are now starting to look more closely at a law student's basic project management skills.[78] According to one lawyer, Jordan Furlong, much to the frustration of clients:

> Lawyers seem pathologically unwilling to estimate time or budget costs (invoking the almighty "it depends" clause) and incapable of creating and managing a plan of action, presumably for fear of failing or being caught shorthanded. But today, everybody project manages: it's [standard operating procedure] in corporate life, and lawyers are the only ones in the business chain who seem to have missed the memo.[79]

But recently lawyers seem to have gotten the memo. For example, the American Law Institute increasingly offers continuing legal education seminars specifically focused on project management for lawyers.[80] New boutique

---

[77] Neil W. Hamilton & Verna Monson, *The Positive Empirical Relationship of Professionalism to Effectiveness in the Practice of Law*, 24 Geo. J. Legal Ethics 137, 160–62, 165 (2011).

[78] Tamara Loomis, *Has the Recession Forever Changed Large Law Firms?*, Am. Law., Oct. 6, 2009, available at http://www.americanlawyer.com/id=1202434302753/Has-the-Recession-Forever-Changed-Large-Law-Firms?slreturn=20141017211303.

[79] Jordan Furlong, *Core Competence: 6 New Skills Now Required of Lawyers*, Law21 Blog, July 4, 2008, http://www.law21.ca/2008/07/core-competence-6-new-skills-now-required-of-lawyers/ (last visited July 15, 2017).

[80] *Project Management for Lawyers*, Am. L. Inst., http://www.ali-cle.org/course/view_email .cfm?htmlfilevcu0622-wwww-alicle.htm (last visited Aug. 1, 2014).

companies such as LegalBizDev now specialize in teaching lawyers and firms about legal project management and legal business development. These companies offer services to help lawyers increase profitability by "improving business development, alternative fees, and project management."[81]

a. Creating Project Management Plans Tailored to Objectives

In recent years, lawyers have used the project management method to form project management plans or project-specific stratagem for accomplishing a specific assignment.[82] While project management methodology is a standardized approach that uses guidelines to help an organization ensure consistency across all projects, a project management plan is unique to a given project and helps a leader incorporate the four basic project management phases into projects.[83] Lawyers tailor project management plans to ensure that the unique objectives necessary for a given final product are implemented smoothly from the beginning.[84]

b. Delineating and Scheduling Requisite Activities for the Project

"If you do not know where you are going, you often end up somewhere else."[85]

It is axiomatic that the clients turn to lawyers for help when they have complex problems that require innovative solutions and highly technical skills. Thus, projects that lawyers help clients with are typically complex matters, and good project managers seek to break them down into smaller, distinct activities from the outset.[86] In order to form an accurate picture of what these smaller tasks are, good legal project managers work with the client (or the assigning attorney) to determine exactly what the objectives of the project are.[87] This involves a rigorous planning phase with many components, including (1) scheduling a meeting to "define sequence, schedule and budget tasks"; (2) prioritizing tasks and determining which activities must be finished before others can start; (3) establishing progress report intervals; (4) agreeing on simple progress review measures; and (5) mapping the project life cycle from beginning to end with a number of milestones.[88]

---

[81] *About*, LEGALBIZDEV, http://www.legalbizdev.com/aboutus/company.html (last visited Aug. 1, 2014).

[82] Furlong, *supra* note 79.

[83] BURFORD, *supra* note 50, at 25.

[84] HASSETT ET AL., *supra* note 40, at 17–18.

[85] Yogi Berra.

[86] HASSETT ET AL., *supra* note 40, at 17–18.

[87] Failure to adequately communicate with the client or assigning attorney about the client's goals can result in one of the biggest problems for a new lawyer: miscalculating the work to be done and billing for time that does nothing to further the client's goals.

[88] HASSETT ET AL., *supra* note 40, at 18.

c. Organizing a Team to Accomplish the Objective of a Project

Because most legal projects involve many team members, it is essential to assign individual team members specific activities. Each activity should be budgeted for a manageable chunk of time so that team members have "the freedom to perform the task as they think best while still ensuring accountability."[89] Good project managers assign goals that can realistically be met by each team member, given their strengths and weaknesses.[90] It is wise to involve the whole team in the early stages of the planning phase to get their feedback and buy-in as well. Before any team meeting, good project managers determine what they want to accomplish in advance, determine whether the meeting is necessary, and take into account how different team members best communicate.[91] Good project managers understand that while the plan is important to follow, it is never set in stone, and they are able to adapt during the implementation phase to accomplish the objectives of the project and deliver the product or service.[92] Being intentional about using the project management methodology to form a project management plan helps ensure the goal of any project: delivering a high-quality product within budget and by the deadline. Of course, as in any other profession, there is a certain minimum level of competent service that a lawyer owes to a client.[93] While project management can help lawyers deliver what lawyer Tom Joyce calls "value for cost," keep in mind that there are minimum levels of service that are owed to any client. Striking the right balance between competent "value" and keeping costs low is a skill learned over time through experience, practice, failure, reflection, and improvement. To the extent that new associates are already versed in using the project management methodology, they will be more valuable to the employer on day one.

4. How Law Students Can Practice Project Management Skills during Law School

Proactive law students have the opportunity to hone and practice basic project management skills and develop evidence of these skills while still in law school. Being intentional about developing project management skills through practice while in law school gives you concrete evidence to make the case to employers that you are proficient in this competency. While there are a variety of projects, tasks, and assignments you must complete while still in law school, they can generally be grouped into two categories: solo projects and multiple-team-member projects. Because associates are frequently charged with completing both solo and group projects, students who are most dedicated to developing project

---

[89] *Id.*

[90] *Id.* at 37.

[91] *Id.* at 38.

[92] *Id.* at 18.

[93] MODEL RULES OF PROF'L CONDUCT r. 1.1 (2014).

management skills will use the three years of law school to practice using these skills for both types of projects. After each section—solo projects and group projects—we will provide a more general project management assessment tool that can be adapted and used for any project. These assessment tools are also available electronically at **http://ambar.org/roadmap**.

a. Applying the Project Management Methodology to Solo Projects

Consider two examples in which a student could apply project management methodology to solo projects.

i. Planning and Executing Research-Based Briefs in Lawyering Skills

Law students are required to learn to write various common types of legal briefs: interoffice memorandums, persuasive briefs, and appellate briefs. The project management method could be helpful to students in each semester but would be particularly useful in effectively using time for the persuasive briefs, where independent research is a primary aspect of the assignment. One of the most challenging aspects of legal research is knowing when to stop researching. Students can be tempted to over-research and keep searching for obscure and off-point conclusions of law well after an adequate amount of research has been completed. Using the project management techniques from the beginning of the research process can help you stay within the scope of the assignment and use time efficiently. By intentionally understanding the scope of the questions presented, you can devise an efficient research plan that will discourage unnecessarily in-depth or unfocused research. Once you begin researching and executing the project, you can continually monitor whether you are sticking to the research plan and determine whether changes to the scope of the project are appropriate. Finally, while bearing the initial plan in mind, you will know when it is appropriate to conclude the research and begin the next phase of the assignment—the actual writing of the brief. Using the project management process not only can help you succeed by turning in a high-quality final product, but it will also give you practice in project management.

ii. Participating in the Law Journal Writing Competition

After the last exam in the second semester of law school, University of St. Thomas School of Law students are invited to sign up for a weeklong writing competition to compete for a position on a law journal. The writing competition consists of two parts: writing an objective memorandum on a given topic and completing a citation exercise—a fictional law journal entry with hundreds of errors in which the student is charged with locating and correcting the errors. These two activities serve to gauge the student's general writing and editing abilities. It is understood that both of these activities are taxing and time-consuming, and, in that way, it also tests the student's endurance.

Table 14 Sample Individual Project Life Cycle

Solo Project: Lawyering-Skills Brief			
Planning	**Build-Up**	**Implementation**	**Closeout**
Activities			
• Determine the main questions presented	• Identify what points of law you need to research	• Complete a draft of the question-presented section	• Evaluate the project and determine whether you answered the question
• Identify the audience you are writing for	• Determine whether to write persuasively or objectively	• Monitor the tone of your paper and keep it consistent in each section	• Ensure that your final paper has the right tone for the audience
• Define the major topics and subtopics you need to address	• Create an outline of the headings/subheading	• Expand the outline and incorporate each heading into the paper	• Do a final review to ensure that the order of the topics flows
• Determine what research tools will be most useful to you	• Evaluate which research tools and sources will be most useful to you	• Return to research as needed throughout the project for a particular point of law	• Evaluate the authorities and sources you used in the project
• Acknowledge time constraints on time to research	• Prepare a schedule for both the research phase and the writing phase	• Implement the schedule and remain aware of the time constraints	• Reflect on the difference between time used versus allotted for future projects

While securing a place on a journal is very helpful for securing meaningful employment, even participating in the writing competition is another perfect opportunity for the student to practice and show evidence of project management skills. As with any project, the writing competition has a fixed start date and due date requiring a final deliverable under time constraints. Students can use the project management methodology to plan and estimate the work that will need to be done by identifying the tasks and creating a schedule with several milestones for each project. For example, a student could set these milestones for the memorandum portion: (1) create an outline, (2) summarize the points of law, (3) create a set of headings and subheadings, (4) compose an initial draft, and (5) set a schedule for a series of edits for the paper. Much like the lawyering-skills briefs, the benefits of applying project management methodologies to the writing competition are twofold: a superior final product and further practice toward competency in project management.

iii. Individual Project Initiation and Planning Template

This template is available online at the following link: **http://ambar.org/roadmap**. **Begin in the following way:**
Make a rough estimate of the total time for the project. If you are doing a zero-to ten-hour project, then answer questions 1–7. If your project will take more than ten hours, then answer questions 1–12.

1. **What problem will the project solve?** *Here you should define exactly what the project will achieve or what problem will be solved.*
2. **What is the vision for the project?** *You should ask yourself, what is the best possible outcome for this project?*
3. **Do you need more guidance in order to clarify your answers to questions 1 and 2?**
4. **What are the constraints on the project?** *Try to think about the best possible outcome of the project. Then think about the constraints. The typical constraints are cost and time.*
   1. *By when do you want to have completed the project?*
   2. *What is the maximum amount of time you have for the project?*
   3. *How much money do you have in your budget for the project?*
5. **What are the most effective solutions for the project?** *You should brainstorm and identify several solutions to the problem. You should also try to identify the strong and weak points of each proposed solution. Include an estimate of how much time each solution will take.*
6. **Out of these proposed solutions, which one is best?** *Try to identify the solution that best balances the result achieved against the time and money spent achieving the result.*
7. **How will you determine whether the project was a success?** *Here you should define the factors for determining whether the project was successful. These factors will allow you to evaluate the success of the project once it is completed.*
8. **What objectives must be completed in order to implement your chosen solution?** *Objectives define what must be completed in order to accomplish the mission. Estimate how long it will take to complete each objective, remembering that objectives are SMART (specific, measurable, attainable, realistic, and time limited). Use table 15 to track your progress.*

Table 15

Objective	Number of Hours Estimated for Completion	Complete? (y/n)	Date Completed	Due Date	Objective Added to Calendaring System?	Date to Check Progress of Objective?

9. **What tasks must be completed for each objective?** *Tasks are a way to break up the work of objectives into smaller, more manageable pieces. If you can see that achieving an objective will require the completion of two or more tasks, then use table 16 to outline and track those tasks. Adding tasks to a calendaring system is a good way to track progress and make the individual and the team aware of upcoming deadlines.*

Table 16

Objective 1:	Task	Number of Hours Estimated for Completion	Task Added to Calendaring System?	Date to Check Progress of Task?

10. **Do you need to communicate with anyone as you work on the project? If so, what is your communication plan (table 17)?**

Table 17

Who needs to know about the project progress?	What do they need to know?	Why do they need to know it?	When/how often do they need to know it?	How should the information be shared with them?	Who is in charge of this communication?

11. **What are the major milestones of the project?** *Here you should define specific goals and when they are to be achieved (table 18).*

Table 18

Milestone	Deliverable	Due date	Date to check progress	Milestones added to calendaring system?
25% Complete				
50% Complete				

12. **What are the risks involved with this project, and how might they be prevented or mitigated?** *You should brainstorm and identify risks that are likely to occur (table 19). You should not be concerned with risks that only have a remote possibility of coming to fruition.*

Table 19

Risk	Probability Occurrence (Low, Medium, High)	Impact if Risk Occurs (Low, Medium, High)	How Can It Be Prevented or Mitigated?

b. Applying Project Management Methodologies to Group Projects[94]

i. Effectively Planning and Executing Speaking Events for Student Organizations

Many students are involved in student organizations. A primary objective of many student organizations is to organize events and bring speakers to the school to address the community on a particular topic of interest. For any one of these projects, using the project management methodology can help ensure a successful result. For example, when scheduling a speaker, the student in charge of that event must be intentional and jump through many hoops to ensure the event goes smoothly. The student needs to contact the speaker in advance, coordinate a space for the event with the appropriate administrators, and publicize the event to increase attendance. Identifying the core subtasks during the planning phases and preparing a schedule during the build-up phase will ensure that the project manager knows exactly what needs to be done before doing it. With a plan in place, the project manager can focus on monitoring successful implementation of the subtasks, knowing that once all the logistical objectives are met, the event will be a success.

ii. Effectively Planning and Executing Law School Fundraisers

Most student organizations have a commitment to service in the community in one fashion or another. Due to the nature of student organizations, most

---

[94] For a further discussion of group projects, *see* "The Basics of Teamwork" in section III.

money-raising efforts will take the form of fundraising events. Even minor, informal events are quintessential projects with definite goals, a start date, and a close. Orchestrating a major event like a student auction inherently has many tasks that need to be planned for and accomplished to ensure the success of the event. Student project managers can use the four-phase methodology to make sure that the event goes off without any major problems. Table 20 is an example of how a student project manager can identify the activities to take place in each phase of organizing a student auction, and the "Master Planning Template," available online, is an example of how to delegate and assign the various activities.

Table 20 Sample Group Project: Planning and Executing a Student Auction

Planning	• Identify who you hope will bid at the auction • Determine what logistical needs you have (table space, school approval of donors, venue) • Choose who will be the team members for the project • Set goals for the amount of funds to raise • Identify what the money will go toward and why • Estimate the total time needed to complete the project
Build-Up	• Set up an initial meeting with your selected team members • Distribute assignments to team members based on their unique strengths and weaknesses • Schedule deadlines for coordinating with school administrators • Create a final list of approved donors • Distribute the list of donors among the team and assign each member a call sheet • Create a script template for contacting potential donors • Establish a schedule for team meetings and criteria to evaluate progress • Come up with ways to publicize the event • Set the date and the time that the auction will take place
Implementation	• Arrange a venue and table space with the school • Call all potential donors to secure gifts for the auction • Properly publicize the event (social media, school e-mail, announcements in class) • Assign team members to coordinate pickup of gifts for the auction • Create templates for signup lists and bidding sheets • Gather all the donated items and find a safe place to keep them • Assign team members to man the auction table during the auction • Inform potential bidders of how the process works

(continues)

Table 20 Continued

Closeout	• Take down the auction tables and remove all materials
	• Identify the winners of certain items and contact them to arrange payment and pickup
	• Have a postauction meeting with team members to determine what went right and what went wrong
	• Compare the total time that was needed with the initial estimate
	• Write thank-you notes to donors
	• Document and save template and donor lists for future auctions
	• Have a social event with your team to celebrate a successful project

iii. Team Project Initiation and Planning Template

This template is very similar to the Individual Project Initiation and Planning template, as it asks the team member to consider some of the same questions and offers identical tables to fill out, with an additional table called the "Master Planning Template." The Team Project Initiation and Planning template is available electronically at **http://ambar.org/roadmap**.

5. Assessment Tools Students Can Use to Gauge Project Management Acumen

"All assessment is a perpetual work in progress."[95]

The project management methodology is new to most students. Fortunately, as discussed previously, there are many opportunities for you to practice applying the methodology. But how can you determine whether you are making progress in successful project management? The answer lies in an ongoing process of evaluation and assessment conducted both by you and your trusted advisors and colleagues.

Assessment is a process of reflecting on the progress, successes, and failures of your performance of a given task. It's all about evaluating how you carried a task into action, with a focus on student learning and development outcomes.[96] There are two reasons assessment of learning is important. First, it is needed for improvement: it establishes ways to measure the degree of your knowledge and skills and gives you an opportunity for self-reflection.[97] Second, it is needed for accountability: it provides evidence of your achievements and acknowledges the successes and failures. Because the project management methodology is a learned skill, it is helpful and appropriate for you to pursue and accept intentional and

---

[95] Linda Suske, Vice President, Middle States Commission on Higher Education.

[96] *Assessment Day*, JAMES MADISON U., http://www.jmu.edu/assessment/Visitor/aboutAday.shtml (last visited July 16, 2017).

[97] *Why Is Assessment of Student Learning Important?*, KENT ST. U., https://www.kent.edu/aal/why-assessment-student-learning-important (last visited July 16, 2017).

supportive ways to measure progress. Remember that assessment is not about berating yourself about failures and shortcoming but about finding ways to continue to improve and grow toward overall professional excellence.

Self-directed students are interested in taking initiative to grow professionally. This includes a willingness to engage in structured critiques of self through a process of self-assessment and by actively soliciting feedback. Self-assessment of project management skills involves three main components: (1) knowledge of the project management methodology, (2) successful application of the project management methodology to a given project, and (3) the success or failure of a given project, including meeting deadlines and producing a high-quality final product. Because self-assessment is inherently subjective and subject to bias, it is important to have a standard and predetermined template to rate the quality of performance. These templates can either be adapted from outside sources or created before the project begins. Table 21 is one example of how a student can

Table 21 Satisfaction Levels for Major Elements of Project Management

	Highly Satisfied	Satisfied	Neutral	Dissatisfied	Highly Dissatisfied	Insufficient Exposure
Accurately defined project goals and objectives						
Satisfactorily delegated assignments						
Managed time well						
Communicated effectively with stakeholders and team members						
Closed out project at appropriate juncture						
Accurately predicted budget and time needs						

self-assess his or her performance of a project. A self-directed student should also ask a trusted advisor to rate his or her project performance using the same rubric. This is just one way for a student to assess project performance. Because projects are by their nature unique, different assessment tools may be appropriate for different projects.

In the business world, many companies use a "scorecard" method of assessing the success of a project. The scorecard method identifies the task to be accomplished during the planning phase, determines the relative "weight" of each task, and, as an assessment tool, gives the performance a score on a 1–10 scale of how well each task was performed. Consider, for example, the research portion of writing a lawyering-skills brief. To write a high-quality brief, you had to accomplish several tasks during the research process before you could begin writing. Table 22 shows a sample way you could measure the relative importance of each task.

Table 22 Scorecard: Researching for the Summary Judgment Brief

Tasks to Be Accomplished	Weight	Score/10
Accurately identifying the question presented	15%	9/10
Selecting credible and citable authority	10%	8/10
Setting accurate estimates of time needed to complete research	10%	6/10
Properly citing sources by *Bluebook*	15%	8/10
Addressing each part of the question presented	25%	9/10
Ensuring cited authority is still "good law"	15%	7/10
Knowing when to stop researching and begin writing given time constraints	10%	7/10

One advantage of the summary judgment brief is that it is a graded event, meaning that there is an assessment at the end of the project. After receiving a grade, you can use the scorecard to determine how well you did in accomplishing each task. Furthermore, you can identify whether you gave appropriate weight to each series of the task. This method of self-assessment gives you an opportunity to learn lessons from the experience, which can be applied to the appellate brief written in the second year.

But no matter how objective you strive to be, it is still only one viewpoint. To ensure accurate assessment, it is critical to develop the habit of seeking outside perspectives on project performance. Any outside assessor should be familiar with both you and the project you were working on. For example, asking team member to use the same assessment templates to rate you gives you a perspective from someone who knows the project intimately. It is also useful to get feedback from a supervisor, professor, or trusted advisor. This varied-perspective approach gives you ways to compare viewpoints to gauge more accurately your true performance. This 360-degree assessment is a great way to learn from a project management experience and is a fitting task to complete after the closeout phase of a project. The sooner the assessment can happen after the closeout, the greater the likelihood you can actually learn from mistakes made during the project.

While there will be different components of an assessment based on the specific project, one aspect of every project that can be assessed is the difference between initial estimates for time and budget needs and the end result. It would be very advantageous for you to be able to explain to a potential employer that you have improved your ability to estimate time and budget needs for a given project by doing assessments after projects conducted in law school. The ability to accurately estimate need and costs up front is invaluable in the legal world, and in fact, new CLE courses on project management focus on estimating how long various tasks should take.[98]

6. Conclusion

So, why should you, as a law student, be intentional about using the principles of project management to handle the various projects while still in law school? The answer is threefold. First, using the proven methods of project management can ensure the success of any project. By determining what needs to be done in the planning and build-up phases, monitoring and controlling the tasks during the implementation phase, and conducting a final assessment of the quality of the product in the closeout phase, you ensure a higher chance of achieving success. Second, using the project management methodology while still in law school gives you practice using a methodology that law firms and employers are increasingly expecting new associates to know. If you have used these methods in law school, you have demonstrable evidence to provide to an interviewer that you have already mastered some of the core competencies that employers desire. Third, project management ability responds to many of the themes seen in section I: (1) it is how organizational clients approach problems; (2) it interferes with machine intelligence; (3) it sends strong messages about efficiency and cost effectiveness; and (4) it fits "hand in glove" with effective teams, including lower -cost providers.

Now that you have read "Project Management Skills: How Law Students Can Learn and Implement the Skills Employers Value," complete the Reflection Dashboard at **http://ambar.org/roadmap** to develop a better understanding of what developmental stage you are at and what steps you will take to grow to the next stage. Also, recall that the project management assessment tools, for both individuals and groups, may be found online, as well.

---

[98] *Project Management for Lawyers, supra* note 80.

Group 2: Competencies Related to "Internalization of Deep Responsibilities to Others (the Client, the Team, the Employing Organization, and the Legal System)"

E. Commitment to Others
F. Trustworthiness: Building Lasting Professional Relationships
G. Dedication and Responsiveness to Clients
H. The Basics of Good Judgment to Help Clients
I. The Basics of Teamwork
J. Commitment to the Employing Organization
K. Building Relationships Based on Trust through Networking
L. Cross-Cultural Competency: Developing Cultural Competencies for the Changing Workplace
M. Listen to Persuade: How Attentiveness Leads to Value

Hand in glove with ownership over a student's own professional development toward excellence in all the competencies needed to serve employers and clients well is an internalized responsibility to others, including clients, the team, the employing organization, and the legal system. Of course the law of lawyering, including the Rules of Professional Conduct, set a floor of fiduciary responsibilities to the client particularly, and conduct below this floor will get penalized. However, compliance with the minimum standards does not differentiate you.

What will differentiate you is to internalize the basic principles in section I's discussion of being a coproducer of legal services with your clients and having an entrepreneurial mindset with respect to your clients (note that your clients in the early years are often senior lawyers). You are an entrepreneur offering service to help clients, your team, and your organization be successful.

Author Neil Hamilton recently had lunch with a former student who graduated in 1983 in about the middle of his class. After eight years as a commercial litigator, he decided that he was not drawing energy from the work. He had been a very good musician prior to law school and had a passion to help musicians with their problems. Over time, he built a highly successful practice representing musicians. His comment to me was, "You have to learn that you are an entrepreneur in a service profession. It is not about you; it is about the client. It is about helping them solve problems, and not just technical legal problems. Over time, try things to find your passion in helping a type of client. They know if you are passionate about helping them. Build trust. The rest will take care of itself."

The next nine chapters look at the competencies that signal to legal employers and clients that you know it is not about you; it is about helping them.

E. Commitment to Others[99]

All legal employers value competencies related to a commitment to others. For example, in ratings across four studies, the following competencies were considered very important to critically important in the decision to hire a new lawyer: (1) *integrity/honesty/trustworthiness*; (2) *dedication to client service/responsiveness to client*; (3) *commitment to firm/department/office, its goals, and its values*; and (4) *ability to initiate and maintain strong work and team relationships*. Among the competencies considered important to very important in the decision to hire: (5) *inspires confidence* and (6) *seeks feedback/responsive to feedback*. In an analysis of eighteen firms' competency models, all firms included *ability to initiate and maintain strong work and team relationships*; sixteen firms included *business development/marketing/client retention* and *dedication to client service/ responsive to client*; and twelve firms included *commitment to firm/department/ office, its goals, and values.*[100] In addition, in a synthesis of competency models from ten state attorney general offices, all offices assessed *ability to initiate and maintain strong work and team relationships*, and almost half assessed *commitment to the firm/department/office, its goals, and its values.*[101]

Some empirical research exists to show corporate clients' definition of lawyer effectiveness and what competencies they want in a lawyer.[102] The central theme found in this research is that exceptional effectiveness moves beyond excellent technical competence and toward excellent relationship skills demonstrating (1) a strong understanding of the client's business and needs, (2) good judgment and problem solving in light of that understanding of the client, (3) strong responsiveness to the client, and (4) a focus on cost-effective solutions that provide value to the client. Note that section I's discussion of changing markets for legal services strongly emphasized that these competencies are very important.

There are few empirical studies of what competencies individual clients want to see in lawyers. One major study shows "listening" and "able to see the world through the eyes of others" are both considered essential factors for attorney effectiveness. The available research also indicates individual clients want to know their lawyers are committed to and responsive to their needs—not excessively focused on money. Caring about the client, keeping the client informed and empowered, and listening skills are critical competencies that individual clients value. Clients want to trust that, above all else, their lawyers are dedicated to caringfor them with all of their ability. In giving their trust to you as a lawyer, clients primarily "want to know that your entire focus is on them and their interests

---

[99] Authored by Neil W. Hamilton and Christopher Damian.

[100] *See* table 2 in section I.D.1 "Assessment Models."

[101] *See* table 1 in section I.D.1 "Assessment Models."

[102] *See* "What Clients Want" in section I.D.4.

and not on you and what you can get from them."[103] Go back to section I to review the competencies that the Schultz–Zedeck empirical study of the competencies that lawyers as clients wanted if they were hiring a lawyer.

Law schools, however, have tended not to prioritize these competencies. As a student, you should focus on the courses and experiences that develop these competencies, but this requires proactive ownership on your part.

A deep commitment to clients is the foundation for successful practice. Professor William D. Henderson says his research "shows that the single best predictor of success and effectiveness as a lawyer is the ability to become truly client focused."[104] Even though you may only interact with clients in clinics or clerkships, there are many ways to gain experience and create evidence to show your competency of a deep commitment to serving others. For example, "Trustworthiness: Building Lasting Professional Relationships" focuses on the competency most emphasized in section I's discussion of what legal employers want. You need to understand that credibility, reliability, and your relational skills build trust, and your own self-orientation (self-centeredness) decreases trust.

"Dedication and Responsiveness to Clients" recommends law students learn and apply the critical skills of dedication and responsiveness to a client by providing their professors with "exceptional service according to their individual needs, wants, and expectations." For example, Meagher & Geer PLLP tells new lawyers to practice client-service skills through interactions with senior attorneys. If students or new lawyers can provide exceptional service to a professor or senior attorney, they will do the same for a client. Thus, the lawyer seeking to gain competency at the level of a senior lawyer should focus on professional development in general, seeking excellence and other-directedness in *every* relationship.

"Building Relationships Based on Trust through Networking" notes that networking is "the single most effective, underutilized, and misunderstood tool to gaining meaningful professional employment." This problem largely stems from a misunderstanding of what networking is. Rather than a self-interested practice in manipulation, networking is best understood as "the formation of professional, ideally long-term, relationships that are mutually beneficial." The chapter provides ways in which law students can create professional contacts based on trust. Among other things, the "expert networker" looks for ways to benefit contacts and develop networking strengths that an employer would value. While the inexperienced networker sees networking primarily as about gaining employment, experienced lawyers will see networking as a means to establish long-term relationships based on trust.

---

[103] Greg Stephens, *Law Practice Today, How to Obtain and Retain Clients*, Am. B. Ass'n L. Prac. Division (Nov. 2012), *available at* http://www.americanbar.org/publications/law_practice_today_home/law_practice_today_archive/november12/how-to-obtain-and-retain-clients.html.

[104] William D. Henderson, *The Client-Focused Lawyer*, Nat'l Jurist, Jan. 2011, at 62, *available at* http://www.law.indiana.edu/instruction/wihender/focus_jan11.pdf.

Likewise, teamwork requires the diminishment of self-interest and a focus on the success of others. "The Basics of Teamwork" begins with Andrew Carnegie's assertion that teamwork is "the ability to work together toward a common vision—the ability to direct individual accomplishment toward organizational objectives."[105] Teams consist of individuals who interact while striving to achieve mutual goals in positive interdependence. The free rider—the team member who cannot or will not do his or her part for the team—is the biggest fear or annoyance when working on teams. The success of a team depends on proactive responses to address the "free-rider" challenge and the pursuit of a commitment to others.

In "Commitment to the Employing Organization: Intraoffice Professionalism and How to Be a Successful New Lawyer," Professor Benjamin Carpenter notes that, as a new lawyer, your initial focus should be on serving those you are working for. Everything you do as a new lawyer should follow from this fundamental principle. In transitioning from a law student to a "go-to" lawyer, your primary focus should be an orientation toward service to the senior lawyers who give you work.

An effective lawyer is not simply someone with competency in networking relationships, team relationships, and organizational relationships. An effective lawyer is someone with excellent relational skills and competencies and who can apply these skills and competencies to *any* relationship. Further, an effective lawyer will be able to anticipate the needs of colleagues, employer/supervisors, and clients and will be *proactive in committing* to their success.

These competencies will be essential for lawyers who desire to take charge of their legal careers. Though a certain degree of doctrinal knowledge and technical skill is a threshold to any legal work, students who have particularly excelled in these areas may not necessarily become lawyers with the greatest degree of power and mobility in their professional careers. Consider a course project that requires a team of your peers: you may want the student with the highest grades in your class as a part of your team, but if this student doesn't interact well with others, you may not necessarily want him or her to be the team's manager or to correspond directly with your supervisor/professor. Rather, you may choose students for such work who are better able to interact with others, build trust among your team members, and instill confidence in others concerning their commitment to the team, the supervisor/professor, and others who will be needed for the project.

Without strong relational competency, the high-ranked student also may not be the best person to interact with clients as a future lawyer. Senior attorneys or supervisors may elect to have other attorneys interact more directly with clients, while the attorney with less relational competency will have to engage clients primarily through these intermediaries. The gatekeeper to the client,

---

[105] Andrew Carnegie, American Entrepreneur.

however, is the gatekeeper to legal work. A lawyer who is unable to develop the competencies needed to become this gatekeeper will be unable to take charge of his or her career. A lawyer without a developed and demonstrated commitment to others will always be relying on others as a gatekeeper to his or her work. The following chapters focus on ways to become this gatekeeper.

F. Trustworthiness: Building Lasting Professional Relationships[106]

Trustworthiness tends to be the criterion employers consider most critical when hiring new attorneys.[107] More importantly, trust is at the heart of a student's or lawyer's own professional ethical identity. The life of the profession is indeed sustained by trust—by each client's trust in his or her lawyer and in the profession itself.

So what builds trust? We often believe that simply becoming skilled in the profession will enable other's trust in us, and it will to an extent. The foundation of trust, though, is our own ethical professional identity upon which we stand while we grow in our competencies and professional formation.

1. A Starting Point for Reflection

The Trust Quotient Assessment is a highly recommended tool, as it will help you understand both your own self-perception of your trustworthiness and others' perceptions of your trustworthiness. Instructions to access this assessment can be found at https://trustsuite.trustedadvisor.com. This assessment gives you both the strongest aspect of your own trust quotient and the aspect that needs the most improvement, then provides suggestions for leveraging the strength and improving the less developed aspect. The Trust Quotient Assessment will give you a good starting point for reflection, both on how you can persuade potential employers and clients that you are trustworthy and on how you can develop toward a later developmental stage of trustworthiness. If others perceive you as highly trustworthy in your professional work, you will be able to build lasting relationships and enjoy greater meaning and success. In *Give and Take: Why Helping Others Drives Our Success,* Wharton Professor Adam Grant argues that others perceive "givers" as more trustworthy.[108] "Whereas takers tend to be self-focused, evaluating what other people can offer them, givers are other-focused, paying more attention to what other people need from them."[109] We all want our service providers—like lawyers—to be givers, not takers.

---

[106] Authored by Neil W. Hamilton and Bradley Yenter.

[107] First for large firms and county attorneys, second for small firms, and fourth for legal aid providers.

[108] The first chapter of the book is available online for free.

[109] ADAM GRANT, GIVE AND TAKE: WHY HELPING OTHERS DRIVES OUR SUCCESS 4 (2013).

2. Implications for Law Students Seeking Employment

The question then becomes, "How do employers assess the trustworthiness of job applicants?" This chapter explores what employers mean by trustworthiness, then suggests ways students can build an affirmative case for this critical competency.

One way to understand the competency of trustworthiness is to consider to whom you would turn in your class if you had a serious legal problem of your own (assume your classmates have acquired the requisite knowledge and experience). Create a table similar to table 23 to list them. What traits or characteristic makes these people trustworthy?

Table 23 Which Classmates Would I Trust with a Serious Legal Problem?

I would trust _____ with my problem   because he/she is_____

Another way to understand trustworthiness is to ask why adults make referrals of service providers (e.g., doctors, dentists, and auto mechanics) to other adults. Ask at least two people that question, and either record their responses in table 24 or create your own table similar to table 24. What traits or characteristics make these service providers trustworthy? Do these adults know the class rank of the service providers?

Table 24 To Whom Do Adults You Know Make Referrals?

_____ refers people to _____   because he/she is_____

The list you generated in table 23 is likely not a ranking of just the technical legal skills of the students you know, and the adults you spoke with likely did not know the class rank of their service providers. That is because trust is dynamic and multidimensional—someone might trust your expertise and intelligence but distrust your relationship skills and motives.[110] Indeed, trustworthiness involves consideration of both integrity and competency—about whether you are able to accomplish a task as well as whether you are motivated by immediate

---

[110] David H. Maister, Charles H. Green & Robert M. Galford, The Trusted Advisor 70 (2000).

self-interest or long-term relationships that involve fairness and loyalty. Furthermore, trust does not remain fixed and static but varies according to our perception of the other person's behavior, integrity, and competence.

According to Maister, Green, and Galford, **Trust = (C + R + I)/S**, where:

"**C**" is credibility (which speaks to your record of demonstrated competence in the skills needed for the work and your ability to communicate that competence);

"**R**" is reliability (which speaks to how others perceive your dependability to constantly perform well the skills or functions that are expected of you);

"**I**" is intimacy (which speaks to how secure others feel in sharing important matters with you); and

"**S**" is self-orientation (which speaks to how self-centered you are, as compared to being focused on serving the client well and fairly).[111]

To be trusted, then, is to score well on all four dimensions (from the perspective of others), unless your performance in one or two dimensions is strong enough to overcome relative weaknesses.[112] Maister, Green, and Galford, however, believe that low self-orientation (i.e., being very other-directed) is the most important element of trustworthiness.[113]

Many service providers, as professionals with specialized training and state licenses, instinctively focus on credibility. They are technically competent (i.e., credible) and want their clients to know as much—that's why doctors, dentists, and lawyers often display their diplomas in their offices. By repeatedly providing quality service, these professionals also demonstrate their reliability.[114] Keep in mind, though, that "most humans—including clients—buy from the heart, and justify it from the head."[115] That means even the most credible, reliable service providers need to work at increasing their intimacy scores and decreasing their self-orientation scores.

They do the former by addressing difficult problems with empathy and tact, by active listening, and by speaking with clients as if they were friends.[116] Empirical data presented in *Give and Take* also makes clear that law students will want to grow toward being givers in professional relationships. The more legal employers and clients perceive a student as a giver, the lower that student's self-orientation score, and the greater the student's trustworthiness. As William Sullivan explains, "Each client or patient needs to trust that her lawyer or

---

[111] *Id.* at 69.

[112] *Id.* at 70.

[113] *Id.*

[114] *Id.* at 74.

[115] Charles Green, *The Trust Equation: A Primer*, TRUSTED ADVISOR, http://trustedadvisor.com/articles/the-trust-equation-a-primer (last visited July 16, 2017).

[116] MAISTER, GREEN & GALFORD, *supra* note 110, at 77–82.

physician is dedicated above all else to care for her with all of the professionals' ability."[117]

Sadly, legal consumers are often disappointed. In a 2001 survey, 69 percent of respondents thought many lawyers are "more interested in making money than serving their clients," are "manipulative," and "do a poor job of policing themselves."[118] An attorney can avoid these perceptions by, for example, sending a message that she or he is aware of the impact of the cost on the person served and is trying to keep costs down. And when mistakes are made, she or he can make lemonade out of lemons (generally gaining trust) by saying, "I will make this right, at no cost to you."

The latter strategy has provided powerful results in other service industries. Take the example of Ryan Companies, a Minneapolis-based construction group whose mission statement is "Building Lasting Relationships."[119] President and CEO Pat Ryan enjoys telling the story about a 1950s project in which his two uncles were building a grocery store.[120] When the structure started to settle, his uncles could have filed for bankruptcy and walked away.[121] Instead "they went across the street, bought the property and built the store all over again—at their own expense." This story cemented the company's reputation for trustworthiness. Several decades later, Ryan Companies employs 800 people across the country and generates $1 billion in revenue.[122]

"Although we often stereotype givers [like the Ryan family] as chumps and doormats, they turn out to be surprisingly successful."[123] Clients reward those who focus on contributing value to them, not on claiming value from them.[124] And as the service sector continues to expand, "more and more people are placing a premium on providers who have established relationships and reputations as givers."[125] To compete in such an economy, new attorneys must emphasize the elements of the trust equation.

3. Trust in the First Five Minutes of a New Relationship

In a new relationship, the first five minutes function as some of the most important moments, as they set the tone for the development of the relationship to come. In fact, the relationship and the other person's perception of you are significantly formed in these first few moments. In *Thinking, Fast and Slow*, Daniel Kahneman names our tendency to lock in a person's trustworthiness or

---

[117] SULLIVAN, *supra* note 11, at xi, xv.

[118] *Id.* at 7–10.

[119] Doug Hennes, *Take Care of Your Customer*, ST. THOMAS MAG., Spring 2014, at 12.

[120] *Id.*

[121] *Id.* at 13.

[122] *Id.*

[123] GRANT, *supra* note 109, at 9.

[124] Hennes, *supra* note 119, at 17.

[125] *Id.*

character in these first few minutes as the "halo effect."[126] Kahneman explains the halo effect in this way: "The tendency to like (or dislike) everything about a person—including things you have not observed—is known as the halo effect."[127] He goes on to signify the importance of the halo effect in our first impressions: "The sequence in which we observe characteristics of a person is often determined by chance. Sequence matters, however, because the halo effect increases the weight of first impressions, sometimes to the point that subsequent information is mostly wasted."[128]

So how do we create lasting trust in such a short amount of time? Research by David DeSteno in *The Truth about Trust* offers us some clues about how *not* to act. DeSteno focuses on an assessment of our body language that helps indicate trustworthiness as perceived by others. He notes that there are four individual cues that, *when taken together*, strongly predict how trustworthy a person will be.[129] The four cues are "crossing arms, leaning away, face touching, hand touching. The more frequently any individual engaged in these behaviors, the less trustworthy he or she acted."[130] He continues, "When combined, these features offer a picture of a partner who doesn't want to engage and is self-conscious or worried about how he or she is likely to act. They mark someone who doesn't want to be your friend and is thinking about acting in a way you wouldn't like."[131]

DeSteno also argues that first impressions can build a sense of expertise in the following way: "Cues to expertise are those directly associated with nonverbal expressions of pride and status: expanded posture, head tilted upwards, arms held open and raised or placed akimbo (i.e., hands on waist with elbows tilted outward), and decreased gazing at others during interactions."[132] Note that the behaviors that signal trustworthiness are highly influenced by cross-cultural biases, and the later discussion of cross-cultural competency is important here. However, in seeking employment, you should be aware of the research on how important these signals are in the first five minutes of building a relationship.

4. Becoming a Trusted Advisor

"The trusted advisor is the person the client turns to when an issue first arises, often in times of urgency: a crisis, a change, a triumph, or a defeat."[133] Most service providers begin their careers as vendors, completing a specific technical

---

[126] Daniel Kahneman, Thinking Fast and Slow 82 (2011).

[127] *Id.*

[128] *Id.* at 83.

[129] David DeSteno, The Truth About Trust: How It Determines Success in Life, Love, Learning, and More 162 (2014).

[130] *Id.*

[131] *Id.* at 163.

[132] *Id.* at 171.

[133] Maister, Green & Galford, *supra* note 110, at 7.

task.[134] Eventually, clients may sense that a certain service provider has additional capabilities beyond the original area of expertise and is trustworthy.[135] They will ask that service provider to solve general problems, including those involving more than technical mastery.[136] If he or she does that well, clients will see the service provider as "having the ability to put issues in context and to provide perspective."[137] The service provider may then start providing advice proactively and, over time, will become a trusted advisor.[138] At that point, virtually all issues are open to discussion.[139] This development, from subject-matter expert to trusted advisor, is depicted in diagram 3.[140]

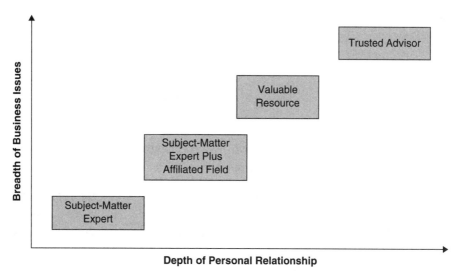

Diagram 3 The Evolution of a Client–Advisor Relationship

We can also track this progression by type of relationship, as in diagram 4.[141]

5. Tips for Law Students

The legal profession's current deficits in terms of trustworthiness present an opportunity for law students to differentiate themselves on this competency. To convey trustworthiness to potential employers, you must assemble evidence

---

[134] *Id.* at 7.

[135] *Id.*

[136] *Id.*

[137] *Id.* at 8.

[138] *Id.*

[139] *Id.*

[140] *Id.* at 7.

[141] *Id.* at 9.

related to each element of trust: credibility, reliability, intimacy, and self-orientation. (Stories help, and so do references—especially because many legal

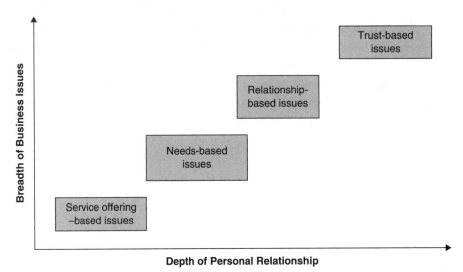

Diagram 4 Four Types of Relationships

employers are beginning to use behavioral interviewing. Be prepared with specific answers to demonstrate the elements of trustworthiness.)

1. *Credibility*: Most large firms start their assessment of candidates with a screen of technical legal skills, such as class rank, but many other legal employers do not. Individual clients care whether you are licensed to practice law and whether other users of your services have had a good experience. The key is to have evidence of the competencies relevant to those two client desires. If you are interested in litigation, for example, you want to present a strong record from experienced lawyers who have observed your work in litigation courses, such as advocacy classes and clinics.

2. *Reliability*: By definition, reliability requires repeated experiences—others need to hear you commit and then see you make good on those commitments. Consider, for example, taking on a leadership role in a student organization where you can set and achieve objectives.

3. *Intimacy*: To improve your intimacy score, take courses like negotiation, client interviewing, and counseling; you need to be comfortable dealing with other people's emotions. Also read the following chapters in the Roadmap: "Initiative, Drive, Work Ethic, and Commitment to Professional Development,"[142] "Commitment to Others,"[143] and "Listen to Persuade: How Attentiveness Leads to Value."[144]

---

[142] *See* "Initiative, Drive, Work Ethic, and Commitment to Professional Development" in section III.

[143] *See* "Commitment to Others" in section III.

[144] *See* "Listen to Persuade" in section III.

4. *Self-orientation*: Practice effective active listening,[145] a skill that demonstrates both intimacy and other-focusedness.[146] By volunteering your time to a service organization (beyond any graduation requirement), you also demonstrate commitment to something larger than yourself.

Simply by seeking a 360-degree assessment of your trustworthiness, reflecting on the results, and changing your behavior, you are sending a powerful message to potential employers of self-improvement. You should also strive to develop a reputation for going the extra mile for others and for correcting mistakes. You'll succeed by focusing on something other than financial success—namely, on building lasting trust-based relationships.

Now that you have read "Trustworthiness: Building Lasting Professional Relationships," complete the Reflection Dashboard at **http://ambar.org/roadmap** to develop a better understanding of what developmental stage you are at and what steps you will take to grow to the next stage. The Trust Quotient Assessment instructions are also available electronically through the link just provided.

G. Dedication and Responsiveness to Clients[147]

1. Client Service

Dedication and responsiveness to clients are extremely important. Clients have many options, and competition for them is fierce. Clients tend to assume that you provide an excellent work product. Therefore, often it is client service that determines whether you obtain and retain business.

Successful attorneys know that relationships are the key to being successful. Clients want to do business with people they know, like, and trust. Successful attorneys are the ones who not only possess the requisite legal skills but also know how to connect and stay connected with clients by providing them with the superior service that helps make the clients successful.

2. A Client-Focused Mindset

Successful attorneys are the ones who have developed a mindset that keeps the focus on the client instead of on them. They have developed the habit of taking a *sincere* interest in the client. These attorneys' words and actions consistently demonstrate that their work is really all about the clients and not what they can get from the clients. Their sole focus is to help and serve their clients.

---

[145] *See* "Listen to Persuade" in section III.
[146] *See* Neil W. Hamilton, *Effectiveness Requires Listening: How to Assess and Improve Listening Skills,* 13 FLOR. COASTAL L. REV. 145 (2012).
[147] Authored by Greg Stephens.

Consequently, they continually ask clients and prospective clients three questions: (1) What are your needs, wants, and expectations? (2) Is there anything that I can do for you? (3) Is there anything that I can do to make your life easier? William Sullivan writes that nearly all of us

> will be vulnerable and in need of medical expertise. We will want the best-prepared and most knowledgeable doctors we can find. But more than that, we will need to be able to trust that our physicians will be dedicated above all else to care for us with all their ability.[148]

The same can be said of clients seeking legal advice. Clients need to trust that, above all else, their lawyers are dedicated to caring for them with all their ability. Successful attorneys are those who have developed this dedication to the client.

3. Needs, Wants, and Expectations

Each client is unique, with specific needs, wants, and expectations. Talk with your clients and listen to them. You need to understand their business and what is important to them. Ask them questions. Discover and understand their specific needs, wants, and expectations.[149] For example, you may discover that one client wants you to try every case to a conclusion, while another client wants you to settle the case as soon as possible. You may discover that one client does not care how you staff a file, while another client wants you to use only one partner and one associate on the file.

But there are some needs, wants, and expectations that all clients have. Clients want a consistent, superior work product that is timely, clear, and decisive. Clients want to work with an attorney who is focused on them and their success. Additionally, clients want to work with an attorney who is committed to excellence in everything that he or she does. And clients want an attorney who is accessible, attentive, caring, ethical, friendly, likable, sincere, and trustworthy.

4. Treat Professors as Your Clients

Unless they have received prior sales training, how can students learn and apply the critical skills of dedication and responsiveness to a client? One firm

---

[148] SULLIVAN, *supra* note 11, at xi.

[149] The skills and preparation needed to have a successful interaction with a client are quite similar to the skills and preparation needed for a successful networking meeting. In preparation for a client meeting, you should research the client; determine what information you wish to convey about yourself, the firm, and the client's issue; and formulate a general idea of different ways to proceed. Just as in the networking meeting, there are four steps in a client meeting. In the meeting, one should (1) be mindful of creating a positive first impression, (2) provide a brief overview of oneself and the client, (3) discuss specific and preprepared questions, and (4) end by expressing your gratitude for the client's time and business. Also like the networking meeting, a meeting with the client is not about the attorney. Be mindful that your main goal is similar to the goal of the networking meeting: to learn from the client and to discover, *from the client's perspective*, the best way to proceed. Essentially, you want to learn *from the client* how best to help the client.

tells its young associates to practice their client-service skills on senior attorneys by treating them as their clients.

Just like each client, each senior attorney is unique, with different needs, wants, and expectations. Firm associates must discover the differences among the senior attorneys and provide them with exceptional service according to their individual needs, wants, and expectations. In addition to learning how to serve the senior attorneys according to their individual needs, wants, and expectations, associates must also provide what all clients expect: a superior work product that is timely, clear, and decisive. Good client service makes clients look good, and good client service makes clients' lives easier. So associates focus on helping the senior attorney look good and making his or her life easier.

While you are in law school, you have a golden opportunity to practice clients-ervice skills on your professors by treating them the same way that you would treat a client. Over the years, I have reviewed important client-service principles with our attorneys. In the November 2012 issue of *Law Practice Today*, the American Bar Association (ABA) published my article "How to Obtain and Retain Clients."[150] I recommend that you read my article and then conduct your own research on client service. Make a list of the principles and skills of client service, and start applying them to your professors. You can start by learning all that you can about your professors. What are their backgrounds? What articles and books have they published? What are they working on now? What are their personal interests? What are their favorite sports or activities? What are their likes and dislikes? What are their unique needs, wants, and expectations?

What are some principles of client service that you can start using to treat a professor as your client? Maybe you read an article that you think your professor would enjoy reading. E-mail it to him or her. This is a great habit to continue using with your clients and potential clients. Maybe you discovered that one of your professors is writing an article and needs help checking his or her footnotes. Volunteer to help. Remember, you are not trying to be a "brownnoser" or the "teacher's pet." You are merely practicing client-service principles, one of which is to help others without expecting anything in return.

Because I want you to think about what principles make up good client service and how you can apply them to your new client, I am going to give you only a few insights. First, you need to develop a new mindset. You need to focus on your professors. Even though they are here to help you learn, they are not here to serve you. On the contrary, good client service dictates that you are here to serve them. President John F. Kennedy once said, "My fellow Americans, ask not what your country can do for you, ask what you can do for your country."[151] Similarly, ask not what your professor can do for you, ask what you can do for

---

[150] Greg Stephens, *How to Obtain and Retain Clients*, Law Prac. Today (Nov. 2012), *available at* http://www.americanbar.org/publications/law_practice_today_home/law_practice_today_archive /november12/how-to-obtain-and-retain-clients.html.

[151] President John F. Kennedy, Inaugural Address (Jan. 20, 1961).

your professor. Second, start asking yourself questions such as: How can I help my professor? How can I make his or her life easier? Third, you need to become committed to excellence in everything that you do. And just as you would do for any client, you can start by being committed to always providing a timely, superior work product.

5. Keep a Journal or Portfolio

When applying for a job, you have many ways to distinguish yourself. One way to distinguish yourself is to mention in your résumé or cover letter that during law school, you gained experience applying client-service principles. And one way that you gained the experience was by treating professors as your clients. In fact, your experience with client service may be the one thing that piques the curiosity of a hiring partner and triggers an interview. In order to provide examples and to tell a compelling story at the interview, you need to keep a journal of your client-service activities.[152] Put the journal into the portfolio discussed previously in section II.F.

Complete a self-assessment using table 25. Be sure to think about what evidence you have that can demonstrate the stage of development you are at. Also consider what steps you need to take to grow to the next stage. Additionally, it

Table 25 Developmental Stages of Dedication and Responsiveness to Client

Junior Attorney	Mid-level Attorney	Senior Attorney
• Interacts with clients under supervision • Responsive to client needs • Understands expectations and deadlines • Only interested in client insofar as is required to complete the project	• Demonstrates empathy • Shows initiative to learn more about client and client's needs • Demonstrates responsibility for high-quality work product • Listens carefully to the client with sensitivity • Demonstrates a more client-oriented focus	• Actively seeks to learn more about the client's context and needs • Shows exceptional empathy • Instills respect and confidence of clients • Holds others accountable for quality of work for the client • Shows commitment to the clients' interests • Shows a sincere interest in the client • Demonstrates a strong focus to help the client be successful • Seeks to expand firm relationship with client

---

[152] Experiences of client service, like all experiences with competencies, should be kept in a portfolio. *See* "Creating Portfolios for Two or Three of Your Strongest Competencies" in section II for further discussion of this habit.

may be useful to go back and look at the material on coproduction with clients presented in section I, as this may guide you on how to move to the next stage of dedication and responsiveness to clients.

Now that you have read "Dedication and Responsiveness to Clients," complete the Reflection Dashboard at **http://ambar.org/roadmap** to develop a better understanding of what developmental stage you are at and what steps you will take to grow to the next stage.

H. The Basics of Good Judgment to Help Clients[153]

There are thousands of works from different disciplines defining good judgment and how a person can grow toward good judgment. Reflection on all these works would be helpful to define good judgment, but our focus here is the *practical* question of how legal employers define and assess good judgment. Our current data defining the developmental stages of good judgment (set forth in table 26) are from five large firms with 67 to 740 lawyers.[154]

We do know that small firms and government employers also look for good judgment in hiring and assess good judgment, but we do not yet have data from those employers to define the developmental stages of good judgment they use to assess new lawyers. A reasonable assumption is that the major elements of good judgment for small-firm and government employers will be similar to the large-firm definition. A synthesis of the four major elements of good judgment from the five law firms is as follows:

1. **Recognition and evaluation of risks and problems, and alternative courses of action, with a recommendation on the most reasonable course of action among the alternatives**. This is a common theme running throughout all five of the columns in table 26.
2. **Creativity and strategic thinking**. Creativity and strategic thinking pair well with element 1 because without creativity and strategic thinking, it is difficult to properly evaluate risks/problems and discover possible alternative courses of action.
3. **Understanding the client's best interests in the larger context of the client's situation and the client's business**. This pairs well with elements 1 and 2. The legal issues the client faces arise in a much larger context of considerations (some of which are equally or more important than a

---

[153] Authored by Neil W. Hamilton.

[154] Categories A, B, and C of this chart come from a study of the 14 largest Minnesota law firms in May and June 2012. Each firm provided Neil Hamilton with associate evaluation forms. Category D comes from Peter B. Sloan, *From Classes to Competencies, Lockstep to Levels* (2007), at B2. Category E comes from SCOTT A. WESTFAHL, NAT'L ASS'N FOR LAW PLACEMENT, YOU GET WHAT YOU MEASURE 37, 46, 55 (2008).

Table 26 Developmental Stages to Assess Associate Attorney Good Judgment

	Firm A	Firm B	Firm C	Firm D	Firm E
Junior Associate	• Demonstrates astute discernment and fitting behavior in interactions with others, even when under stress • Uses diplomacy and tact routinely • Knows when to ask for guidance and direction on work assignments • Demonstrates professionalism in personal appearance and attire • Accepts constructive feedback with maturity	• Recognizes potential risks involved in clients' situations	• Uses common sense and creativity in applying the law	• Able to identify risks involved in alternative courses of action	• Consistently grasps complex legal issues and applies the law effectively • Is intellectually curious and a creative problem solver • Is able to identify and analyze issues independently • Thinks strategically • Can assimilate a large volume of complex legal or factual information and synthesize it carefully
Mid-level Associate	• In addition: • Able to grasp complex facts and aspects of law as well as practical aspects of matters	• Identifies and evaluates risks involved in alternative courses of action	• Uses both common sense and creativity in applying the law	• Able to identify and evaluate risks involved in alternative methods of action and to recommend sound courses of action	• Participates with others in formulating strategy and responding to significant developments • Consistently exercises excellent discernment in complex transactions, drafting pleadings, or discovery matters with some partner oversight

• Understands the business issues concerning the matter and client priorities • Anticipates clients' needs • Shows astute discernment in personal client intake decisions	• Recommends appropriate course of action based upon evaluation of the relevant facts, issues, and risks	• Identifies and articulates alternative courses of action and strategies for consideration by the supervising lawyer, and identifies risks involved in such courses of action	• Evidences creative problem solving and reliably resolves difficult issues • Is building a reputation for depth of thought and intellectual rigor • Is starting to exercise good business common sense
Senior Associate In addition: • Is a role model for, and can mentor new associates • Can recommend creative alternatives to shareholders and clients in addressing clients' concerns (legal and business)	• Evaluates the relevant facts, issues, and risks; distinguishes among various options; and prepares and executes effective strategies to achieve the clients' objectives	• Uses both common sense and creativity in applying the law • Identifies and evaluates facts, issues, and risks involved in alternative courses of action; recommends sound course of action to supervising attorney; and effectively articulates bases for recommendation	• Able to recommend proper course of action based upon evaluation of the relevant facts, issues, and risks; to distinguish among various options; and to prepare and execute effective strategies to achieve the client's objectives • Able to first-chair a contested proceeding or case or to lead and manage a transaction or a significant portion of a complex transaction or other client matter • Has ability to apply legal principles and his/her experience to solve problems and develop approaches that add real value for clients • Has excellent business common sense that inspires partners' confidence • Is well regarded by partners, peers, and clients for intellectual rigor, strategic thinking, and creativity

simple technical legal analysis) that the lawyer needs to understand in order to exercise good judgment to help the client. The lawyer must, in particular, have a strong understanding of the client's business.

4. **Asking for guidance or help/seeking feedback and dialogue with other lawyers to gain insight**.

1. Good Judgment Is Developmental

The first important practical message from table 26 is that legal employers recognize that a new lawyer grows toward these elements of good judgment through developmental stages. Another implicit message is that clients are also going to be in the process of developmental growth toward the elements of good judgment, and a lawyer who is a good counselor can help a client grow toward good judgment by asking good questions and helping the client think through the issues. The challenge is how to intentionally foster your own developmental growth in good judgment through these stages. To further understand how to foster your development of competencies, such as good judgment, it may be useful to read "Entrepreneurial Mindset" in section I.C.2 and pay particular attention to self-directed learning in sections II.C and II.D.

2. Understanding the Overall Context of the Client's Issues and the Client's Business

The second important practical message from the synthesis of the four major elements of good judgment is that all four elements are closely interrelated. For example, a good place to start developing good judgment to help a client identify and analyze risks and to develop creative alternative courses of action is to begin by spending time and energy understanding the overall context of the client's issues, particularly how the client's business works and what the client's business challenges are. Even if the time spent informing yourself is not billable, by doing so, you are sending strong messages about dedication and responsiveness to the client, which is another important competency. To increase your understanding of the overall context of the client's issues, develop your listening and observational skills. Become someone your clients recognize as a strong listener. See "Listen to Persuade: How Attentiveness Leads to Value" in section III for further ways to develop your listening skills.

Additionally, it may be helpful to approach each situation with Professor Ken Goodpaster's creative problem-solving template in mind. The template includes seven steps to help solve any problem. The steps are as follows:

1. Identify the relevant stakeholders, and try to articulate what is truly motivating each stakeholder in the situation in terms of motivations, concerns, interests, and fears. What are the benefits and costs the stakeholders face in the situation? What critical facts does the client need to know to do a competent stakeholder analysis?

2. Identify the principles, norms, and duties (of the client and then of the lawyer) most applicable to the facts.
3. Articulate the principal issue(s) in the problem.
4. Articulate the principal realistic options the client has to address the problem.
5. Tentatively select the best option.
6. Test the client's reasoning at each stage through hypothetical fact situations and, if possible, feedback from others.
7. Give as much time as is practicable for reflection during this process.

3. Internalizing the Habit of Actively Seeking Feedback, Dialogue on the Tough Calls, and Reflection (FDR)

To develop toward later stages of recognizing and evaluating risks and problems and the discovery of creative alternative courses of action, element "D" from the FDR synthesis—asking for guidance or help and seeking feedback and dialogue with other lawyers—is the most important step. "The Competencies Legal Employers Want and Each Student's Professional Formation" in section III analyzes all the empirical data on the most effective pedagogies to foster each student's professional formation, particularly the development of moral reasoning. The empirical studies strongly support fostering each students' internalization of the habit of actively seeking feedback from others, dialogue with others on the tough calls, and reflection. We called this the FDR habit. Coaching and mentoring are particularly effective pedagogies to help a student internalize this FDR habit, in which the coach/mentor asks stage-appropriate questions and tells stage-appropriate stories to promote the student's thought and reflection on a dilemma.

4. A Personal Board of Directors

You should seek out coaches and mentors who can challenge you to reflect and help the student internalize the FDR habit. Jim Collins, author of *Good to Great* (2001) and *Great by Choice* (2011), suggested over a decade ago that a decision maker who exercises good judgment needs a personal board of directors that embodies the core values and ideals the decision maker aspires to achieve. The best board members care enough to give honest and candid feedback, ask the tough questions, share stories of others' experiences handling similar situations, draw analogies, engage in moral dialogue, and foster personal reflection and self-assessment. They do not judgmentally dictate answers; they foster growth of the lawyer's own professional judgment and moral core. You should, over time, recruit a personal board of directors. These trusted advisors will provide the same independent judgment and candid advice for you that you aspire to provide to future clients as their lawyer.

So, how does a junior lawyer go about developing a personal board of directors who can provide counsel on the difficult judgments every lawyer has to make? To begin, Jonathan Haidt, author of *The Righteous Mind: Why Good*

People Are Divided by Politics and Religion (2013), emphasizes the benefits of a diverse board of directors. To further understand diversity, it may be useful to read "Cross-Cultural Competency: Developing Cultural Competencies for the Changing Workplace" in section III.L. It is also wise to include veteran lawyers, as they have an abundance of experiences to draw from. Additionally, we asked three senior lawyers for advice on how to develop a personal board of directors.[155] Collectively, these conversations suggested six skills young lawyers should use to develop a personal board of directors.

- First, be observant. Watch for ethical and moral issues to present themselves to others in your environment, and then see to whom others turn. Usually, individuals who are willing to thoughtfully discuss these dilemmas are sought out for that specific reason and may have a reputation for being open to dialogue.
- Second, build relationships. The legal profession is driven by those whom you know. Personal relationships are already used as a source of knowledge, to locate clients, and to secure employment. This same network should be used to find your personal board of directors.
- Third, choose your board members wisely. Young lawyers should be looking for a particular type of person, not just someone in an advanced position or with certain credentials. Seek out individuals who are respected for their interactions with subordinates and their genuineness, as well as who align with your personal values. These individuals need to be trustworthy and see you in the same light.
- Fourth, humbly approach the conversation. Remember that you are there to learn. You have asked an individual for his or her time, and you should respect it. When approaching the conversation, you need to convey an overt willingness to learn, that you take these issues seriously, and that you are thankful for the person's time.
- Fifth, be candid. During conversations with a board member, explain the dilemma, and be candid about your concerns. In order to be effective, discussions need to be open, honest, and sincere.
- Sixth, reflect on your conversations. Set aside time to candidly reflect on the issues and advice presented during your conversation(s). Without reflection, any guidance and information provided are without context and can easily become lost. The practice of law presents many difficult issues; self-reflection about these topics will help young lawyers develop personally and professionally.

In general, section III.I on "The Basics of Teamwork" also notes extensive empirical evidence that team approaches to problem solving deliver more insight,

---

[155] Neil W. Hamilton & Kurtis Young, *Do You Have a Personal Board of Directors?* MINN. LAW. 8 (Dec. 19, 2011).

more creativity, more testing of ideas, and more diverse thinking that all contribute to good judgment. Organizational clients increasingly work in teams to address challenges, and they expect that the organization's lawyer will be effective in teams.

5. Learning from Bad Judgment and Mistakes

You may have heard the story about the lawyer (or client) who wanted to know how to live a good life. She heard of a guru in Nepal who could answer the question. After trekking for weeks, she found the guru. She asked, "How does a person live a good life?" After thoughtful silence, the guru answered, "Good judgment." The lawyer followed up with, "How do I learn good judgment?" After more reflection, the guru answered, "Bad judgment."

The guru's paradox that from bad judgment, we learn good judgment rings true in Neil Hamilton's experience. Moreover, life offers abundant opportunities to learn good judgment from bad judgment, starting with childhood incidents like sticking a tongue on a swing in winter to colossally stupid decisions in junior high and high school in terms of risk assessment.

Eleanor Roosevelt said, "Learn from the mistakes of others. You can't live long enough to make them all yourself." It is clear that lawyers need to learn everything they can from the mistakes of others, and early in our career, we need the help of coaches and mentors to reflect and borrow their stories of mistakes made. Note that in many ways a lawyer counsels a client by telling stories about the mistakes of others in situations similar to that of the client's. One of the central themes of leadership courses is that, by definition, leaders take risks and will make some mistakes and experience failure. In fact, an important aspect of exercising good judgment is acknowledging that mistakes will occur. The question then becomes whether they learn from the mistakes and failures. A lawyer can make a great contribution to a client's good judgment by sharing stories of what has worked and has not worked in the past when people faced similar situations to the one the client is in now. The lawyer can ask questions that help the client think things through carefully.

Life brings many lemons for both clients and their lawyers, many of which are caused by the person's own errors of judgment. The question is whether or not we make lemonade out of the lemons by helping our clients and ourselves to learn good judgment from bad judgment.

6. Thinking, Fast and Slow, for Lawyers and Clients

Can we improve our abilities both to make good judgments for ourselves and to help clients make better judgments? Psychologist Daniel Kahneman, a Nobel Laureate in economics, published a book, *Thinking, Fast and Slow* (2011), that synthesizes many decades of empirical work on how the mind works. The book provides a wealth of insight both on how each lawyer can improve his or her decision making and how, in the lawyer's counseling role, a lawyer can help clients to improve their decision making.

Kahneman and his deceased coauthor Amos Tversky spent their careers exploring how the human mind works in predictable ways to make errors of judgment. The good news is that they conclude humans are fundamentally reasonable and rational. While our judgments are quite useful and not irrational, they often have errors and need help.[156] The good news here is that there are abundant opportunities to make better decisions for ourselves and to help clients make better decisions.

A general theme of Kahneman's book is that we are overconfident in how well we think and make judgments. We have an exaggerated sense of how well we understand the world. Empirical research consistently shows that we make many systematic errors of judgment from cognitive biases, fallacies, and illusions.[157]

So what does Kahneman's empirical work have to do with our work as lawyers? A good lawyer wants both to minimize errors of personal and professional judgment and, as a counselor, to help clients minimize their errors of judgment. If a lawyer understands the systematic errors of judgment that the human mind makes, he or she can take steps to minimize them.

a. System 1 and System 2 Thinking

From his empirical research, Kahneman argues that human reasoning is distorted by systematic biases, and one major source of such errors is the distinction between what he calls System 1 and System 2 thinking. System 1 and System 2 are metaphors or contrivances—not anatomical places or pathways—that Kahneman has created to help us understand how the mind works. The intuitive, largely unconscious, and automatic System 1 does the fast thinking, and the effortful System 2 does the slow, evaluative, and reasoned thinking. System 2 monitors System 1 and exercises control over System 1 as best it can with its limited resources. System 1 develops over time as a product of learned patterns of association and retained memory to enable a person to create quick drafts of reality and to act in real time. It is especially sensitive to threats where immediate action may be necessary. So, System 1, for example, can immediately detect fear in others' eyes and anger in the voice of others. Essentially, System 1 is the ability, developed over a lifetime, to recognize patterns and causal interpretations of events in a fraction of a second so that the person can produce an adequate solution to a challenge in real time.[158]

System 2 thinks slowly; it evaluates and it reasons. It is essential for tasks that require comparisons, ordered reasoning, and choice. Kahneman's empirical data indicates that although we believe our System 2 is principally in control making reasoned judgments, in reality, our System 1 thinking is more common. The problem is that System 2 has limited resources for concentrated cognitive work

---

[156] KAHNEMAN, *supra* note 126, at 10 and 411.

[157] *Id.* at 415–18.

[158] *Id.* at 20–25.

and self-control, and it gets depleted. As System 2 gets depleted, it weakens in its ability to monitor and control the thoughts and actions suggested by System 1. A depleted System 2 regularly provides overly quick rationalizations for System 1 intuitions and biases.

b. System 1 Errors of Intuitive Judgment

While System 1 as "a machine for jumping to conclusions" gets it right most of the time, its quick and automatic search for causal interpretations of events is sometimes quite wrong. It often creates causal stories out of very dubious raw material. Kahneman's empirical research reveals a great number of systematic errors of System 1 judgments from cognitive biases, fallacies, and illusions. Examples include anchoring effects, the optimistic bias and the planning fallacy, framing effects, the halo effect, the "Florida" effect, the focusing illusion, outcome bias, and availability bias. Only the first two of these biases are discussed here in order to give you a sense of the errors we often make.[159]

i. Anchors or Arbitrary Reference Points

One of the most robust and reliable results of experimental psychology is that when people consider a particular value (called an anchor) for an unknown quantity before estimating that quantity, the estimates of the unknown quantity tend to be close to the particular value (the anchor) they heard before the estimate occurred. For example, the experimental data are clear that even if people are aware of the effects of an anchor, the anchor still influences them more than they know or want. For example, in an experiment, real estate agents were asked to assess the value of a house that was coming on the market, but the agents did not know the actual listed price. They visited the house and studied a comprehensive booklet of information that included an asking price. Half of the agents saw an asking price that was substantially higher than the eventual listed price, and half saw an asking price that was substantially lower. Each agent was then asked to give his or her opinion about a reasonable buying price and the lowest price at which the agent would sell the house if the agent owned it. The agents were then asked about the factors that affected their judgment. The agents took pride that the asking price was not one of the factors they considered. They said they ignored it. Yet the anchoring effect index was only slightly lower than the anchoring effect index of the asking price in the same study of business students with no real estate experience. Moving first to create an anchor in a single-issue negotiation over price has a powerful effect. A lawyer needs to know that any initial number on the table from the opposing side has had a strong System 1 effect on the client, the lawyer, and the decision maker, like a judge. If the stakes are high, the lawyer has to mobilize System 2 to combat the anchoring effect.[160]

---

[159] *Id.* at 39–49. *Id.* at 119–28.
[160] *Id.* at 119–28.

ii. The Optimistic Bias, the Planning Fallacy, and Inside and Outside Views

Kahneman finds:

> Most of us view the world as more benign than it really is, our own attributes as more favorable than they really are, and the goals we adopt as more achievable than they are likely to be. We also tend to exaggerate our ability to forecast the future, which fosters optimistic overconfidence. In terms of its consequences for decisions, the optimistic bias may be the most significant of the cognitive biases.[161]

The planning fallacy, one of the manifestations of the optimistic bias, describes the phenomenon that, in making plans and forecasts for future projects, we tend to overestimate benefits and underestimate costs. We tend to make forecasts and plans that are "unrealistically close to best-case scenarios."[162] For example, in 2002, a survey of Americans remodeling their homes reported that, on average, they had expected the job to cost $18,618, and they ended up paying an average of $38,769. The solution is again to enlist System 2 to consult statistics of similar situations and projects to take the "outside view" rather than to assume the "inside view" that uses meager initial evidence about a project to extrapolate optimistically about the future.[163]

c. A Lawyer's Role in Thinking, Fast and Slow

Kahneman provides an empirical map and language to understand distinctive patterns of System 1 errors of judgment for both lawyers and clients. Although humans are not irrational in most cases, "they often need help to make more accurate judgments and better decisions."[164] Specifically, each lawyer should have a personal board of directors to provide this help to make an accurate diagnosis of possible System 1 judgment failures and to suggest System 2 interventions that limit the damage of bad judgment. Of course, this is the independent, candid, and honest counsel that lawyers give to clients. Lawyers can give particularly valuable counsel in situations where the client's System 2 resources are depleted, which will cause System 2 to endorse the client's System 1 response too quickly without careful checking and reasoning.

Kahneman also suggests that experts like lawyers can improve their System 1 skills to minimize judgment errors through (1) careful attention to minefields like the anchor effect where System 1 judgments are most prone to error and (2) practicing System 1 decisions and then seeking immediate feedback on the decision to learn from mistakes.[165] For example, a trial will require many System 1 decisions for a litigator, but whenever possible, a newer lawyer can ask for

---

[161] *Id.* at 119–28.

[162] *Id.* at 255. *Id.* at 250. *Id. Id.* at 411. *Id.* at 241–42, 265.

[163] *Id.* at 241–42, 265.

[164] *Id.* at 241–42, 265.

[165] *Id.* at 241–42, 265.

immediate feedback on System 1 decisions. A lawyer can also counsel his or her client about both of these strategies.

7. Developing a Portfolio of Examples of Good Judgment

Section II.F covers the creation of a portfolio for your strongest competencies. A portfolio is basically a file in which you keep a record of your experiences and achievements with respect to a particular competency so that you can tell a story about how you have developed the competency. With respect to the competency of good judgment, some employers are asking candidates in an interview to explain a crucial moment in life, including those caused by the candidate's own mistakes, how the candidate handled the mistake, and what the candidate learned. If you are keeping a portfolio of your experiences, you will have a good story to tell.

Your portfolio could include stories of how senior people—members of your personal board of directors, for example—have evaluated your good judgment in challenging situations. These senior people can also give a reference about your internalized habit of FDR.

Finally, if you have counseled clients in a clinic or counseled others in non-client settings, a story about how you have developed your counseling skills to ask good stage-appropriate questions and tell stories to help the other person think through his or her problems also speaks to your own habits of developing good judgment. It also speaks to your competency of dedication to a client/responsiveness to a client.

Now that you have read "The Basics of Good Judgment to Help Clients," complete the Reflection Dashboard at **http://ambar.org/roadmap** to develop a better understanding of what developmental stage you are at and what steps you will take to grow to the next stage.

I. The Basics of Teamwork[166]

"Teamwork is the ability to work together toward a common vision—the ability to direct individual accomplishment toward organizational objectives. It is the fuel that allows common people to accomplish uncommon results."[167]

Attorneys operate in a fast-paced, pressure-filled environment. The practice of law has become a collaborative endeavor to meet a client's needs, requiring knowledge of experts from a wide range of disciplines and backgrounds. Given this reality, it is important to understand that one of the best tools a lawyer can have in his or her toolbox is the life skill of teamwork. During law school, knowing how to be a good team member and how to operate effectively within a team will give a law student the knowledge necessary to operate in the new legal economy. In the business world, teams tend to outperform individuals acting

---

[166] Authored by Neil W. Hamilton and Patrick Lucke.

[167] Andrew Carnegie, American Entrepreneur.

alone, especially when the goal or performance requires "multiple skills, judgments, and experiences."[168] Author Patrick Lencioni stated that teamwork is the ultimate competitive advantage, saying, "if you could get all the people in an organization rowing in the same direction, you could dominate any industry, in any market, against any competition, at any time."[169]

Teamwork is an invaluable life skill for succeeding in the legal economy.[170] In fact, in a survey of the fourteen largest law firms in Minnesota, every single firm responded that it evaluates associates in terms of their ability to initiate and maintain strong work and team relationships.[171] The firms use the following criteria to assess and evaluate new lawyers in teamwork acumen. For junior associates, the firms valued the following skills: (1) *effectively communicating and collaborating with others as part of a team*, (2) *working effectively with others to address client needs*, (3) *interacting well with staff*, (4) *demonstrating cooperation and respect including respectful candor*, and (5) *being respectful to all team members and staff*. For mid-level associates, the firms additionally required the following: (6) *accepting leadership responsibilities*, (7) *effectively supervising and setting a positive role model for other team members*, and (8) *being able to delegate assignments appropriately to junior members*. For senior associates, the firms additionally required the following: (9) *demonstrating strong leadership capabilities and responsibility over teams*, and (10) *being able to deal effectively and maturely with interpersonal conflicts with team members*.[172]

The benefits of teamwork are also apparent in education. Effective teams are associated with higher levels of academic achievement and productivity.[173] But despite all the evidence pointing to both the importance of teamwork in the legal profession and its benefits in education, law schools historically have not facilitated opportunities for students to work in teams, thus not allowing them to learn what makes an effective team. Because legal employers and clients value teamwork, an opportunity exists for law students to distinguish themselves from their competition by being willing to engage in intentional professional team formation. If a law student can begin to develop the core competency of teamwork while still in law school and then be able to marshal evidence of how the student applied his or her knowledge of teamwork, the student will stand out to a potential employer.

---

[168] *See generally* Jon R. Katzenbach & Douglas K. Smith, The Wisdom of Teams: Creating the High-Performance Organization (2006).

[169] Patrick Lencioni, The Five Dysfunctions of a Team: A Leadership Fable (2002), at vii.

[170] *See generally* Neil W. Hamilton, Verna Monson & Jerome M. Organ, *Empirical Evidence that Legal Education Can Foster Student Professionalism/Professional Formation to Become an Effective Lawyer*, 10 University of St. Thomas L.J. 11 (2012).

[171] *Id.*

[172] Hamilton, *supra* note 38, at tbl.1.

[173] David W. Johnson & Roger T. Johnson, *An Educational Psychology Success Story: Social Interdependence Theory and Cooperative Learning*, Educ. Researcher (June/July 2009), at 5.

It's quite common for law students to react with fear or annoyance when presented with a team task or project for a class. Team assignments require students to be held accountable for their team members' performance. Teams also require a certain level of personal interaction with classmates, which can be outside some students' comfort zones. But regardless of these fears, empirical evidence overwhelmingly suggests that law school graduates must be good at teamwork to succeed in the professional world. Therefore, students dedicated to differentiating themselves should commit to overcoming their fear of working in teams and developing competency at teamwork.

The biggest fear or annoyance when working on teams is the free rider, a team member who cannot or will not do his or her part for the team. While the free rider is often discussed in the abstract, in practice, a free rider almost always exists on any team. It is an unfortunate reality that every lawyer or law student must realize is inevitable. Each team member must learn to effectively deal with the free rider to succeed in team projects as a lawyer. One former CEO of a Fortune 500 company explains that a common interview question is asking the interviewee to explain a time when he or she handled a free rider while working on a team.[174] That former CEO subscribes to the theory that past behavior is the best predictor of future behavior and expects a potential employee to have already developed effective ways to handle free riders in a positive and professional way.[175]

1. Teams

A team consists of two or more individuals who (1) are aware of their positive interdependence as they strive to achieve mutual goals, (2) interact while they do so, (3) are aware of who is and is not a member of the team, (4) have specific roles or functions to perform, and (5) have a limited life span of membership.[176] This chapter discusses teams in general, as well as managed and self-managed teams specifically. Table 27 sets forth five attributes applicable to both managed and self-managed teams.

a. Clear and Relevant Group Goals

First, a team must have clear and relevant group goals that give the team a compelling direction. Each team member should understand these goals. If done correctly, the team's goals can help create cooperation and evoke a high level of commitment from every member.[177] A team's purpose must be clear, challenging, and consequential. A clear purpose orients the group in the correct

---

[174] Holloran, *supra* note 32.

[175] *Id.*

[176] David W. Johnson Jr. & Frank Pierce Johnson, Joining Together: Group Theory and Group Skills 532 (11th ed. 2013).

[177] *Id.* at 567.

Table 27 Five Attributes Applicable to All Clearly Established Teams

Attribute	Purpose
A clear, challenging, and relevant group goal	• Gives the team direction • Evokes a high level of commitment to the team goal • Can help create cooperation • Is important for people to know the purpose • Engages members' talents
Effective, accurate, and clear two-way communication	• Allows members to speak openly and candidly • Allows for disagreement and decreases groupthink • Promotes creative decision making • Makes empathy important for this skill
Clear distribution of leadership and power sharing	• Ensures commitment from all team members • Ensures resources of each team member are fully utilized • Ensures an equal level of power for all team members
Clear rules for conduct and expectations	• Defines meeting times, work to be done by each member, and expectations • Increases team member buy-in • Leads to better outcomes because of shared norms • Tends to preempt spending time and energy dealing with behavioral problems later
Measurements of team progress	• Keeps team members accountable to each other • Provides opportunities for feedback, dialogue, and reflection (FDR) • Keeps team on plan

direction and guards against an excessive amount of time and effort that would be expended if the group were unsure of its purpose. A challenging goal energizes the team, builds excitement, and compels the team to strive to achieve it. Finally, a consequential goal engages members' talents. Members will be more willing to work toward a meaningful end rather than an ill-conceived solution to a problem.[178] It is also important to structure positive interdependence among team members and allow them to engage in the process of redefining the mission into team-specific goals. This allows each team member to take ownership of the project.[179]

b. Clear Communication

The second necessary attribute of teamwork is that effective, accurate, and clear two-way communication must be established among team members. Clear and

---

[178] J. Richard Hackman, *Six Common Misperceptions about Teamwork*, Harv. Bus. Rev. (June 2011), at 69.

[179] Johnson& Johnson, *supra* note 176, at 547.

open communication allows group members to speak openly and candidly with each other.[180] This allows team members to disagree and challenge others' assumptions, conclusions, and reasoning. It also promotes creative decision making and problem solving and decreases groupthink within the team.[181]

To ensure clear and open communication, team members need to be aware of cultural differences, as cross-cultural competency improves trust, communication, and group problem-solving abilities. See section III.L, "Cross-Cultural Competency: Developing Cultural Competencies for the Changing Workplace," for deeper discussion on this issue. Empathy is a key skill in communication within a team. Misunderstandings can be avoided by actively listening to teammates, paying attention to their thoughts, and attempting to understand their feelings, ultimately leading to better team chemistry and a better work product.[182] Review section III.M, "Listen to Persuade: How Attentiveness Leads to Value," for discussion on active listening to enhance your communication skills.

c. Power Sharing

The third attribute of effective teams is a distributed-leadership and power-sharing structure. Distributing leadership among all members of the group ensures that the members are involved in the team's work and are committed to implementing the team's decisions. It can lead to greater satisfaction in the team as well. Distributing leadership ensures that the resources of every member are fully utilized.[183] It is also important to structure the team in a way that promotes a consistent and, for the most part, equal level of power and status across the entire team.[184]

d. Clearly Established Group Norms

Clearly established group norms are the fourth aspect of effective teams. Clear rules of conduct and group norms should be established early on in the team's life span (including expectations, meeting times, punctuality, amount of work to be done by members, etc.). Self-defined team norms, created through group discussion, can increase member buy-in.[185] Having clear norms set up from the outset allows for more time and energy to be spent on achieving the team's goal rather than on correcting behavioral issues.[186] Shared norms focus behavior and lead to better outcomes.

---

[180] Eileen Scallen, Sophie Sparrow & Cliff Zimmerman, Working Together in Law: Teamwork and Small Group Skills for Legal Professionals 30 (2014).

[181] Johnson & Johnson, *supra* note 176, at 567.

[182] Neil W. Hamilton, Effectiveness Requires Listening: How to Assess and Improve Listening Skills, 13 Flor. Coastal L. Rev. 145 (2012).

[183] Johnson & Johnson, *supra* note 176, at 556.

[184] *Id.* at 549.

[185] Hamilton, Monson & Organ, *supra* note 170, at 15.

[186] Hackman, *supra* note 178, at 103.

The team's rule of conducts should be revisited and refined after the team encounters a problem, such as a team member who consistently stares at his computer screen instead of giving his attention to other team members.[187] This problem could be addressed by implementing a new rule such as "be open to others' suggestions" or "contribute to the discussion."[188] The templates "Considerations for Drafting Team 'Rules of Conduct'" and "Considerations in Running an Effective Team Meeting." Both templates are available at **http://ambar .org/roadmap**.

e. Progress Criteria

The final attribute of effective teams is having a way to measure the team's progress. This includes having frequent and regular meetings that provide opportunities for team members to interact face-to-face and promote one another's success.[189] Additionally, one member should be designated to track which team members are working on specific team objectives. Refer to the Project Initiation and Planning template found in the section III.D.). It is also available electronically.

Measuring progress can also include frequent processing sessions. These should be used to go over the timeline and debrief how the team is functioning at various points throughout its life span.[190] They are opportunities to give FDR.[191] Frequent celebrations are another effective method by which teams can measure progress and recognize the contributions of team members.[192] These celebrations should focus on getting results and celebrating small wins while pursuing broader purposes.[193]

Keep in mind that each of these attributes and necessary team behaviors must be built on a foundation of trust, which can be the most difficult trait to develop on a team. It is *impossible* to get the full results of effective teamwork if members do not trust each other. Absence of trust hampers effective communication and

---

[187] Sophie M. Sparrow. *Can They Work Well on a Team? Assessing Students' Collaborative Skills*, 38 WM. MITCHELL L. REV. 1162, 1167 (2012).

[188] *Id.* at 1168.

[189] Technology can be an important part of any group work and can enhance a team's ability to communicate. Using technology such as Skype, Dropbox, and Google Docs allows for a faster exchange of ideas and materials among group members. But it is important to remember the value of face-to-face meetings to share ideas and feedback as well. Depending too much on technology can result in a breakdown of interpersonal communication that may damage team chemistry. *Virtual Meetings and Virtual Teams Using Technology to Work Smarter*, PENN. STATE U., http://www.opia. psu.edu/sites/default/files/insights009.pdf (last visited July 16, 2017) (Innovation Insights Series No. 9).

[190] *See* "Project Management Skills: How Law Students Can Learn and Implement the Skills Employers Value" in section III.

[191] Hamilton, Monson & Organ, *supra* note 170, at 15.

[192] JOHNSON & JOHNSON, *supra* note 176, at 547.

[193] *Id.* at 549.

feedback. It also prevents constructive criticism. In essence, trust requires team members to be vulnerable to one another and to be confident that those vulnerabilities will not be used against them. Vulnerabilities may include weaknesses, skill deficiencies, interpersonal shortcomings, mistakes, and requests for help.[194]

While feedback should be given often, team members should have at least one official qualitative assessment about halfway into the team's life. Several options exist to provide such an assessment, but all feedback should be anonymous. Team members could list one thing that each member is doing well and one thing that each member could do to improve team performance.[195] Better yet, teams could conduct a 360-degree assessment of each team member's performance to provide a holistic view of each individual's performance. This assessment should be conducted about halfway into the team's life and again at the completion of the team. After conducting the midpoint review, the team should revisit and possibly refine its rules of conduct created at the onset of the team. Visit **http://ambar.org/roadmap** to access the 360-Degree Assessment form your team can use to provide feedback to individual team members.

2. Self-Managed Teams

A self-managed team is unsupervised or nominally supervised by a manager. Instead of being directed toward its goal, the team takes on supervisory and decision-making responsibilities as a group in order to reach its goal in the team's own way. Along with the essential team attributes discussed previously, a self-managed team should develop a flexible decision-making process that can meet the needs of any given situation in order to be successful.[196]

One major issue most self-managed teams face is holding team members accountable for their actions and work product. In other words, how does a self-managed team deal with free riders? The first step in addressing a problem team member is confronting that person about his or her unacceptable performance. It is important to make sure that the problem being confronted is framed as a work or performance-related issue, not a personal issue and personal attack. This will focus the conversation toward finding solutions instead of trading hurtful insults. When confronting a team member, the team should remove obstacles that may be preventing the confronted team member from achieving full performance and provide that person with the resources necessary to succeed.[197] The emphasis during these discussions should be on a win-win scenario. The team benefits from each member contributing, and the individual benefits from the enhanced work product that the team will produce with full participation. Finally, teams should use the confrontation to grow into

---

[194] LENCIONI, *supra* note 169, at 351.

[195] Sparrow, *supra* note 187, at 1171.

[196] JOHNSON & JOHNSON, *supra* note 176, at 567.

[197] This tactic is equally useful for resolving problems faced by managed teams.

a stronger, cooperative team by reaffirming individual team members and the norms set by the team.[198]

3. Managed Teams

A managed team is formed and directed by a manager or supervisor, as opposed to a self-directed team that determines its own norms and procedures. For example, in a law firm, a senior attorney acting as a project manager picks the team members and manages them. A quasi-managed team, however, could be a professor-assigned team for a law school course. While the professor assigns the team, the team bears many characteristics of a self-managed team.

There are a number of enabling conditions for creating a successful managed team. First, it is important to create a real team. On the one hand, a real team uses positive interdependence to build commitment toward the common goal. This leads to increased cooperation and a mentality of "sink together or swim together." The group will be evaluated as a group and not as individuals. A pseudo-group, on the other hand, is a group that is made to work together but has no interest in doing so because they will be evaluated individually. Instead of working together, team members are competing with one another, which can lead to inefficiencies. In essence, they would be better off working alone. Similarly, a traditional work group is assigned to work together but interacts only occasionally. The members believe they will be graded individually, so there is no reason to assist other members in their success.[199]

Second, a manager must assemble the right number of the right people for a team. Usually smaller is better. As a team grows larger, a smaller percentage of individuals will contribute to its efforts, the free-rider problem will increase, and more members will feel anonymous. This leads to less involvement and members feeling less responsible for the team's success. Large teams also have more difficulty interacting constructively as a group and are less able to work through their problems. Practically, it is more difficult to handle a large team logistically, including, for example, finding the resources to accommodate everyone, making sure everyone can meet at the same time, and fitting into a good space.[200]

A manager should consider forming a heterogeneous team that can force team members to interact with diverse teammates. This compels one to challenge one's assumptions and expand one's sensitivity to diverse perspectives. Working in a diverse group also reduces stereotypes among members. This will help develop empathetic and compassionate ways of reaching others.

Finally, the team must be given adequate resources and adequate coaching. This provides the necessary background support for the team to succeed in

---

[198] Dean Tjosvold & Mary M. Tjosvold, Psychology for Leaders: Using Motivation, Conflict, and Power to Manage More Effectively 212 (1995).

[199] Johnson & Johnson, *supra* note 176, at 19.

[200] *Id.* at 537.

achieving its goal.[201] Appropriate coaching can help a team move through difficult periods in the team's life span by reinforcing the skills necessary to overcome obstacles that team members may have in working together. After the team is formed, in many ways, the level to which the team members buy into the team and its goals often determines the success of a team. Aside from setting up a team using the enabling conditions described previously, it is important for the manager to be a compelling symbol of accomplishment in order to motivate and energize the team.[202]

4. Teamwork in the New Legal Economy

"Some young associates come to a firm planning on holing themselves in their office and pouring over documents. While that type of work is needed sometimes, more often a firm needs them in the conference room, working closely with their colleagues to accomplish the client's goals."[203]

Successful law students have to be self-driven and willing to work hard in their various assignments. They must study hard and jump through the many hoops of the law school experience to get a job. The vast majority of these tasks are solo projects, requiring foremost a dedication to individual excellence. Many law students think the same values that led them to succeed in law school will be sufficient to make them excellent in the legal workplace. A student may think, "As long as I work hard, learn fast, and bill enough hours, I will succeed at the firm." While all of those virtues are necessary for success, the notion that those attributes are all that is needed is misguided. In reality, most of the work done in the modern law firm involves some degree of teamwork.

A shift is occurring in the legal marketplace. Growth in the new legal economy requires low-cost and high-value legal services. This shift has created a need for a new kind of lawyer with specific competencies.[204] While traditional legal services like courtroom advocacy or transactional work will continue to be an important part of the legal-services market, the primary area of growth in the market is not in artisan or tailored services provided by solo expert trusted advisors. The growth in the market for tomorrow's lawyers will be in other areas, such as organizing complex legal content and distilling it into systems and standards that can be used to solve a variety of legal problems.[205]

In addition, in the new legal economy, lawyers will not only represent corporate clients and other organizations as a legal practitioner but also as a general problem solver. The problem-advisor lawyer needs to be able to use many teamwork skills—clear communication, empathy, fostering cooperation— to achieve successful results for clients. Lawyers in this role will need to provide nonlegal insights as well as legal opinions. Put simply, "lawyers who prosper [in

---

[201] Hackman, *supra* note 178, at 131–147.

[202] JOHNSON & JOHNSON, *supra* note 176, at 549.

[203] Holloran, *supra* note 32.

[204] *See* "The New Legal Economy and Transferable Competencies" in section I.

[205] *See* Henderson, *supra* note 104.

organizational representation] will be those who can make themselves the best available go-to person in a combined law-and-substantive field and who market themselves accordingly."[206]

When lawyers and clients team up, they coproduce solutions that are responsive to the changing legal market. More often, clients are viewing lawyers as partners rather than as service providers.[207] Lawyers, therefore, must work to develop a partnership with their clients. "A frank conversation on goals and expectations is the first step to a successful and lasting relationship," and transparency is key in this conversation.[208] Just like in an in-firm team setting, lawyers should seek feedback from their clients and make adjustments based on that feedback.[209] Lawyers should implement the same team elements in teaming up with a client, including a clear communication structure and group norms. Refer to section I for further discussion regarding coproduction.

Teamwork is also a necessary skill for a large portion of project management competencies.[210] Teamwork is a primary competency that lawyers are going to use in the new legal economy, and to the extent that a new lawyer is comfortable working with others and knows how to practice good teamwork, that lawyer will be more valuable to the employer on day one.

5. Opportunities to Practice Teamwork in Law School

Students have opportunities to experience positive teamwork in the classroom. In some classes, teachers use team assignments to reinforce learning concepts. Team assignments give the students the opportunity to understand the material better by explaining it to each other.

As an example, a class can be structured with students placed into teams. These teams may remain in effect for the full length of the course, with teamwork and discussions assigned periodically. To reinforce learning and foster discussion, the professor will pose a question to the class and ask each group to volunteer an answer to the question. While these exercises are not graded, they lay the groundwork for the skills necessary to complete a second teamwork component of the course—graded group midterms. For each of this professor's midterms, students are required to complete a short examination independently for the first half of the examination period and then complete the exact same examination in their respective teams. Each portion—the group examination and the independent examination—are weighed equally in determining each student's examination grade.

---

[206] Thomas Morgan, The Vanishing American Lawyer 134–36 (Oxford Univ. Press 2010).

[207] Eilene Spear, *Strategic Partnerships between Law Firms and Clients: The New Rules of Collaboration*, The National Law Review (Jan. 16, 2017), *available at* http://www.natlawreview.com/article/strategic-partnerships-between-law-firms-and-clients-new-rules-collaboration.

[208] *Id.*

[209] *Id.*

[210] *See* "Project Management Skills: How Law Students Can Learn and Implement the Skills Employers Value" in section III.

For the independent portion of the examination, the student simply needs to determine the correct answer to each of the multiple-choice questions. For the group portion, there is an added challenge: the group must determine the right answer by consensus but then must also write a short statement explaining why each other option was wrong. While the single most important factor in determining the grade for the group portion is the group's substantive knowledge of the course material, several aspects of good teamwork are essential for a successful result.

The biggest challenge facing groups of students answering difficult questions is agreeing which answer is correct; therefore, communication is a key skill for doing well on the tests. Because of the obvious time constraints of a test, the group further needs to be able to know when to stop discussing which answer is correct, respond to the question fully, and then move on to the next question. Keep in mind that the law being tested is difficult, and usually there is more than one answer that looks correct. Successful teams need to have firm, fair, and consistent ways of deciding how to come to consensus for answering a question, even when not everyone agrees on the answer selected. When team members disagree as to why the wrong answer is wrong, they are still under time constraints and must select a reason the wrong answer is incorrect to move on before they run out of time.

Due to the difficulty of the material, the high likelihood of some disagreement, and the stringent time constraints, it's axiomatic that bad teamwork skills can spell disaster even for a group of talented students who know the material well. As such, bad teamwork is not an option for students who want to succeed. By being intentional about learning what it takes to form a good team and practice good teamwork, a team taking one of the professor's midterms could employ some strategies and tactics to ensure good decision making and communication.

First, have an initial meeting at the beginning of the semester to determine the standards and expectations the team wants to employ over its life. It is much easier to agree on standards of behavior before those standards need to be upheld than to formulate them in the heat of a disagreement. Second, make a commitment to share talking time and power with each member of the team. If some team members routinely dominate discussion, and others rarely speak up, then the result will be the team not getting a full range of views and opinions. Third, set expectations for levels of preparation. Nobody likes to have the impression that one of their team members is a free rider, and if the team gets that impression, it can lead to mistrust, ineffectiveness, and bad communication. By setting expectations early on, teams can avoid the pitfall of free riders.

Finally, a strategy for success for teams that are highly motivated to improve their teamwork is having periodic team meetings throughout the life of the team. The purpose of meeting at regular intervals is to discuss how the team itself is doing. The conversation should include a process of reflection and discussion about how well the team is doing in general. Are team members behaving by the agreed-upon standards of behavior and preparation? Are power and speaking time being distributed fairly, or is there disproportionate participation among team members? An agreed-upon short, but dedicated, team meeting addressing these subjects not only can help teams identify room for improvement but can also serve as an extra "stick," motivating team members to uphold standards lest they be held accountable and brought to task at the meetings.

This is just one example of many in-class or assigned team projects that law students will have to grapple with in their three years of law school. Each student has to make a conscious choice about how he or she approaches team projects. Many students will view team projects begrudgingly, resenting that they are being asked to be accountable for other students. They will go through the motions and suffer through teamwork as best they can. However, for students interested in their own professional development, they can use these group assignments as a testing ground to practice good teamwork skills to prepare for the professional world. Students can add these team exercises to their ongoing law school portfolios and use the assessment tools discussed throughout this chapter, which are all accessible electronically, to construct evidence of teamwork competencies.

6. Conclusion

Most of the new competencies—teamwork, project management, good judgment, good listening—that empirical research has shown employers look for in new hires can be learned and applied in conjunction with one another. Many projects involve teams, and most teamwork relies on good judgment and good listening. For students who decide that it is in their interest to practice and hone these core competencies of professionalism, being active and motivated participants in team assignments is a good place to start. See table 5 in section I to determine which stage of teamwork development you are at and to examine what steps you can take to advance toward the next developmental stage.

Now that you have read "The Basics of Teamwork," complete the Reflection Dashboard at **http://ambar.org/roadmap** to develop a better understanding of what developmental stage you are at and what steps you will take to grow to the next stage. Recall that the assessment tools discussed throughout this chapter are also available through the link just provided.

J. Commitment to the Employing Organization[211]

First impressions at a job can be very sticky. Unfortunately, many bright, perfectly capable new lawyers get off to a rocky start simply because they do not appreciate the professional environment within most legal offices and the expectations of those they are working for. With that in mind, the following tips will help you to transition from being an excellent law student to a "go-to" lawyer (or a "must-hire"

---

[211] Authored by Benjamin Carpenter.

summer associate)—starting on day one. First, ten general principles to guide your interactions with those you work for are presented, followed by nuts-and-bolts advice for receiving and turning in work, then some final thoughts regarding the longer view.

1. Ten Core Principles

a. Rule 1: The Golden Rule—Make Your Colleagues' Lives Easier

People want to work with those who make their lives easier. Whenever you are unsure about how or whether to do something, ask yourself, what will make my colleague's life easier? If you can consistently add value for the person you are working for, in ways big and small, you will get more work. The day will come when people are working for you, but that time is not during the first year or two of your legal career. Your initial focus should be on serving those you are working for. Everything that follows flows from this fundamental principle.[212]

b. Rule 2: You Are Not as Busy as the Person You Are Working For

The classic myth among new lawyers is that life is easier for their employers and supervisors. It isn't (not for many years, at least). Few appreciate the various demands established lawyers have to juggle, both in and out of work. They constantly have other responsibilities pulling at them, demanding their time. They may be up throughout the night with infants or sick children, up early to get children ready for school or daycare, picking their children up after work, attending (or missing) school functions, taking care of an elderly parent, and so forth. Indeed, when lawyers leave at 6:00 p.m., rarely is their day done. They likely left "early" so they could see their kids for a couple of hours (which really means feeding, changing, bathing, reading to them, etc.) and then will work late after the kids are in bed. They, literally, may not have ten minutes to themselves all day, day after day. For most established lawyers, working late affects their family life—and causes significant stress in the home. As a student or new associate, when you work late, it likely will affect only you. In addition, more senior lawyers have pressure to bring in new clients, to manage numerous existing clients, and (in many offices) to serve on community boards, bar association committees, and so forth—and to *supervise you*. On top of that, they *still* will be billing the same number of—if not more—hours than you. Never complain to them about how busy you are. You will not get their sympathy, but you will annoy them. And even if you are in fact busier, keep this in mind: they have paid their dues, and now they expect you to. Fair or not, that's a fact.

A similar pitfall that summer law clerks fall into is that they feel "too busy" to attend firm social functions. While you should never miss a deadline to go to a company baseball game, you should plan to attend as many events both during

---

[212] For ways of practicing this as a law student, *see* "Dedication and Responsiveness to Clients," section III.F.4 ("Treat Professors as Your Client").

the day and in the evening as possible. Many high-level associates make time to attend these events, and you should as well.

c. Rule 3: Your First Client Is Your Employer

As a new lawyer, you will rely primarily on your colleagues for your first projects. Many new lawyers complain about doing nonbillable work or that they are just "behind the scenes." This is the wrong attitude. As a first-year lawyer, the person who assigns you work *is your client*. If you prove yourself, soon enough, you will be working directly with the "real" clients. Even if asked to work on a nonbillable matter or to prepare materials for a CLE your colleague will be presenting, treat it with the same attention and care you would for a paying client. Again, refer to rule 1.

d. Rule 4: Never Turn Down a Project

Just as you would never tell a good client that you are too busy to help, never do so to your employer or supervisor (see rules 1, 2, and 3). If you *truly* are so busy that you cannot meet the deadline (and not because of an evening cooking class), discuss whether there is any room to reshuffle the priority list for the various projects on your plate. But keep in mind that *someone* has to do the project. If your supervisor is up at 2:00 a.m. writing a brief because you were "too busy," this will not make life easier. And you may soon find yourself not busy at all. *Never, never* turn down a project because you don't "want" to do it. Again, somebody has to do the work—and if you don't want to, you can be sure your employer or supervisor doesn't.

e. Rule 5: Never Miss a Deadline

Few things will aggravate a busy supervisor more than a late assignment. Never simply miss a deadline. You will have less resilient colleagues who complain about the grave injustice of a supervisor's "false" deadlines. But you won't, because you understand this: *there is no such thing as a false deadline.* Your project may be a building block for someone else's next step. Or a supervisor may have only a small window available to review your work, even though it may not be filed until a bit later. But the reason doesn't matter; the supervisor is your client, and you don't set the deadlines. If a project is taking longer than expected, you find yourself being pulled in too many directions, or something intervenes beyond your control, tell the attorney immediately and well in advance of the deadline. The supervisor may extend the deadline, find another lawyer who can help, or reduce the scope of the project. Don't just leave the problem with the supervisor, though; tell your supervisor what you can do instead, then deliver. And make sure this does not become a pattern for you.[213]

---

[213] As you seek to effectively manage your time to complete a project, you may want to consider the skills and practices discussed in section III.K on "Project Management Skills: How Law Students Can Learn and Implement the Skills Employers Want."

f. Rule 6: Understand Your Role

In most instances, your role as a new lawyer is to provide support to your supervisors. You may do this by researching the law for them, writing first drafts of briefs, preparing documents for depositions they will conduct, assisting with document review or due diligence, and in dozens of other ways. Through these experiences, you gain experience and exhibit your ability and potential to the supervisors. Always understand, though, that the supervisor is ultimately responsible for the client relationship. Do the absolute best job you can, but if a supervisor rejects your suggestions, heavily edits your work, or accepts credit from a client for work you have done, do not take it personally. Do not sulk. There may have been other considerations at play that you were unaware of (or, just perhaps, your suggestions were a bit off-base). In any event, learn from the experience and find a way to continue to contribute.

g. Rule 7: Accept Responsibility

Eventually, you will make a mistake. Everybody does. When this happens, supervisors will be much more interested in how you respond than in why it happened. Frankly, they likely will not care why it happened; they are more interested in whether you are mature, honest, and self-confident enough to take responsibility. In fact, many employers look specifically for this trait, resiliency, during the interview process. If you take responsibility for your mistakes—including mistakes of those whom you supervise—almost any mistake will be forgiven. If you assign blame elsewhere, you will lose others' respect and confidence. Two caveats: (1) take responsibility and apologize, but do not grovel—it does not come across as professional—and (2) you will be expected to *learn* from your mistakes; don't make the same mistake twice.[214]

h. Rule 8: Be Responsive

For better or worse, you are now connected almost 24 hours a day through e-mail and smartphones. If you will be out of your office for an extended period of time (30 minutes or more), be sure your assistant knows where you will be and how to reach you. Return all voicemail and e-mail messages promptly. Some employers have a policy that all messages must be returned within an hour. If your employer does not, adopt that as your own policy. Even if you respond simply to inform your supervisor that you are headed to a meeting and will get back to him or her later, your supervisor will appreciate the response. It will ease anxiety. It will make life easier.

i. Rule 9: Keep Client and Employer Confidences

Do not discuss your employer's business with people outside of your office. Do not discuss client business with anyone who doesn't need to know (even within

---

[214] *See* "Trustworthiness: Building Lasting Professional Relationships" in section III.

the office). Be sensitive to your surroundings, particularly in bathrooms, elevators, at lunch, on a plane, and so forth. It is your duty to protect your clients' and your employer's confidences. This is the one area where the failure to do so just once could cost you your job. This is not discretionary.

j. Rule 10: Treat Everyone with Respect

The original Golden Rule. Although the previous advice refers only to your relationship with supervisors and employers, this advice applies to anyone with whom you work. Keep in mind that even lawyers one year your senior may be asked to evaluate you, and they will be your supervisors when you are eligible for promotion. And treat *all* assistants with respect, not just those who may work for you. You can learn a lot about how the office works from staff, and their support (or lack thereof) can make or break you. Moreover, many assistants have worked for years, if not decades, with certain lawyers. If you disrespect an assistant, his or her supervisor—and all the other assistants—will hear about it. And, most importantly, of course, it's just the right thing to do.

2. Getting Work: Nuts and Bolts

a. Receiving Projects

Take notes and ask questions. Always bring a pad and paper to every meeting. (In fact, take one with you anytime you leave your office.) Listen carefully and take extensive notes. If you are unclear about anything, ask questions until you are sure. Be persistent. It is okay if you don't understand something at first. It is not okay, however, to go back the next day with questions because you neglected to clarify or write something down. This will not make your supervisor's life easier.[215] If you do need to ask additional questions, be sure to do your initial research first. This will avoid the possibility of needing to go to your supervisor multiple times with questions.

Understand the exact issue. Before you leave the meeting, restate precisely the issue you are being asked to research. Do this even if you feel it is clear to you. Often, upon hearing again what they have asked you to do, supervisors will realize they were not completely clear and revise their initial instructions. If you do not ask, however, they will not recall later that they were unclear. Rather, they will think you were not listening carefully.

Understand the scope. Be sure you understand the scope of your project. Is the supervisor looking for a full-blown memo for the file, a simple answer in an e-mail, or (often) both? Can you use Lexis or Westlaw? Should you research the law only in one state, or should you look at outside jurisdictions as well? Is there a specific form or template the supervisor would like you to start from (depending on the project)? These questions make you

---

[215] This will involve essential listening skills, which are discussed in "Listen to Persuade: How Attentiveness Leads to Value" in section III.

look thoughtful and detail oriented—and may prevent a supervisor from having to write off your time.

Get a deadline. Do not leave until you have a clear deadline. If the supervisor doesn't give you one, ask for one. If your supervisor says "sometime next week," clarify if that means by next Friday. In your supervisor's mind, "sometime next week" may mean midweek. Again, if you do not ask for specificity, the supervisor may remember the conversation differently days later. You will not annoy a supervisor by seeking a clear deadline. Instead, he or she will appreciate that you are being detail-oriented and responsible. He or she may have more confidence in you. Now, go and deliver.

b. During Projects

Take ownership of a project. For your first few assignments, you likely will be asked to help with a small piece of a larger project. It may be reviewing a contract, summarizing deposition transcripts, or writing one section of a larger brief. While doing that piece as well as you can, demonstrate an interest in the larger project. Ask how that piece fits into the bigger picture. Ask what the next steps will be. Take the initiative to review other parts of the file (for instance, the legal and correspondence spindles) to get a sense of the client's backstory and history with the office. (Note: Consider this an investment in yourself—do not bill for work you are not asked to do!)

Provide updates. Keep your supervisors updated as to the status of the projects you are doing for them. In this regard, no news is not good news. Long stretches with no communication may lead supervisors to assume you haven't made progress (and may create anxiety for them). That said, respect their time and update them appropriately. While a weekly update may be reassuring, daily updates may become annoying. Find out what each supervisor prefers (daily, weekly, e-mails, voicemails, etc.). Importantly, the purpose of this is to reassure the supervisor, not to get affirmation that you are doing a good job. Do not ask the supervisor to review what you've done so far—this will make you look like you need your hand held. I once did, and the supervisor simply asked, "Can you swim on your own yet?" Point taken. You don't ever want a supervisor to ask you that.

Be proactive. If, however, for any reason the project is not going according to plan, address it immediately with the supervisor. For instance, if the project is taking longer than anticipated or if you've reached a fork in the road on strategy or research-wise (that you cannot resolve yourself), seek guidance well before the deadline.

Prepare for meetings. If you need to (or are asked to) meet with a supervisor during a project, prepare for that meeting—no matter how informal it may seem. Show the supervisor that you respect his or her time. Research any issues that are mentioned, and write down your questions in advance. This won't make you appear dull, but conscientious. Leave your laptop in your office (unless essential for the meeting); come prepared to engage in a discussion. Be prepared to explain where you have looked and why you have not been able to find the answer already. Bring copies of statutes or cases for both of you if you may be discussing them. Whenever possible, bring proposed solutions, not just problems.

Adopt your working style to that of the supervisors you work with. Your job is to work well with your supervisors; it is not their job to work well with you. Supervisor may have individual preferences about how they prefer to communicate (what medium and frequency), how they like to receive work, and so forth. Find out what those preferences are from other lawyers in the office, and take notes about each supervisor's preferences after you have worked with him or her.

c. Handing in Projects

Hand the project *to* the supervisor. Whenever possible, hand your work product to the supervisor in person and ask if he or she would like to discuss your conclusions (and be prepared to do so!). Do not simply e-mail the supervisor your work, leave it in the inbox, or ask your assistant to give it to the supervisor. Handing your work to the supervisor shows respect, maturity, and confidence, and it provides you an opportunity for further interaction. Then, follow up with an e-mail so that the supervisor has it in electronic format as well. Now your supervisor can access it from anywhere if he or she desires to. If the supervisor is out of the office, wait until he or she returns. If you cannot, e-mail it *and* leave a hard copy on his or her chair with a brief note offering to discuss the document at your supervisor's convenience. If you are out of the office, e-mail it to her or him and ask your assistant to print out a copy and provide it to the supervisor.

Provide complete materials. If your memorandum or brief relies on cases or statutes, provide copies of those with your memorandum, along with the KeyCite summary for each case (preferably clean copies, with key aspects highlighted, clipped to the back of the memorandum or brief). If the supervisor would like to review a source you have cited, this will make life easier. Even if he or she does not, it will demonstrate that you are detail oriented and respect your supervisor's time. Few others will take this extra step. But you will—and you will stand out because of it.

Never turn in a draft. You may be asked to prepare a draft, or told that "a draft is fine." This just means "be prepared to be edited." It does not mean expectations are lower. Everything you submit to a supervisor should be well organized, accurate, properly formatted, and typo-free and should include proper citations. Draft pleadings should include the caption. Draft letters should include a heading, date, direct dial, and so forth. Take pride in your work product. Act as though you expect it to go out as is, even if you know it will not.

d. Follow Up

Always ask "What's next?" When you turn the project in, always ask if there is anything else you can do. Even if you never want to touch the project again, ask the question. It will reflect that you view yourself as part of the team.[216] Finally, a week or so later, follow up one last time to confirm that nothing else has come up relating to the project that the supervisor would like your help with.

Seek feedback. You should seek feedback for every major project you do. If you don't receive any feedback after a reasonable time, don't just wait passively; take the initiative to seek it out. This expresses humility and a desire to improve. Respect that the supervisor is busy, though, and may not have the time to provide feedback. Ask once, but don't pester. Seek out constructive criticism, too, not just compliments. And when you do get feedback, handle it gracefully. Remember that perception is reality; if a supervisor thinks you did it wrong, don't debate the supervisor. Rather, focus on what you can do next time to prevent that perception.

Let supervisors know your interests. If you particularly enjoyed a project or the subject matter that you worked on, let the supervisor know about your enthusiasm. They may think of you for similar projects that come up.

Build a portfolio of your work. As you are working, you are also growing your skillset and writing ability. When permissible, keep copies of your completed projects for self-reflection. Some firms also let your keep redacted copies of work as writing samples. Be sure to know firm policy on the issue before starting your record keeping.

3. Final Thoughts

a. Roll Up Your Sleeves

The only way to learn the law is to read the law. A secondary source may help you understand it, but *you* must roll up your sleeves, reread cases, reread statutes, reread regulations, get out a pencil, and take notes as you do so. If it still isn't clear, reread it all again. There is no substitute for this. Don't expect anybody else to do this work for you, and don't expect anybody else to swoop in and fix a problem for you. You are a professional now. Act like one. Dress like one. Treat others like one. Be self-sufficient, responsible, and reliable.

b. Be Enthusiastic!

Always show enthusiasm for even the mundane and menial tasks, as well as the big, exciting projects. People are drawn to those who have enthusiasm. Exhibit pride in your place at the office by diving into projects and striving to do even

---

[216] For the skills and perspectives necessary for a successful team member, *see* "The Basics of Teamwork" in section III.

seemingly trivial tasks to the best of your ability. Establish a reputation for being a team player who is not afraid to do whatever needs to get done. This is how you get the opportunity to work on great projects.

c. Be Open-Minded

Some projects on the surface may seem mundane, uninteresting, or outside your comfort zone. Treat those projects with the same zeal as any other work, and you may be pleasantly surprised. Mundane projects can open new doors and expose you to areas you may have not otherwise explored.

d. Build Genuine Relationships

Understand that the relationships you have with those you work with will determine your job satisfaction more than the work itself. Law, ultimately, is about people—those you serve and those you work with. Ask questions of those around you (and not just attorneys!) about their work, their career, their experiences, their families, and their own goals. Show interest in them, not just in what they can do for you, and they will do the same.

e. Be Vulnerable

There are no shortcuts to becoming an effective, respected lawyer. Ultimately, the only way to improve significantly and become comfortable is through experience. If you want to get better at taking depositions, you have to take more depositions. If you want to become more effective at negotiating contracts, you have to negotiate contracts. *Seek out these experiences; do not avoid them.* And don't let any bumps in the road deter you. You will not be perfect at first, and neither were the supervisors you work for. Strive to be thorough, and prepare, prepare, prepare—but don't beat yourself up over mistakes. Learn from them and look forward to your next opportunity. Draw inspiration from the great Teddy Roosevelt, who urged us all to dare greatly over a century ago:

> It is not the critic who counts; not the man who points out how the strong man stumbles, or where the doer of deeds could have done them better. The credit belongs to the man who is actually in the arena, whose face is marred by dust and sweat and blood; who strives valiantly; who errs, who comes short again and again, because there is no effort without error and shortcoming; but who does actually strive to do the deeds; . . . Who spends himself in a worthy cause; who at the best knows in the end the triumph of high achievement, and who at the worst, if he fails, at least fails while daring greatly[.][217]

f. Take the Long View

Finally, you may find that your first job is not what you had hoped for. Indeed, few people today retire from the same employer they start their career with.

---

[217] President Theodore Roosevelt Jr., Speech in Paris, France, Citizen in a Republic (Apr. 23, 1910); *see* BRENÉ BROWN, DARING GREATLY 1 (Penguin 2012).

Don't let this affect your effort. Approach your work as though it is your dream job. Build strong relationships, acquire as much experience as possible, seek out more responsibility, and set yourself up for the future. You never know when your break may come—which client may offer you an in-house position, which supervisor may leave and take you with her or him, or which employer may have an opening. The single most effective thing you can do to set yourself up for future opportunities is to do outstanding work today. Indeed, that is the only thing you can control—focus on that, find value in doing your work well, and your break will come.[218]

Now that you have read "Commitment to the Employing Organization," complete the Reflection Dashboard at **http://ambar.org/roadmap** to develop a better understanding of what developmental stage you are at and what steps you will take to grow to the next stage.

K. Building Relationships Based on Trust through Networking[219]

"Networking is the formation of professional, ideally long-term, relationships of trust with others; it is a critical skill for a student to develop in order to be an effective lawyer."[220] Too often the term "networking" is thought of as "a giant cocktail party with inexpensive wine and hundreds of people I don't know all looking for a job."[221] So to emphasize the strategy of developing long-term relationships through networking, we will instead use the term "relationship building." You should recognize, however, that many people will still refer to the process as "networking."

Relationship building is the single most effective, underutilized, and misunderstood tool for developing one's skill as an effective lawyer and gaining meaningful professional employment. Some students' reluctance to engage in the practice of networking stems largely from a lack of clarity regarding what networking *is*. It is not seeking out immediate offers of employment, manipulating others into assisting you, or making small talk with people in whom you are really not interested and won't ever talk to again. Rather, networking is the formation of professional, strategic relationships that are mutually beneficial and ideally long term.

---

[218] A large part of "taking the long view" is seeing your work as part of ongoing professional development in which you consider yourself as a "project." For more information on managing the project of your professional development, *see* "Lessons from Entrepreneurship" in section I.E and "Initiative, Drive, Work Ethic, and Commitment to Professional Development" in section III.

[219] Authored by Neil W. Hamilton, Colin Seaborg, and Robert Maloney.

[220] E-mail from Steven Tourek, Senior Vice President & Gen. Counsel, Marvin Windows and Doors, to author (Dec. 21, 2014, 13:48 CST) (on file with author).

[221] James Citrin, The Career Playbook: Essential Advice for Today's Aspiring Young Professional 47 (2015).

Strategically building relationships with senior people—professors and senior lawyers—who have enough evidence of your strengths and differentiating competencies to support a strong reference ought to be a student's first priority. These relationships make a tremendous difference in the hiring process and will be exceedingly important for students' early years of practice because these veteran lawyers can provide invaluable advice when faced with a new and complex problem.

Networking as understood in this manner relates directly to what lawyers do and how a lawyer is effective and successful. Lawyers counsel clients to help them understand their best interests in a situation and then influence others to benefit their clients' best interests in the public and private forums of society. Networking is central to how a lawyer creates client relationships built on trust and then successfully influences others on the clients' behalf.

The most important networking objective for you is to have strong trust relationships with professors and senior lawyers who have enough evidence of your strengths and differentiating competencies to support a strong reference. Some of these relationships may develop into active mentors, coaches, and even sponsors during law school and the early years of practice. You should also recognize that your law school's faculty and staff, your mentors, and your classmates are your professional legal colleagues. Having a good reputation among these colleagues for trustworthiness can lead to future referrals and other opportunities.

1. Proven Performance

In the current economic climate, students seeking meaningful professional employment cannot afford to turn a cold shoulder to relationship building. But you're an intelligent and skeptical (to a healthy degree, of course) law student, and you need to see the proof. According to the National Association of Law Placement (NALP), relationship building through self-initiated contact with the employer, referral by a colleague, or starting up a practice or business accounted for 34.5 percent of the pregraduation employment offers received by law students graduating in 2013.[222] This number increases to 54.4 percent for postgraduation employment offers. [223] Translation: relationship building accounts for more postgraduation employment offers than all other methods combined).[224]

Even students who are among the privileged few who obtain employment through on-campus interviews (OCIs) and who may be tempted to think that they need not concern themselves with networking must recognize the importance of relationship building to their future success as a lawyer—both in representing clients and in the path to partnership. In the words of Katherian Roe, chief federal public defender for the District of Minnesota,

---

[222] Nat'l Ass'n Law Placement, Jobs & JD's: Class of 2011, at 111 (2012).

[223] Id.

[224] Id.

In law school, I disliked networking because I am an introvert and I thought those other people are not like me and we have nothing in common. This was a serious misunderstanding on my part. After I started practicing criminal defense, I realized that in order to achieve good results for my clients and to create the changes I hoped for in the law, I had to have a wide network of people who knew me and trusted my work. I had to become a seed planter in as wide a circle of people as I could. It is not easy, but it is absolutely necessary.[225]

In addition, the authors of a 2016 empirical study of the factors that influence the promotion to partner in a big law firm include being highly networked. According to the book *Accelerating Lawyer Success: How to Make Partner, Stay Healthy, and Flourish in the Law Firm,*

We found that lawyers who make partner within 10 years tend to have certain characteristics in common. For starters, they are highly networked within their firms. They are not just connected personally to their colleagues; they also know how to use others' expertise. In other words, partners don't just know people. They know who knows what and are able to strategically leverage that information to get their work done effectively and efficiently. Beyond having a strong sense of where expertise lies in the firm, partners tend to develop more effective informal mentoring relationships than those who do not make partner.[226]

Lawyers who make partner are more likely to report having multiple informal mentors who played a role in their career development; 57 percent of lawyers who made partner reported having three or more informal mentors who influenced their careers, compared to only 26 percent who did not make partner. In other words, having one mentor is simply not sufficient to excel. Having multiple mentors will boost your chances of getting that brass ring.[227]

And remember that it is not enough to merely have informal mentors; it is up to you to be proactive and develop those relationships so that you get as much out of them as possible. Your mentors won't know what you need until you ask them; so ask![228]

So, if you want to make partner, spend time working on your interpersonal skills. Most important, never forget how crucial relationships are to success.[229]

2. Networking Not Working?

Given the importance of effective relationship building to a student seeking meaningful employment, why are some students so reluctant to engage in the

---

[225] Katherian Roe, Dist. of Minn. Chief Fed. Pub. Defender, at a University of St. Thomas Law Employment Advisory Committee Meeting (May 17, 2013).

[226] BERMAN et al., *supra* note 3, at 7.

[227] *Id.* at 10–11.

[228] *Id.*

[229] *Id.*

practice? Students may point to several excuses for avoiding strategic relationship building: (1) being "too busy," (2) introversion, (3) distaste for the perceived "instrumental" nature of networking, and (4) not knowing how to begin. This section will give you some strategies to overcome all of these obstacles.

a. Introversion as an Obstacle to Effective Strategic Relationship Building

Students may be reluctant to build relationships because they perceive themselves to be ill-prepared to engage in conversation with professionals due to shyness or reserved personalities. These fears of the shy or reserved students are largely the result of a misperception of what networking is and how it is conducted. The prototypical mental image of networking is interacting at an event with professionals with whom the student is not acquainted. Students should recognize that relationship building is about developing enduring professional relationships—lacking the ability to "shoot the breeze" in a carefree manner with a stranger is by no means a prerequisite to success in that venture. While a networking event with a large number of professionals present might be effective for more outgoing and gregarious students, those who are more introverted have alternative means of achieving the same result.

Students who are uncomfortable introducing themselves to professionals with whom they have no prior connection may (1) contact professionals with whom they are already acquainted; (2) request a referral from a professional with whom the student is acquainted to a professional practicing in areas in which the student is interested; (3) request contact information for alumni of the student's legal and undergraduate educational institutions from the career-services offices; or (4) join professional, civic, volunteer, or student organizations for the opportunity to form relationships with senior people who are involved in areas of common interest. These forms of contacts can provide you with a greater sense of commonality with the practicing professional and thus reduce your reservations or introversion. Using these methods of meeting contacts provides you with the sense that you have a "reason" to initiate a relationship with the professional.

Second, students who are introverted should not be deterred from long-term relationship building because they feel unable to make small talk. To the extent that having the "gift of gab" may detract from the ability of the outgoing networker to direct a networking (or "informational") meeting in an organized, thoughtful, and concise manner, being naturally talkative is not an inherently helpful quality when networking intentionally. If you are a student who is quiet, you should not be deterred from networking because of feeling uncomfortable or unable to make small talk. You can prepare a short introduction or question to get conversations started with attorneys at these events. For example, you can ask a question about what the attorney finds most interesting in his or her work. With the appropriate research and planning prior to the meeting, you can also plan and construct an organized and concise informational meeting by using active listening skills and asking thoughtful questions. This will not only provide you with valuable information but will also demonstrate your organization and professionalism, which will leave a greater positive impression on the contact than would a meeting filled with pleasantries and small talk that progressed slowly or in a disorganized manner and appeared to be inconsiderate of the contact's time.[230] You can build off small positive steps to develop the enduring relationships with attorneys and professionals needed to gain meaningful employment.

Additionally, you may take measures to choose when and where you engage in relationship building. If you are entirely uncomfortable interacting with or introducing yourself to a professional at a networking or social event, you may be able to network in other situations. For example, you may choose to participate in civic associations, volunteer events, or committees in a professional association.[231] Such events provide a common goal for the group and the opportunity for the student to interact with a smaller group of people. You may also attend CLE seminars to meet attorneys in your field of interest.

Finally, you may choose to attend a professional event and set a goal to meet and engage in meaningful conversation with just one or two attorneys or professionals, obtain their business cards, and follow up with an informational meeting at a later date. Not only does a one-on-one informational meeting enable you to build a deeper relationship with the attorney, but as you gain more confidence in the competency of building relationships, you will begin to feel more comfortable interacting at larger networking and social events. You can build off small positive steps to develop enduring relationships with professionals. In addition, you can use visualization techniques by imagining a scenario over and over again where you initiate a conversation at a networking event to feel familiar with that situation. Often the most difficult part of networking is simply getting out that first sentence. You can visualize and practice a short introduction to get conversations started at networking events. For example, ask a question about what the lawyer finds most interesting in his or her work. You should approach every networking event as an opportunity to develop the skills you will be using to counsel your future clients in an effective and successful manner. Each of these methods puts you in control of your networking.

b. "Manipulative" Nature as an Obstacle to Effective Strategic Relationship Building

For other students, the primary opposition to strategic relationship building is the view that networking is fundamentally "instrumental" or "manipulative"

---

[230] Marcia Ballinger & Nathan A. Perez, The 20-Minute Networking Meeting 33, 34 (2012).

[231] Several points in the networking discussion are borrowed from an earlier version of this document: *Networking*, U. St. Thomas Career & Prof'l Dev. (June 3, 2013), http://www.stthomas.edu/media/schooloflaw/careerandprofessionaldevelopment/NetworkinginaNutshell.pdf.

in nature. Networking, though, should be more correctly viewed as a means of forming a long-term professional relationship—based on trust—that will benefit both parties. Although networking may be done with the objective of using the contact solely for the networker's benefit (which should not be the aim of the networker), it is more correctly viewed as a means of forming a long-term professional relationship based on trust that will benefit both parties. At times, when you are networking with the professional, you may feel as if you are unable to assist or benefit the professional in any meaningful way. However, you need to remember that many veteran lawyers have an intrinsic desire "to pay forward" the help that they received earlier from veteran lawyers and to improve the profession. It also means a great deal to many experienced professionals to make a positive difference in a new lawyer's life, especially if the new lawyer expresses gratitude.

In addition to the benefits that the professional can gain from the relationship while you are in school, the professional has the opportunity to benefit from the relationship as you begin a career. The relationship between you and the professional will ideally continue beyond your education, which enables the professional to extend her or his network to the next generation of professionals. At some point in the future, you may be prepared to assist the professional in a way that benefits the professional's career. Adopting a thoughtful, intentional, and gracious attitude toward forming long-term professional relationships can eliminate any concerns you may have about the "instrumental" or "manipulative" nature of relationship building.

c. Being "Too Busy" as an Obstacle to Effective Networking

Law students have many demands on their time, which can make it difficult to find opportunities to engage in networking. Unfortunately, this tends to lead students to attempt to juggle all of their other obligations while ignoring what is most likely to result in meaningful, professional employment for them in the future. Part of this may stem from students being uncertain of where to begin networking and thus feeling as though the process of networking will take much more time than it does. This chapter aims to provide you with information regarding how to network most effectively and thus provide a realistic picture of how much time is required.

The excuse of being too busy may also result from a poor analysis of how you should spend your time in law school to achieve the greatest long-term benefits to your career. Because networking accounts for nearly 37 percent and 60 percent of pre- and postgraduation employment offers, respectively, it is the single most effective tool to achieve meaningful professional employment. Rather than recognizing networking for its true value, students tend to view it as an "optional" activity that they can engage in if, and when, they happen to have time (which generally equates to never). If, however, students were to view networking as an opportunity to invest in their future careers and dedicate even *one to two hours per week* to networking activities (e-mailing contacts; researching contacts with whom the students have informational meetings; meeting with contacts; attending professional, civic, volunteer, or student events; etc.), students would greatly increase their future employment prospects by diversifying the investment of their time.

Take, for example, Student A, who engages in two hours of networking activities per week, 40 weeks per year for three years of law school (40 weeks because there will be times where other demands will not leave any opportunity for the student to network). Compare Student A to Student B, who averages 30 hours of networking activities per year over three years of law school. Upon graduation, Student A will be *150 hours* ahead of Student B in the single most effective tool to gaining meaningful professional employment. Even if Student B has achieved a higher GPA than Student A, the statistics regarding the effectiveness of networking tend to show that Student A will have a significant advantage over Student B in searching for employment.[232] Student A has a much greater likelihood than Student B of being considered for jobs, which may never be formally advertised, because Student A has developed relationships with the decision makers—or people who know the decision makers—while Student B may never learn of the opportunity to be able to apply for it. Even more likely is that Student B's résumé and cover letter will be lost amidst the chaos of applications for a position, while Student A will have people specifically looking for his or her application materials.

Due to the effectiveness of networking, the thoughtful and future-focused student will recognize the value of making room in his or her schedule for networking now, even if it is only small (but consistent) bits of time. To put off networking is to fail to realize the full value of one's time in law school. To put it simply (even if predictably), students do not have the time *not* to network if they wish to gain professional employment before, or soon after, graduation.

d. Not Knowing Where to Begin as an Obstacle to Effective Strategic Relationship Building

For many students, the idea of contacting professionals in an attempt to form professional relationships is overwhelming because they do not know where to begin. Nevertheless, it is always beneficial to have an intentional relationship-building plan to use to form long-term relationships with attorneys who will provide valuable insight about your employment areas of interest. In fact, the students who intentionally form relationships with attorneys and professionals discover and open doors to employment in the areas of their most promising employment options, not close them.

---

[232] *See* the statistics in the discussion at notes 79–80 in the discussion of proven performance earlier.

Fortunately, after completing the Roadmap, you have identified three of the most promising employment options at this moment. Initially, your relationship-building efforts should concentrate on building long-term relationships with professionals within these most promising employment options. As you explore potential career opportunities, you will gain information to confirm, eliminate, or add to career options and refine your relationship-building plan based on experiences.

As you begin or continue to build relationships, you should maintain focus on what your big-picture goal is: to develop a strong professional network and the skills that creating a professional network fosters. Employers know that building relationships is a highly transferrable skill, and you should always be mindful about developing these types of skills to differentiate yourself.[233]

3. How to Build Relationships Effectively

The following sections—which are largely a synthesis of *The 20-Minute Networking Meeting*[234] and insight about adding the most value to your networking relationships—help illustrate how to network most effectively. Additionally, your law school's career services office will have additional information on networking and building long-term relationships. Informational meetings are an effective way to start building long-term relationships and to explore your most promising employment options. Essentially, building an effective long-term relationship has eight steps: (1) identifying your most promising employment options and target relationships, (2) preparation, (3) initiating the relationship, (4) the meeting, (5) follow-up, (6) growing the relationship, (7) expanding your network, and (8) building evidence of your professional development and networking competency.

a. Steps to Building Long-Term Relationships

i. Identifying Your Most Promising Employment Options and Target Relationships

The first step in developing an effective relationship-building plan is to identify your most promising employment options (subject to change as you gain more experience). These are the potential areas of employment identified in your Roadmap template. Next, as best as you can, you should identify the various strategic relationships you will need both to test whether your most promising employment options are the best fit for you and to gain experience in these areas of employment. Through strategic relationship building, your plan should focus on building long-term relationships with specific people, especially senior people, in the areas of your most promising employment options. These groups include both the people you want to serve (e.g., future clients) and the employers who

---

[233] *See* "The Importance of Transferable Skills" in section I.

[234] *See generally* BALLINGER & PEREZ, *supra* note 230. This section also borrows substantially from the University of St. Thomas School of Law Office of Career and Professional Development webpage at http://www.stthomas.edu/law/students/careercenter/.

serve these clients. Understanding the specific competencies that your potential employers look for in the hiring decision will enable you to create an intentional networking plan that focuses on building the long-term relationships needed to gain meaningful employment within your most promising employment options.

Your networking plan should also focus on deepening existing relationships and creating new ones with senior-level people, *especially professors and at least two outside senior lawyers,* who can provide a strong reference for you in the future on an array of your strongest competencies. For example, if you are a student who wants to emphasize effective teamwork[235] and project management skills,[236] you should identify one person who will know your development of your teamwork competency and another who will know your development of your project management competency. Each should know you well enough to tell a story about your development of that specific competency. Ultimately, once you have demonstrated that you have developed a specific competency that is wanted by one of your potential employers, senior-level people can influence decision makers on your behalf by referencing your progression at that competency either through a letter of recommendation or a phone call.

Once you have identified both your most promising employment options and the various types of long-term relationships that will be necessary for successful service in these areas, you must write down and implement a relationship-building plan that will achieve the long-term relationship goals you have outlined. Your written networking plan should include the steps you are going to take in each semester to build long-term relationships with the specific people and specific groups of people you have identified. It should also include specific benchmarks and a clear timetable for each month so that you can assess whether you are succeeding on your networking plan. For instance, set a specific goal to conduct a certain number of informational meetings each month. Remember, while you are a student and early-career lawyer, your objective while networking is to create and sustain a professional network and develop the skills necessary to become a successful professional. At this stage in your development, informational meetings with professionals are extremely useful because they provide you with the opportunity to form a meaningful relationship, gather information about the practice of law, obtain additional contacts, and explore your most promising employment options.

ii. Preparation

Preparing for an informational meeting involves determining what information you wish to convey to prospective contacts, creating opportunities to network, and researching your contacts and their employers. The information you

---

[235] For information about developing your teamwork competency, *see* "The Basics of Teamwork" in this section.

[236] For information about developing your project management skills, *see* "Project Management Skills: How Law Students Can Learn and Implement the Skills Employers Value" in this section.

communicate with future contacts should include relevant information regarding your academic, work, and volunteer experiences, as well as information regarding what direction you hope to go with your career. These skills, personal characteristics, and aspirations are your "value proposition."[237] Defining your value proposition is how you will market your unique skills and background to employers.

You need to prepare two versions of this information: a one-minute summary of the most important of this information (i.e., your "elevator speech") and a slightly more detailed five-minute discussion of your skills and background. Having both of these versions prepared will help you adjust to a variety of situations in which you might meet someone with whom you wish to build a relationship and make a positive impression. These summaries, however, are not your end goal because they are unlikely to leave an enduring impression with your contacts. These short summaries give you talking points when you meet a new contact (such as at a bar association event) that you can use to obtain the contact's business card so that you have the opportunity to set up an informational meeting with the contact.

Once you have prepared your value proposition, you need to create opportunities to network and put the information to use. Determining who is already in your network is an important step of preparation. Your network includes friends, relatives, current and former colleagues, lawyers, professors, classmates and alumni of both your law school and your undergraduate institution, and members of your faith community and volunteer, civic, or professional associations.[238] From the network that you already have in place, you should determine who is most likely to be able to provide helpful information regarding the practice areas in which you are interested and referrals to other contacts in those areas. In addition to identifying the people who are already in your network, you should also look for opportunities to get involved in bar association committees, professional or civic organizations, CLE seminars, and student organizations. This will create opportunities for you to meet professionals who are actively engaged in areas in which you are interested.

As your career progresses, you should also get involved in business and industry associations. This will help you to provide greater value to the clients that you, or your firm, already represent (by knowing their business or industry) and to meet potential contacts and clients. As a student, these types of networking events are where your value proposition is going to be put to use to meet professionals and obtain their contact information so that you can initiate informational meetings with the professionals. Remember, meeting a professional and obtaining his or her contact information will not do you, or the professional, any good if you don't put the information to use!

---

[237] *See* the introduction to the Roadmap for Employment template in section II.

[238] *Networking*, U. St. Thomas Career & Prof'l Dev., at "Step 1" (June 3, 2013), http://www.stthomas.edu/media/schooloflaw/careerandprofessionaldevelopment/NetworkinginaNutshell.pdf.

After you have identified someone you wish to contact, whether through your preexisting network, meeting at an event, or a referral by another person in your network, the next step is to research that contact's background (e.g., what area of law, any recent awards or recognition the contact has received, etc.) and the contact's firm or employer (e.g., what practice the firm specializes in, major clients, recent awards or recognition the firm has received, etc.).[239] You can begin your research on the website of the contact's employer, the contact's LinkedIn profile, and Google. You will need to use the information you gather from your research to ask the contact *specific* and *relevant* questions at the meeting.[240] You do not want to go to the informational meeting unprepared and ask the contact generic questions (e.g., "What do you do?"), to which you could—and should—have already known the answer.[241] This will simply display your lack of interest, preparation, and professionalism to the contact, as well as give you very little useful information.[242] Rather, if you come prepared, knowing your contact's background and areas of expertise, you will be able to simultaneously craft thoughtful questions, resulting in more specific and useful answers, and leave a positive impression on your contact.[243]

Your school's office dedicated to career and professional development may have additional information to help you in your preparation to become a successful relationship builder as well. If you do not feel comfortable engaging a professional in an informational meeting, make an appointment with a representative from such an office to practice. This will give you an opportunity to prepare, determine how you can most comfortably direct the meeting, and establish a relationship with your school's staff. They will also most likely have suggestions of individuals you can contact if you don't know where to begin. From here, you can begin networking effectively with your contacts. The resources and individuals who make up your school's office dedicated to career and professional development are there to assist you as you prepare for your career. Get to know their staff so that they can help you to develop into a professional who adds value to prospective employers and clients.

iii. Initiating the Relationship

If you discover a potential contact through your research or networking, it is a valuable use of time to determine whether you have any other contacts in common with that person who are able to provide you with an introduction or referral to the potential contact. The potential contact is more likely to be willing to meet with you if you know people in his or her network. If you use LinkedIn to research your prospective contact, you may discover that you have a contact

---

[239] *Id.*; *see also* BALLINGER & PEREZ, *supra* note 230, at 91–95.

[240] BALLINGER & PEREZ, *supra* note 230, at 97–98.

[241] *Id.* at 90–96.

[242] *Id.*

[243] *Id.*

in common with your prospective contact of which you were not aware. Even if you do not have any contacts in common with the potential contact, it is still appropriate for you to initiate a meeting, but it may be more difficult to get the potential contact to find time for you. However, don't let this discourage you from trying to connect with a potential contact!

When initially contacting a professional to set up an informational meeting, it is often helpful to use both e-mail and phone because the professional may prefer one method of communication over the other. Regardless of how you contact the professional, the message should include information regarding who you are, your connection with the professional, and a *specific* question relevant to the professional's expertise that you wish to discuss with the professional (your prior research on the professional is essential here).[244] In addition, your message should be error-free, maintain a professional tone, and express gratitude for the professional's time. If you do not receive an immediate response to your initial contact, do not be concerned. It is generally appropriate to contact the professional again in one or two weeks.[245] If the professional is too busy or otherwise unable to meet with you presently, you may ask whether you may contact her or him in a month or two to attempt to set up an informational meeting at that time. If the professional agrees, be sure to contact her or him within the stated time.

iv. The Meeting

Once you have successfully set up a time to meet, you need to prepare to run a meeting that will leave a positive impression on the professional. Your goal is to make such a positive impression that the professional becomes a "sponsor" for you—someone who takes affirmative action on your behalf through introductions and recommendations to members of his or her network and provides recommendations to decision makers on your behalf when career opportunities arise. Gaining a sponsor will not happen every time you meet with a contact, but when you do gain a sponsor, it will be invaluable to your career. For instance, if the student gets one of his or her sponsors to place a voluntary call to a potential employer on the student's behalf, then it will make a much greater impression on decision makers than the student who simply stands by waiting for decision makers to call someone on the student's reference list. *The 20-Minute Networking Meeting* offers an excellent structure for how to effectively direct an informational meeting and make the greatest positive impression on a contact by outlining the meeting into four categories: (1) the first impression, (2) the overview, (3) the discussion, and (4) the ending.[246]

The suggestions that follow on how much time to spend in a given portion of the meeting are flexible, but you should aim to spend only about 20 minutes in

---

[244] *See Networking, supra* note 231, at "Step 3."
[245] *Id.*
[246] *See* BALLINGER & PEREZ, *supra* note 230, at 52–149.

an informational meeting.[247] If the meeting is going very well and your contact is directing the conversation to last longer (or if the meeting is for lunch), you can allow the meeting to run longer, but you need to do your best to take only as much time as you requested from your contact.[248] Because you are forming a lasting relationship, you will have more chances to talk with the professional. Better to leave the professional wanting more than less.

A. The First Impression

You only get one chance to make a good first impression. Arrive to the meeting several minutes early, knowing where you are meeting, how to get there, and where to park. You should also have the professional's phone number on hand in case you run into an unavoidable delay. If you are meeting at the professional's office, do not check in more than 10 to 15 minutes early because the professional may feel unnecessarily rushed or uncomfortable having you wait. If you arrive too early, find a place to wait where you can review the questions you wish to discuss. Remember that you begin making first impressions the moment you arrive, so be respectful and courteous to everyone you meet. If you do not act professionally toward support staff, word will get back to your contact and likely damage the otherwise positive impression you made.

Once you are in the meeting with the contact, remember to run it efficiently. Twenty minutes is sufficient to establish a positive connection, engage in a thoughtful discussion, and show consideration for the professional's time by not using more of it than is necessary.[249] You should use a couple of minutes to establish a connection with the professional and make a good first impression by being confident, positive, and professional (and make sure you know how to pronounce the contact's name).[250] This includes expressing gratitude for her or his time, highlighting your mutual connections, and giving a summary of what you wish to discuss with the contact.[251] Throughout the meeting, you should make good eye contact and use active listening skills[252]—show the professional that you enjoy listening to him or her. You should also bring a legal pad and pen to write down notes for the follow-up.

B. The Overview

Next, take one minute to provide a brief overview of your educational and work experiences and career interests.[253] Yes, this is a short amount of time to cover everything you've done, but this is an informational meeting, not a job interview.

---

[247] *Id.* at 64–65.

[248] *See id.* at 80.

[249] *See id.* at 64–65.

[250] *Id.* at 72.

[251] *Id.* at 75–79.

[252] Hamilton, *supra* note 182, at 145.

[253] *Id.* at 82.

Use your value proposition for a *couple* of your strongest competencies. What do you most want the person to remember about you? You do not want to bog down the contact with all of the little details of your background; rather, you want to give enough information to provide a general sense of your background while being efficient with your use of the contact's time.[254] Try to consider two strengths that will help your target audience of top employment options that you want them to remember about you.

Because this is an informational meeting and not a job interview, *do not* ask the contact for a job.[255] Unless you have a prior relationship with your contact, you do not have sufficient trust built with the professional to request a job—especially if you set up the meeting claiming to be seeking only information.[256] If your contact is aware of a job opening at which he or she believes you would excel, your contact will mention it.[257]

C. The Discussion

Following the summary of what you wish to discuss and your background, you should spend about 12 to 15 minutes engaging the professional in a thoughtful discussion.[258] This is where your research about the professional and the firm or company is essential. You should prepare several questions that are both specific and relevant to the contact's experience.[259] A good way to format such questions (and display the effort you put into researching and preparing for the meeting) is to pair an *observation* that you gained through your research of the contact with a *relevant question* to that observation.[260] For example, a question may be phrased: "I see that you work in your firm's energy regulation department. What steps should I be taking while in law school to gain experience in this area of law?" Leading with an observation provides the contact with a "heads-up" regarding the topic of your question and will help you ask a question that is specific to her or his experiences and expertise.[261]

After several questions specific to the professional's areas of expertise, you should also ask if he or she has any referrals for you to contact in your relationship-building endeavors. Although it may feel forward to request contacts from the professional you are meeting, this is a generally accepted practice and is of vital importance to expanding your network in an intentional and effective manner. There are several reasons not to avoid this question: your contact understands the value of networking; your contact agreed to meet with you and

---

[254] *Id.* at 83.

[255] *Networking, supra* note 231.

[256] *Id.*

[257] *Id.*

[258] BALLINGER & PEREZ, *supra* note 230, at 89.

[259] *Id.* at 98.

[260] *Id.*

[261] *Id.* at 100.

is likely expecting you to request additional names; your contact may have come prepared with names for you; and your contact may not give you the names unless you request them.[262] In addition, most job offers are not the result of relationship building with one's original contacts but rather result from networking to the "third ring" of contacts (i.e., contacts of contacts of contacts).[263] An informational meeting that is conducted in a professional, well-organized, and thoughtful manner is likely to inspire the professional's trust, which may mean he or she is more willing to give you contacts because he or she has reason to believe that you will conduct yourself in a similar manner with any contacts provided.[264] This question will yield the best results if it is phrased specifically, as opposed to one broadly phrased: "Do you know anyone I could contact?" For example, you could ask, "Although you work in your firm's financial services regulatory department, do you know anyone in your firm's securities litigation and enforcement department whom I could contact?"[265] Phrasing the question specifically will not only help you to develop contacts who have experience in areas in which you are interested but will also assist your contact to think of specific names rather than drawing a blank.[266] If your contact does not have any names with which to provide you, simply thank the contact graciously and proceed to the final question of the meeting.[267]

The final question recommended by *The 20-Minute Networking Meeting* is to ask your contact, "How can I help you?"[268] This question reflects the reciprocal nature of relationship building and also displays thoughtfulness and gratitude for the time and knowledge that the professional has shared with you (think about it: if the attorney you meet with bills at $250/hour, your 20-minute meeting was an $83.33 gift).[269] Although the question from *The 20-Minute Networking Meeting* is intended to be asked by business executives, law students should also seriously consider ways in which they may be able to assist a contact.[270] For instance, if the contact heads a professional or charitable association, bar section, or a similar organization (information you can gather through your prior research on the contact), you may volunteer for or offer to promote upcoming events.[271]

Asking the question "How can I help you?" will only be effective if it is genuine and sincere.[272] Even if you are currently unable to help the professional

---

[262] *Id.* at 102–03

[263] *See id.* at 54–55.

[264] *Id.* at 105.

[265] *Id.* at 103–04.

[266] *See id.* at 104.

[267] *Id.* at 103.

[268] *Id.* at 105.

[269] *Id.* at 106; *see generally Networking, supra* note 231.

[270] Taken from an earlier version of *Networking, supra* note 231.

[271] *Id.*

[272] BALLINGER & PEREZ, *supra* note 230, at 107.

as a student, a sincere offer of future assistance will leave the professional with a positive final impression of you as a thoughtful and considerate person (i.e., the type of person that everyone likes to know and help when possible).[273] This is the question that is most likely to make your contact a sponsor. If you feel uncomfortable with or insincere about asking how you can assist the professional, consider how you can increase the intrinsic and extrinsic benefits the professional gains from the relationship.[274] First, you can increase the extrinsic benefits to the professional through expressions of gratitude for the professional's assistance in the meeting.[275] Second, because contacts value students' professionalism and are more willing to vouch for a professionally mannered student, you may increase the benefit to the contact by demonstrating a high degree of professionalism when conducting the informational meeting and interacting with the contact.[276] Finally, and most importantly, you should focus on following through with any advice and referrals that the professional provides and updating the professional when you do follow through with the advice and referrals because the professional intrinsically benefits from the personal satisfaction of helping you to grow professionally.[277]

D. The Ending

The final step of the meeting is to take two minutes to express your gratitude for the professional's time, advice, and assistance. Review any action you promised to take on her or his behalf, such as forwarding a scholarly article that might be helpful in her or his research, and thank your contact for any actions she will take on your behalf, such as providing you with another's contact information.[278] Thank the professional again for his or her time as you leave. If you met in the professional's office, be sure to thank the assistant or any other helpful staff. Very often the assistant has a close relationship with the professional and the professional will take into serious consideration the assistant's impression of you. Also, many times, it will be easier for you to contact the professional, in the future if you know the assistant's name and contact information because the assistant often sets the professional's schedule and may have a better idea of when the professional is available than the professional does. You want to exit the meeting leaving a positive final impression on everyone because information will travel back to your contact if your behavior is less than professional. Be sure to stick the landing.

---

[273] *Id.* at 109.

[274] Neil W. Hamilton, *Initiating and Building Mentor Relationships,* MINN. LAW. 2 (April 16, 2007) http://minnlawyer.com/2007/04/16/initiating-and-building-mentor-relationships/.

[275] *See id.* at 3.

[276] *See id.*

[277] *See id.* at 2–3.

[278] BALLINGER & PEREZ, *supra* note 230, at 112–14.

b. Follow-Up

Within 24 hours of the meeting, you *must* contact the professional with a handwritten card, typewritten letter, or e-mail offering gratitude for the assistance.[279] Waiting for a longer period of time to contact the professional with your thanks will appear ungracious and can tarnish the positive impression you made on the professional.[280] You should also record any key points from your discussion with the contact within 24 hours of the meeting so that you can use the information to reconnect with your contact at a later date.[281] You do not want to forget what you discussed because specific messages will leave a much greater impression of sincerity.[282] If you received the professional's contact information from another member of your network, you should also write a note or send an e-mail thanking the person who referred you.[283] Doing so will strengthen your relationship with that person as well because people enjoy knowing that any assistance they provided was put to use.[284]

c. Growing Your Relationships: Continuing Contact

Conducting informational meetings with attorneys and professionals will help you explore and refine your most promising employment options. At the same time, however, be mindful that the aim of networking is to create long-term relationships, so you should look for ways to reconnect with professionals and grow your relationships.[285] You can find opportunities to reconnect with contacts by informing them when you follow advice they provided you or meet someone they connected you with, informing them when your contact information or employment status changes, looking for individuals whom you have previously met when you attend events or seminars, forwarding scholarly articles or other information that you think would interest them, contacting them to further discuss something mentioned in an informational meeting further; and so forth.[286] You should generally attempt to reconnect with a contact once every six to twelve weeks.[287] Avoid reconnecting with attorneys and professionals through mass e-mails; overly frequent updates with minor changes in your situation; and stories, quotes, or platitudes—keep it professional.[288]

    Asking the professionals in your network for advice is an effective way to influence them to share more information and opportunities with you while also

---

[279] *Id.* at 121, 123; *see also Networking, supra* note 231, at "Step 4."

[280] *Id.* at 120.

[281] *Id.* at 118; *see also Networking, supra* note 231, at "Step 5."

[282] Ballinger & Perez, *supra* note 230, at 118.

[283] *Id.* at 121; *see also Networking, supra* note 231, at "Step 5."

[284] Ballinger & Perez, *supra* note 230, at 122.

[285] *Networking, supra* note 231, at "Step 5"; *see also* Ballinger & Perez, *supra* note 230, at 124.

[286] *Networking, supra* note 231, at "Step 5"; *see also* Ballinger & Perez, *supra* note 230, at 124–25.

[287] *Networking, supra* note 231, at "Step 5"; Ballinger & Perez, *supra* note 230, at 128.

[288] Ballinger & Perez, *supra* note 230, at 127.

growing the relationship.[289] Seeking advice from the professional encourages greater cooperation because you are showing that he or she has valuable insight you are interested in hearing.[290] If you are genuine when asking the professional for advice, it shows that you care about the professional's insight and makes him or her feel helpful and important.[291] When you use a professional's advice, acknowledge the contribution to your personal or professional growth.[292] It is rewarding for professionals to watch you grow as a person, knowing that they contributed to your development, even if it was only in a small way.[293] Asking for advice can also encourage the professional to make an even greater investment in you because the professional is more likely to continue the commitment to you once the professional has invested some time and energy into helping you.[294] If you show the professional that the relationship is not all about you, the professional will be more likely to support you in return.

In addition, adopting a mindset of giving rather than taking will help you build the long-term relationships needed to achieve your networking goals. Remember that relationships built on trust ought to be mutually beneficial. You can build trust in your networking relationships by always demonstrating a high level of professionalism.[295] If you are consistent with your words and how they translate into actions, the professional will come to know you as a "go-to" person who always delivers.[296] You can foster even more trust in your relationships by demonstrating an interest in your contacts as people, not only as professionals. For example, pay close attention not only to the professional background of your contacts but also their personal lives as well. Write down the names of their spouses, children, and support staff. In addition, you can keep track of the contact's professional activities or hobbies to make your next meeting more meaningful. The professional will likely take notice of your commitment and will be more likely to make an investment in you as well.

You can deepen existing relationships by appointing specific people to your "board of directors"—mentors, sponsors, and coaches in your network—who are willing to give you trustworthy and genuine feedback about tough ethical and professional calls that you confront.[297] Be intentional when selecting whom

---

[289] *See id.* at 150.

[290] *Id.* at 151.

[291] *See id.* at 152–53.

[292] *See generally id.* at 1–2.

[293] *See id.*

[294] *Id.*

[295] *See id.*

[296] For more information about building relationships, *see* "Trustworthiness: Building Lasting Professional Relationships" in section III.

[297] *See* Neil W. Hamilton & Kurtis Young, *Do You Have a Personal Board of Directors?* MINN. LAW. (Dec. 16, 2011), *available at* http://minnlawyer.com/2011/12/16/do-you-have-a-personal-board-of-directors/.

to appoint to your board of directors.[298] For instance, select board members who share the same values and passions as you.[299] Seek out individuals you believe are genuine and trustworthy and reciprocate the same beliefs about you.[300] When engaging one of your board members in a discussion, you should show that you are taking the issue seriously and are willing to learn from his or her feedback.[301] Do not simply ask a board member, "What should I do?"[302] Rather, ask your board member for specific thoughts about what he or she thinks of your analysis of the issue.[303] Remember to be humble and candid; the discussion should be open, honest, and sincere.[304] Additionally, you *must* set aside time to reflect on the issues and advice you receive from your board members. Self-reflection will add meaning to your conversations and help you develop both personally and professionally. At the same time, the people on your board will derive a deep sense of meaning from making a difference in your life.

Finally, remember that you should make an effort to stay connected not only with the strong ties in your network but the weak ties as well.[305] Your strong ties are the people with whom you have close relationships, such as your friends, family, and colleagues.[306] Your weak ties, however, are the people you are not as close to, such as casual acquaintances.[307] The common assumption is that your strong ties will provide you the most leads to connections and employment opportunities.[308] Because your strong ties tend to know the same people as you, however, they probably know about the same opportunities as you.[309] Conversely, your weak ties tend to have greater access to different networks and information leading to other employment opportunities.[310]

d. Expanding Your Network

As you become more proficient at building relationships, your network will naturally grow. To assist your network's growth, look for opportunities to meet attorneys and professionals with experience in your fields of interest. These opportunities can include, but are certainly not limited to, performing legal and nonlegal volunteer work, joining a student organization or bar association section or committee, and attending CLE seminars and other professional

---

[298] *See id.* at 3.

[299] *Id.*

[300] *Id.*

[301] *Id.*

[302] *Id.*

[303] *Id.*

[304] *Id.*

[305] GRANT, *supra* note 109, at 47.

[306] *Id.*

[307] *Id.*

[308] *Id.*

[309] *Id.*

[310] *Id.*

events. Volunteer work can provide you with opportunities to meet others in a low-key, small-group setting. Getting involved in student groups can give you opportunities to meet and work with professionals in areas of practice in which you are interested. Joining and becoming involved in a bar association will enable you to meet attorneys because members will begin to recognize you if you attend regularly, and if you volunteer to help with projects or events, you will demonstrate professionalism and dependability.

These events will give you opportunities to meet professionals who have experience in areas of law that you are interested in. Set a goal of meeting and having meaningful conversations with a specific number of professionals at these events. Even one good conversation means an event has been a success. Once you have introduced yourself to a professional and obtained his or her business card, you can make contact to set up an informational meeting. While you are networking, keep in mind that your casual relationships have the potential to provide access to new information and open doors to new opportunities because they have access to a different network.[311]

Another key to expanding your network with senior lawyers is to develop relationships with "nuts-and-bolts" people. These people include court staff, library staff, dean's assistants, and more. They are invaluable. For example, they often act as the gatekeepers to your senior lawyer or judge, as well as the ones to whom you ask questions that you would otherwise be uncomfortable or unlikely to ask of your veteran lawyer or judge. This group, moreover, can help you navigate the legal system when you are unsure where to file papers, wait for appointments, and so forth.

One helpful way to develop relationships of trust with "nuts-and-bolts" people is to carry with you a list of their names and information to your workplace, courthouse, and so forth. Remembering them and placing them in your networking radius will make your practice and your life much simpler. Recent graduates of the University of St. Thomas School of Law have echoed the importance of this process in their own stories. For example, three graduates who built their own firm from scratch outside of the Twin Cities approached this challenge by developing relationships with court staff and the regional law library staff. The staff knew the nuts and bolts of the legal system and effectively answered their questions. Their help proved to be of immense importance to the graduates in their litigation practice.

e. Demonstrating Evidence of Your Professional Development and Relationship-Building Competency

The last step to effective relationship building involves demonstrating your professional development in the specific competencies that employers look for in the hiring decision. You must always keep in mind how you will back up

---

[311] *See Id.*

your story about developing specific competencies, such as your relationship-building competency. To do this, you must be attentive to the challenge of presenting good evidence to potential employers about your relationship-building plan (and also your success in implementing your plan).

In the process of building long-term relationships based on trust, you will have demonstrated concrete evidence of your development of this competency. This evidence is significant in two ways. First, demonstrating evidence of your competencies enables you to tell a detailed story to potential employers about how you developed a specific competency the employer wants in its associates. When speaking to potential employers about your competencies, remember to talk in terms of what you *do*, not what you *are*.[312] For example, do not merely tell potential employers that you are a law student; rather, you should describe your development of a specific competency by saying, "I research, I analyze, I advocate in trial advocacy."[313] More importantly, however, demonstrating evidence of your strongest competencies to senior-level people enables these professionals to give a very strong reference on your later-stage development of that competency, thus increasing your chances of gaining meaningful employment.

You can also create evidence of your professional development and other specific competencies by being intentional when selecting your classes. For example, you should select an upper-level paper topic that will demonstrate the competencies compatible with your most promising employment options. Not only will your upper-level paper topic be useful as a basis for discussion with potential employers, but it will also be a good example of your research and writing abilities.[314] Furthermore, intentionally selecting your upper-level paper topic will provide you with a potential professor who will know your writing and revision skills well enough to write a letter of recommendation.[315] By the end of your third semester, you should develop a relationship with at least two professors who will know your work well enough to write a good letter of recommendation about a *specific* competency.[316] In addition, by the end of your third semester, you should also have at least two senior-level professionals outside of your law school who can write strong letters of recommendation for you about other specific competencies you want to emphasize. These references are invaluable to you when seeking meaningful employment because senior-level people (including professors) who have seen evidence of your professional development of specific competencies will be more likely to take action on your behalf if they have witnessed your progress firsthand. Also, consider the experiences in student organizations, clinics, pro bono work, and paid and unpaid

---

[312] Kimm Alayne Walton, Guerilla Tactics for Getting the Legal Job of Your Dreams 1315 (2d ed. 2008).

[313] *Id.*

[314] *See* "Timeline for Roadmap Steps" in section II.

[315] *Id.*

[316] *See id.* at 1–2.

clerkships and externships that will best demonstrate evidence of your strongest competencies.[317] You should complete at least two of these experiences during your second year. Read "Supporting Your Value Proposition with Evidence" in section IV for a discussion about demonstrating good evidence of other specific competencies.

Finally, you should reflect on the successes and failures you experience as you develop various competencies.[318] Ask professors and other professionals for feedback regarding your progress in a specific competency so that you can demonstrate strong evidence of the competencies you want to emphasize to them.[319] Keep track of these experiences so that you have a story to tell about your development of the specific competencies that legal employers want.[320] At the end of the year, you should refer to the assessments provided through **http://ambar .org/roadmap** to reassess what stage you are at in terms of professional and networking skills development. There are also materials available through the link provided to assist you in setting networking benchmarks. Likewise, ask other professionals whom know you well for a genuine assessment of where they see you in terms of your developmental stage. If their assessment differs from yours, discuss the reasons for the differences, and make any changes that will enable you to demonstrate sufficient evidence of your development. Building evidence of your professional development and networking competency may also be viewed as a return to the preparation stage of networking and repeating the remaining stages. As you expand your network, your confidence and effectiveness in building relationships will improve and thus increase the value to you and your contacts through your networking.

4. Conclusion

Strategic relationship building is your most effective tool for gaining meaningfulprofessional employment. By creating a network of long-term professional relationships founded on trust, you will form connections with people who can attest to your strongest competencies and the value you can bring to an employer. Recognize relationship building as a valuable investment in your future career, not only for gaining your first job but also for achieving long-term professional success. It is an investment that you must make.

Now that you have read "Building Relationships Based on Trust through Networking," complete the Reflection Dashboard at **http://ambar.org/roadmap** to develop a better understanding of what developmental stage you are at and what steps you will take to grow to the next stage. Recall that the self-assessments and planning tools are also available through the link.

---

[317] *Id.* at 3.

[318] *See generally id.* at 2–3.

[319] *Id.* at 2.

[320] *Id.* at 2–3.

L. Cross-Cultural Competency: Developing Cultural Competencies for the Changing Workplace[321]

No matter a lawyer's practice area, it is extremely important that each lawyer must possess the ability to interact and communicate effectively with people from other cultures. Cargill general counsel Laura Witte emphasizes, "To be truly effective counselors in today's global marketplace, it is not enough to know the law. We must be able to communicate, build relationships, interpret and apply the law in the context of applicable cultural norms, norms that may be very different from our own."[322] In a litigation context, law professor Susan Bryan urges that "[l]awyers who explicitly examine the cross-cultural issues in a case will increase client trust, improve communication, and enhance problem-solving on behalf of clients."[323] It is strongly in a lawyer's self-interest to develop cross-cultural competence in his or her everyday work.

Cross-cultural competence can be broadly defined as the ability to "effectively connect with people who are different from us—not only based on our similarities, but also with respect to differences."[324] Accordingly, it is necessary for a lawyer to first identify the various cultures to which he or she belongs in order to understand which cultures are different from the lawyer's own. Indeed, "[a] broad definition of culture recognizes that no two people have had the exact same experiences and thus, no two people will interpret or predict [culture] in precisely the same way."[325]

Culture is defined in this context as "the body of customary beliefs, social forms and material traits constituting a distinct tradition of a racial, religious or

---

[321] Authored by Neil W. Hamilton and Jeff Maleska. Substantial parts of this discussion of cross-cultural competency were first published in Neil Hamilton & Jeff Maleska, *Helping Students Develop Affirmative Evidence of Cross-Cultural Competency,* 19 St. Mary's L.Rev. On Race & Social Justice 187–215 (2017).

[322] E-mail from Laura Witte, General Counsel, Cargill, to author (Sept. 29, 2015, 16:33 CST) (on file with the author).

[323] Susan Bryant, *The Five Habits: Building Cross-Cultural Competence in Lawyers,* 8 Clinical L. Rev. 33, 49 n. 53 (2001).

[324] Ritu Bhasin, *Cultural Competence: An Essential Skills for Success in an Increasingly Diverse World,* LawPRO Magazine, Vol. 13, No. 2, 9, 10 (2014); *See* Mitchell Hammer, Milton Bennett, Richard Wiseman, *Measuring Intercultural Sensitivity: The Intercultural Development Inventory,* International Journal of Intercultural Relations 421, 422 (2003) ("We will use the term 'intercultural sensitivity' to refer to the ability to discriminate and experience relevant cultural differences, and we will use the term 'intercultural competence' to mean the ability to think and act in inter-culturally appropriate ways."); *See* Association of American Colleges & Universities, *Intercultural Knowledge and Competence VALUE Rubric,* http://www.aacu.org/value/rubrics /intercultural-knowledge ("Intercultural Knowledge and Competence is 'a set of cognitive, affective, and behavioral skills and characteristics that support effective and appropriate interaction in a variety of cultural contexts.'") (citation omitted).

[325] Bryant, *supra* note 323, at 41.

social group."[326] Culture, for example, can include a person's age, gender, ethnicity, sexual orientation, or physical ability. Even if the lawyer shares all of those categories with the other person, different regions of the same country may have different cultures. Different organizations may also have different cultures.

For a lawyer to truly provide competent representation to his or her clients, the lawyer must not only understand the law but also understand the culture of the client, of the teams and other groups with whom the lawyer works to advance the client's interests, and of adversaries and decision makers whom the lawyer seeks to influence. Without awareness of the various cultures of these stakeholders in a lawyer's work, a lawyer cannot see how culture affects the representation. For example, not considering a client's culture could cause a misunderstanding of the client's goals, needs, and personal preferences. If a lawyer chooses to ignore the cultural differences between the lawyer and his or her clients, it is likely that the representation will not be as effective as it should be. The inability to understand a client's culture can also make it more difficult for the lawyer to build trust in the relationship.[327]

Beyond the client context, attorneys also encounter many different cultures when interacting with coworkers, other firms, opposing counsel, judges, support staff, and so forth. It is equally as important to be cognizant of how different cultures affect the lawyer's encounters with these individuals. Failing to recognize how different cultures may affect these interactions can lead to confusion, misunderstanding, and even broken relationships. In contrast, cross-cultural competence improves trust, communication, and problem solving among both peers and clients while also acknowledging the inherent dignity of each person.

In our view, empathy is at the heart of developing cross-cultural competency. Empathy is an ability to understand the other's experiences and perspectives combined with an ability to communicate this understanding and an intention to help. In simpler terms, empathy is the ability to walk in another person's shoes, to view life from his or her perspective, and to communicate that understanding and an intention to help.

In response to this ever-increasing diversity, law schools are beginning to recognize the need to better prepare students for the realities that they will face when dealing with clients and peers in practice. Some law schools have implemented policies that specifically focus on developing cross-cultural competency in their students. For example, the University of St. Thomas School of Law faculty adopted a learning outcome that reads:

> Graduates will demonstrate competence in initiating and sustaining professional relationships and working with others towards common goals. *Graduates will also demonstrate competence in interacting effectively with people across cultural differences.* (emphasis added)[328]

---

[326] *Culture*, WEBSTER'S THIRD NEW INTERNATIONAL DICTIONARY (2001).

[327] Bryant, *supra* note 323, at 42.

As several scholars have noted, "in today's multicultural world, students must develop into culturally sensitive lawyers who understand how their own cultural experiences affect their legal analysis, behaviors, and perceptions."[329]

This chapter will establish that cross-cultural competency is an affirmative competency that both law students and legal practitioners can develop throughout their careers. Further, this chapter will also show that it is in the law student and legal practitioner's enlightened self-interest to become culturally competent. With practice, the legal practitioner can come to identify and understand when his or her cultural lens, biases, and stereotypes are affecting the relationship with clients and others. Through this affirmative approach, legal practitioners can better and more effectively serve their clients and ensure a result that best suits the client's needs. Finally, this chapter will give practical advice and techniques as to how the law student and lawyer can begin to improve his or her cross-cultural competence.

1. The Effects of Cross-Cultural "Incompetence"

A good starting point for a discussion on why it is important to develop cross-cultural competence is to examine first the negative effects of being cross-culturally "incompetent." One of the most common reasons a lawyer is culturally incompetent is because the lawyer fails to recognize that a need for cultural competence exists in the situation. Susan Sample better illustrates this point:

> Cultural differences can be easy to miss . . . It is particularly important for professionals because they very well may be the person with the highest status in the room, and people with higher status do not necessarily have a lot of experience at looking for cultural differences and adapting to them. For example, if a person is U.S. American, or male, or upper middle class, or European American, or any combination of those things, they may not recognize all the cultural differences in the room because they are inadvertently making everyone conform to them, and thus, their cultural norms.[330]

It is in instances like the this one above where problems arise as a direct result of a lack of cultural awareness and competency.

One major problem that a culturally incompetent attorney may encounter is the difficulty establishing trust in the attorney–client relationship.[331] Without trust, a relationship between the lawyer and client cannot work well. Trust is not

---

[328] *Learning Outcomes*, UNIVERSITY OF ST. THOMAS SCHOOL OF LAW (October 4, 2015, 17:36 CST), https://www.stthomas.edu/law/about/.

[329] Andrea Curcio, Teresa Ward, and Nisha Dogra, *A Survey Instrument to Develop, Tailor, and Help Measure Law Student Cultural Diversity Education Learning Outcomes*, 38 NOVA L. REV. 177, 232 (2014).

[330] Susan Sample, *Intercultural Competence as a Professional Skill*, 26 PAC. MCGEORGE GLOBAL BUS. & DEV. L.J. 117, 118 (2013).

[331] Bryant, *supra* note 323, at 42.

established simply because the client chose the lawyer to represent him or her; rather, the lawyer must work to establish trust in the relationship.[332] Being culturally competent can help the lawyer to accurately understand the client's goals and behavior and use this information to create a trusting relationship.

A culturally incompetent attorney will also likely miss important information because of failed or misunderstood communication.[333] In particular, because we interpret our surroundings and encounters through our own lens, there may be a gap between our own understanding and another person's understanding.[334] When the lawyer interprets the client's messages through his or her own lens, communication can easily break down. As a result of the lawyer's failure to recognize the inherent differences and nuances of each culture, he or she may make decisions that the client may not have chosen. Communication failures can have a detrimental effect on the attorney–client relationship. In fact, "[s]tudies show that client satisfaction often relates as much to how lawyers communicate as to actual results achieved in a given case. Effective lawyers must be able to recognize, and appropriately respond to, their own and others' cultural perceptions and beliefs because these often play a central role in lawyer-client communications."[335]

Last, cultural incompetence "may impede lawyers' abilities to effectively interview, investigate, counsel, negotiate, litigate, and resolve conflicts."[336] Not recognizing the impact that culture has on a lawyer's interactions with another can lead the lawyer to ask the wrong questions, suggest an unfavorable course of action, take a bad settlement offer, or even to an inability to resolve a conflict.

2. Developmental Stages

Many scholars have attempted to classify the various "stages" that a person may fit into on a spectrum of cross-cultural competence. While not every model can perfectly describe the nuances of the process of developing cross-cultural competence, the models do provide useful guideposts that allow a person to self-reflect and gauge where he or she may fall on the spectrum. While we do not view any one of these models as "best" or "complete," each model we have chosen to discuss is representative, relatable, and applicable in regard to the process of developing cross-cultural competence.

When reading through the descriptions and examining the charts for each of the models, the law student or lawyer should do a self-assessment (using tables 29—32) and estimate his or her developmental stage. Once he or she has

---

[332] Bryant, *supra* note 323, at 42.

[333] Sample, *supra* note 330, at 118.

[334] *See* Bryant, *supra* note 323, at 40.

[335] Curcio, Ward, & Dogra, *supra* note 329, at 192.

[336] *Id.*

completed this self-assessment, we suggest taking these grids and asking at least two others—who have previously observed him or her working in a cross-cultural context—to assess the law student or the lawyer using the same assessment. By completing both the self-and peer assessment, the reader will have an indication of how others perceive his or her cross-cultural abilities, which in turn gives the law student and lawyer a basis to self-reflect on cross-cultural aptitude. From there, the law student and lawyer can use the information gathered to find areas for improvement and to develop a plan to enhance his or her cultural competence.

a. Milton Bennett's Model of Cross-Cultural Competence

Dr. Milton Bennett created one of the most notable and widely used cultural competency models, the Developmental Model of Intercultural Sensitivity (DMIS), which is summarized in table 28. Within Bennett's model, the underlying assumption is that cross-cultural competency can be developed over a period of time as a person continues to experience more culturally diverse situations.[337] The DMIS is made up of six stages: three ethnocentric stages, where one experiences his or her own culture as "central to reality," and three ethnorelative stages, where one experiences his or her own culture as relative to other cultures.[338]

Bennett's three ethnocentric stages include denial, defense, and minimization.[339] Denial is the stage in which a person does not recognize any cultural differences and believes his or her culture is "correct."[340] Next, a person in the defense stage recognizes that other cultures exist but does not acknowledge that these other cultures are valid.[341] Third, those in the minimization stage tend to overemphasize the universality of cultural beliefs and minimize the actual differences between different cultures.[342]

People in an ethnorelative stage are considered to have developed more cultural competency than those in an ethnocentric stage. The first ethnorelative stage in Bennett's model is acceptance. A person in this stage recognizes and views other cultures as valid and sees his or her own culture as just one option among many. Generally, people at this stage tend to be accepting of cultural differences.[343] The second stage is adaptation. This stage is one in which people

---

[337] J. M. Bennett, *Towards Ethno-relativism: A Developmental Model of Intercultural Sensitivity*, in CROSS-CULTURAL ORIENTATION: NEW CONCEPTUALIZATIONS AND APPLICATIONS 24–28 (R.M. Paige ed., 1986).

[338] Milton Bennett, *Becoming Inter-culturally Competent*, in TOWARD MULTICULTURALISM: A READING IN MULTICULTURAL EDUCATION 62, 62 (Wurzel, J ed., 2004).

[339] *Id.* at 62.

[340] Milton Bennett, *A Developmental Model of Intercultural Sensitivity*, INTERCULTURAL DEVELOPMENT RESEARCH INSTITUTE 1, 1 (rev. 2011), http://www.idrinstitute.org/page.asp?menu1=4.

[341] Bennett, *Towards Ethno-relativism*, *supra* note 337, at 3.

[342] *Id.* at 5.

[343] *Id.* at 7.

Table 28 Milton Bennett's Developmental Model of Intercultural Sensitivity[344]

	Stage	Description	Examples
Ethnocentric Stages	**(1) Denial of Difference**	People in this stage are in denial about cultural difference and cannot differentiate culture as a category. They have an inability to perceive or construe data from differing cultural contexts.	"As long as we all speak the same language, there's no problem." "With my experience, I can be successful in any culture without any special effort—I never experience culture shock."
	(2) Defense Against Difference	People in this stage tend to experience culture as "us vs. them." They generally feel threatened by those who are different. Generally, they exalt their own culture and degrade the other's with negative stereotypes.	"Why don't these people speak my language?" "When I go to other cultures, I realize how much better my own culture is."
	(3) Minimization of Difference	People in this stage recognize cultural differences but overemphasize human similarity and universal values. As a result, they tend to believe that it is sufficient to "just be yourself" in cross-cultural situations.	"Customs differ, of course, but when you really get to know them, they're pretty much like us." "If people are really honest, they'll recognize that some values are universal."
Ethnorelative Stages	**(4) Acceptance of Difference**	People in this stage accept all values, behaviors, and cultures. They recognize the alternatives to their culture. Acceptance does not mean agreement with alternative values or cultures.	"Sometimes it's confusing, knowing that values are different in various cultures and wanting to be respectful but still wanting to maintain my own core values." "The more difference the better—it's boring if everyone is the same."
	(5) Adaptation to Difference	People in this stage apply their acceptance of difference and recognize the need to interact effectively with people from other cultures. They act in culturally appropriate ways in different cultural contexts.	"I know they're really trying hard to adapt to my style, so it's fair that I try to meet them halfway." "To solve this dispute, I'm going to have to change my approach."
	(6) Integration of Difference	People in this stage are no longer defined by any one culture but are often multicultural. They have made a sustained effort to becoming competent in a variety of cultures.	"Whatever the situation, I can usually look at it from a variety of cultural points of view." "Everywhere is home if you know enough about how things work there."

[344] We created this chart based on Milton Bennett's *A Developmental Model of Intercultural Sensitivity*.

view cultural differences as a good thing and try to consciously adapt to the cultural norms of the surrounding environment.[345] The last stage is integration. At this stage a person does not feel that he or she belongs to any specific culture but rather can adapt and shift between various cultures and worldviews.[346] The integration stage, however, is not per se better than the adaptation stage; rather, it describes the cultural integration process experienced by "many members of non-dominant cultures, long-term expatriates, and 'global nomads.'"[347]

b. William Howell's Model of Cross-Cultural Competence

William Howell developed another model of cross-cultural competence.[348] This model is less detailed than Bennett's and is generally applied within the context of students. This particular model consists of four stages: (1) unconscious incompetence, (2) conscious incompetence, (3) conscious competence, and (4) unconscious competence.[349] Each stage is discussed in table 29.

Table 29 William Howell's Model of Cross-Cultural Competence

Stage	Name	Description
1	Unconscious incompetence[350]	Characterized by a student's total lack of awareness of the impact of culture and a failure to recognize cultural differences
2	Conscious incompetence[351]	A student is aware of the role that culture plays in his or her interactions with others but does not possess the skills needed for competent cross-cultural interactions with others.
3	Conscious competence[352]	A student possesses the skills necessary to effectively communicate across cultures but must consciously recognize and implement these skills in his or her cultural interactions.
4	Unconscious competence[353]	A student is able to unconsciously implement and use his or her cross-cultural competency skills in all of the student's interactions with others.

---

[345] *Id.* at 9.

[346] *Id.* at 11.

[347] Hammer, Bennett, Wiseman, *supra* note 324, at 425.

[348] Curcio, Ward, & Dogra, *supra* note 329, at 206 (citing William S. Howell, THE EMPATHIC COMMUNICATOR 29–33 (1982)); Bryant, *supra* note 324, at 62–63.

[349] *Id.*

[350] *Id.*

[351] *Id.*

[352] *Id.*

[353] *Id.*

c. Model of Cross-Cultural Competency Borrowed from the American Board of Internal Medicine

We borrowed from the American Board of Internal Medicine's (ABIM) Milestone Project that defined the key competencies for internal medicine residents and stages of development of each competency. This project defined developmental stages of "Responding to Each Patient's Unique Characteristics" and "Professional and Responsible Interaction with Others." Tables 30 and 31 show both of these stage development grids adapted for the practice of law.

Table 30 Developmental Stages in Responding to Each Client's Unique Characteristics and Needs (Adapted from the ABIM Model Applicable to Residents)

Responds to each client's unique characteristics and needs.

Critical Deficiencies	Early Learner	Advancing Improvement	Ready for Unsupervised Practice	Aspirational
• Is insensitive to differences related to culture, ethnicity, gender, race, age, and religion in the client/lawyer encounter • Is unwilling to modify representation to account for a client's unique characteristics and needs	• Is sensitive to and has basic awareness of differences related to culture, ethnicity, gender, race, age, and religion in the client/lawyer encounter • Requires assistance to modify representation to account for a client's unique characteristics and needs	• Seeks to fully understand each client's unique characteristics and needs based upon culture, ethnicity, gender, religion, and personal preference • Modifies plan to account for a client's unique characteristics and needs with partial success	• Recognizes and accounts for the unique characteristics and needs of the client • Appropriately modifies representation to account for a client's unique characteristics and needs	• Role models professional interactions to negotiate differences related to a client's unique characteristics or needs • Role models consistent respect for client's unique characteristics and needs

d. The Roadmap's Model of Cross-Cultural Competency

We borrowed from the Bennett, Howell, and internal medicine models to synthesize our own developmental model of cross-cultural competency in an attempt to define stages of cross-cultural competency where a student or practitioner could

Table 31 Developmental Stages in Professional and Responsible Interaction with Others (Adapted from the ABIM Model Applicable to Residents)

Has professional and respectful interactions with clients and members of the interprofessional team (e.g., peers, ancillary professionals, and support personnel)

Critical Deficiencies	Early Learner	Advancing Improvement	Ready for Unsupervised Practice	Aspirational
• Lacks empathy and compassion for client and the team • Disrespectful in interactions with client and members of the interprofessional team • Sacrifices client needs in favor of own self-interest • Blatantly disregards respect for client privacy and autonomy	• Inconsistently demonstrates empathy, compassion, and respect for clients and the team • Inconsistently demonstrates responsiveness to client's and the team's needs in an appropriate fashion • Inconsistently considers client privacy and autonomy	• Consistently respectful in interactions with clients and members of the interprofessional team, even in challenging situations • Is available and responsive to needs and concerns of clients and members of the interprofessional team to ensure strong representation • Emphasizes client privacy and autonomy in all interactions	• Demonstrates empathy, compassion, and respect for clients and the team in all situations • Anticipates, advocates for, and proactively works to meet the needs of clients and the team • Demonstrates a responsiveness to client needs that supersedes self-interest • Positively acknowledges input of members of the interprofessional team and incorporates that input into the plan as appropriate	• Role models compassion, empathy, and respect for client and the team • Role models appropriate anticipation and advocacy for client and team needs • Fosters collegiality that promotes a high-functioning interprofessional team • Teaches others regarding maintaining patient privacy and respecting client autonomy

demonstrate affirmative evidence of the competency (table 32). The Roadmap model also recognizes that it is possible to be at a later stage of cross-cultural competence in a particular area, such as gender, while also being at an earlier stage in another area, such as age or race.

There are four stages to the Roadmap development model of cross-cultural competency: (1) lack of awareness, (2) recognition, (3) conscious implementation, and (4) proficiency. A person in the first stage, lack of awareness, does not recognize that he or she lacks cross-cultural competency. Someone in this stage may stereotype people of other cultures or feel uncomfortable interacting with others who are different from him or her. In general, this stage reflects ignorance of the role that culture plays in his or her life.

At the second stage, recognition, a person acknowledges a lack of cross-cultural competency but may be unsure of how to develop this skill. A person may notice the role that culture plays and reflect on how his or her culture affects decisions. At this stage, a person begins to see the need to develop cross-cultural competency.

At the third stage, conscious implementation, a person takes affirmative steps to develop cross-cultural competency by engaging in self-reflection and refraining from making on-the-spot judgments in unfamiliar situations. In addition, the person is open to culturally diverse experiences. While there may be some difficulty or discomfort in these interactions, the person reflects on the difficulties and discomfort and seeks greater understanding. It is the affirmative steps taken to become more cross-culturally competent by a person in this stage that are important.

At the final stage, proficiency, a person has become educated about a particular culture and could be considered "cross-culturally competent" in that area. A person at this stage is able to interact freely and genuinely within another culture and understands the differing viewpoints and customs of that culture. Interactions with those who belong to the other culture reasonably approximate those with someone from the person's own culture. There is a genuine respect and appreciation for the other culture, although this need not be marked by agreement with it.

3. Developing Cross-Cultural Competence

Inherent in each of the models discussed is the idea that a person is able to develop skills to become more cross-culturally competent and grow in understanding through the several stages. This idea, however, raises a question: What are the most effective strategies for becoming more cross-culturally competent? While there is no clear-cut answer to this question, there are many pathways for a person to become more culturally aware and to develop the skills needed to become cross-culturally competent.

One of the most important pathways to become cross-culturally competent is through careful observation. Observation is the basis for recognizing

Table 32 The Roadmap's Developmental Model of Cross-Cultural Competency

Stage	Description	Affirmative Evidence	Examples
(1) **Lack of Awareness**	People in this stage are entirely unaware of their insensitivity to other cultures around them; they cannot comprehend the importance of becoming cross-cultural competent or what it even means.	• Accepts one's own beliefs as superior to others • Negatively stereotypes others who are different from him- or herself • Refuses to interact with others who are different or in culturally diverse social situations	Accepts one's own beliefs as superior to others Negatively stereotypes others who are different from him- or herself Refuses to interact with others who are different or in culturally diverse social situations
(2) **Recognition**	People in this stage recognize that they lack cultural competence but are unsure how to develop this into an affirmative skill; they begin to recognize the importance of understanding and accepting other cultures.	• Sees the wide variety of cultural diversity around oneself • Recognizes the need to be able to interact with anyone in any situation • Begins to seek out information on how to develop cultural competency	"I wish I could speak another language." "I think studying abroad would give me a different perspective on the world." "I always go to lunch with the guys and need to try other groups too."
(3) **Conscious Implementation**	People in this stage begin to take affirmative steps in developing their cross-cultural competency; they now place themselves into cultural situations that they would not have before.	• Places him- or herself in culturally diverse situations • Researches and learns more about other cultures • Begins to break-down previously held stereotypes of different cultures.	"I should try to remember that everyone has differing opinions and that they all deserve my understanding and respect." "Even though I might not agree, I can see why they think that way."
(4) **Proficiency**	People in this stage take affirmative steps on a regular basis to understand others and ensure cross-cultural competence; they recognize and account for the unique characteristics and needs of others.	• Experience with working in multicultural team on projects • Continuing/strong relationships with people from other cultures • Experience living in cultures very different than one's own culture	"It is important to look at the situation from someone else's shoes." "We need to understand and respect others' differences to work together most effectively."

differences and the beginning to an understanding of another culture's norms, traditions, and behaviors. It is important to ask, "'[W]hat is going on here that I do not understand?' It must be a constant question in a person's mind."[354] Without first observing and understanding the cultures around us, it is unlikely that a person can become culturally competent.

Hand-in-hand with the need to observe is the need for self-reflection. What types of reflection, then, are most helpful? As Bryant notes, "[e]ffective cross-cultural interaction depends on the lawyer's capacity to self-monitor his or her interactions in order to compensate for bias or stereotyped thinking and to learn from mistakes."[355] First and foremost, then, self-reflection includes identifying a person's own culture, stereotypes, and biases. Through this process of self-reflection, a person can observe other cultures and identify the similarities and differences between different cultures. Moreover, this process of comparative reflection will promote an understanding of misperceptions of others and how different cultures may clash.

Empathy was defined earlier as an ability to understand others' experiences and perspectives combined with an ability to communicate this understanding and an intention to help. Being empathetic thus requires that a person puts him- or herself into another's shoes in order to feel what it is like to be that person.[356] An important part of walking in another person's shoes involves looking at his or her perspective in an unbiased and neutral manner—viewing the other person's situation in this way can help further understanding of his or her behavior.[357] An empathetic worldview also focuses on similarities people share rather than differences. A focus on similarities, bypassing the superficial differences, acknowledges the basic humanity of each person.[358]

Empathy is demonstrated by active listening.[359] According to Hamilton, "effective listening requires not only technical proficiency but also an empathic ability to connect with the speaker."[360] For the lawyer to be an effective, empathic listener, then, it is best he or she uses active listening techniques because it allows the lawyer to show clients that he or she understands them.[361] Moreover, active listening allows the lawyer to orientate "the conversation to the client's world, the client's understandings, the client's priorities, and the client's narrative."[362] Through this focus on the client, the lawyer is able to gather culturally sensitive information and then use that information to ensure respect for the client's

---

[354] Sample, *supra* note 330, at 119.

[355] Bryant, *supra* note 323, at 56.

[356] *Id.*

[357] *Id.*

[358] *Id.*

[359] Hamilton, *supra* note 182, at 145, 151.

[360] *Id.*

[361] *Id.* at 157.

[362] Bryant, *supra* note 323, at 73.

culture and wishes.[363] This process of gathering and using culturally specific information helps the lawyer to develop his or her cross-cultural competency capacity and to retain culturally specific information to guide conduct in similar situations in the future. Taken as a whole, the habits of observing, listening, self-monitoring, and undertaking self-reflection will help develop empathy.

Each law student and lawyer must practice cross-cultural competency in order to improve. Indeed, "like the learning of other lawyering skills, learning cross-cultural lawyering skills occurs through incremental learning and by practice."[364] Like all other learned skills in your life, becoming cross-culturally competent is not something that will be automatic or easy; rather, it is a career-long endeavor that requires patience and diligence. Through the course of this conscious implementation process, a lawyer will still certainly encounter difficult or uncomfortable cultural situations. In these types of cross-cultural situations where a person is unsure what to do, an effective strategy is to *"simply ask others about their perspective or even their feelings regarding a specific situation or occurrence."*[365] By asking someone to clarify when the lawyer or law student is unsure, he or she ensures respect for the other's cultural practices. Overall, addressing these new and uncomfortable situations prevents miscommunication and helps the lawyer develop the knowledge of how he or she can approach a similar situation in the future.

4. Conclusion

There is no doubt that today's world is increasingly multicultural. Now, more than ever, it is important that law students and lawyers alike develop cross-cultural competency and understand how culture affects their everyday practice of the law. As noted at the outset of this chapter, legal employers are continually focusing on building cultural competency in their employees and are looking to hire people who can affirmatively demonstrate some capability in this area. Today, "a culturally sensitive lawyer understands culture is multi-faceted, and that everyone's worldviews, conduct, perceptions, and actions are based upon a complex compilation of numerous cultural factors and experiences. A culturally sensitive lawyer is aware of the need to be self-reflective about the role culture plays in his or her interactions."[366]

Cross-cultural competence is a career-long endeavor that requires dedication and perseverance. When law schools encourage students to develop cross-cultural skills while they are still in school, students benefit in the long run.

---

[363] *Id.* at 73–74.

[364] *Id.* at 62.

[365] Steve Muller, *Developing Empathy: Walk a Mile in Someone's Shoes*, PLANET OF SUCCESS BLOG (October 4, 17:31 CST), http://www.planetofsuccess.com/blog/2011/developing-empathy-walk-a-mile-in-someone%E2%80%99s-shoes/.

[366] Curcio, Ward, & Dogra, *supra* note 329, at 228.

Developing cross-cultural skills will help students to be successful attorneys in the future by improving communication and ensuring understanding in their interactions in all cultural contexts. Failing to recognize the importance of being cross-culturally competent denies the realities of the rich cultural heritage of clients and other stakeholders in each lawyer's professional life.

Now that you have read "Cross-Cultural Competency: Developing Cultural Competencies for the Changing Workplace," complete the Reflection Dashboard at **http://ambar.org/roadmap** to develop a better understanding of what developmental stage you are at and what steps you will take to grow to the next stage. Additionally, tables 28, 30, and 32 are available electronically through the previous link to assist you in determining your developmental stage of cross-cultural competence.

M. Listen to Persuade: How Attentiveness Leads to Value[367]

"If I can persuade, I can move the universe."[368]

Legal employers greatly value effective persuasive communication skills, and clients greatly value a lawyer who listens well and understands the client's context, challenges, and opportunities, not just the client's technical legal issues. As a law student, you can use written and oral communication with potential employers to demonstrate persuasive communication and listening skills and an understanding of what competencies the legal employer needs. You are signaling that this is how you would similarly approach meeting client needs.

Many law students use a standard résumé, cover letter, and reference letter approach in which they do not make clear their strongest competencies and their specific value proposition. Many simply repeat in interviews what employers have already seen on résumés, cover letters, and letters of recommendation. Some students believe that these are the only things they have to offer—the same things everyone else has to offer. But this isn't true. This chapter will focus on how to persuasively communicate your own unique value—value that sets you apart from your competition and, sometimes, that employers don't even know existed.

The first step in becoming a persuasive communicator, however, is listening. To gain information that you can use in persuasive communication, you'll need others to trustfully provide you with information. Active listening sends a message of commitment and care to other people. The more they know you care, the more they will share with you, and the more they will trust you. This chapter provides advice on how to prepare to be a good listener, how to practice strong listening skills, and how to turn these skills into persuasive communication, all in the context of the employment-search process and in

---

[367] Authored by Neil W. Hamilton and Christopher Damian.
[368] Frederick Douglas quoted in KEVIN HOGAN, THE PSYCHOLOGY OF PERSUASION: HOW TO PERSUADE OTHERS TO YOUR WAY OF THINKING 22 (1996).

the interview process in particular. As you read through the following pieces of advice, consider how they are interrelated and mutually reinforcing.

1. Prepare to Question

It does not happen often, but it does happen. The experience is awkward for the students, frustrating for the professor, and embarrassing for the person who does it. This thing, which every law student should seek to avoid, is asking a question in class that demonstrates you did not do the readings. For example, if your readings for a particular class included the rule of perpetuities, when your professor mentions the rule in class, you should not ask what the rule is.

Completing the reading assignment for a class not only prepares you to answer questions, but it also prepares you to *ask* questions. A good question will demonstrate both your preparation and your curiosity. For example, if you raise your hand in class and state that you did not understand how the rule of perpetuities applies to a problem presented earlier in the book, you not only show that you understand the basics of the rule, but you also show that you have completed the reading and that you read thoroughly enough to engage with the material.

In the same way, the interview process should never reveal a lack of preparation. As Robert Miller puts it, "In this game, the only dumb question [in an interview] is one that is readily answered by a law firm's publicity materials."[369] Asking a question that can be answered by a quick Google search shows the interviewer either that you are not prepared or that you are unable to prepare well. Knowing about the potential employer in detail, however, shows that you are capable of preparing for a client meeting or interview. This preparation also evidences a variety of differentiating competencies to a potential employer, including initiative, project management, and dedication to the client, among others.

The "readings" for an interview are the potential employer's publicity materials, including information sent to law schools and students, as well as the employer's website and social media pages. Seeking out more detailed information[370] can help you understand how you can fit into your potential employer's

---

[369] Robert H. Miller, Law School Confidential: A Complete Guide to the Law School Experience: By Students, for Students 267 (3d ed. 2011).

[370] Robert Miller includes the following among the information you should know: "how many lawyers the firm has, in what cities it currently has offices, what its practice areas are, and what its specialty areas of practice are. I would find out who the firm's largest clients are. If the firm is large, I would know where the firm ranked in the city and in the country in the annual poll of associates' satisfaction, and where the firm is ranked in the annual poll of summer associates. I'd find out the latest information about starting salary, bonus structure, vacation time, partner track, and billable-hour requirements, and how those numbers compared to the numbers of comparable firms in the same city. I'd also want to know whether the firm has a multi-tiered partner track. Finally, I would go to the placement office a day or two before the interview, get the name of the lawyer conducting my interview, then find out a few things about her from Martindale-Hubbell. Determine where she went to college and law school, how long she has been with the firm, what areas of practice she is involved in, and what a couple of her interests are." *Id.* at 267.

office and how you can add unique value to the employer's work. Search online for profiles and reviews of the employer and lawyers currently in the firm or office. Ask your career services office to connect you with anyone currently in the firm or office, especially an alum, and ask that person about his or her work, the office culture, changes to the firm or office in recent years, and what the expectations are for new lawyers. If you can meet that lawyer at his or her office, take a look around at what the other lawyers are wearing, and make use of this information as you are preparing for your interview.

Once you have done your research, you can use this information to form nuanced questions for your interviewer, demonstrating your sincere interest in the potential employer and your serious preparation for the interview. Rather than asking about where the employer does most of his or her business, you can ask, "Given that much of your business comes from practice area X, do your attorneys attend the industry conferences and meetings? I would love to really get to know the businesspeople." You have demonstrated preparation skills and dedication to the client.

As in a networking meeting,[371] in a job interview, you will want to prepare questions specific to the employer. In a job interview, you will most likely be asked if you have any questions. This will probably happen at the end of the interview, so a few thoughtful questions that demonstrate thorough preparation and a sincere interest in the employer can be a strong finish. For example, ask if the employer has a mentoring program to help you develop your client-relationship skills.

2. Practice Active Listening Skills

In a study of what clients want, Shultz and Zedeck found "listening" to be among the most effective factors. This competency relates to other differentiating competencies, including responsiveness to the client.[372] In the context of client meetings, active listening is essential.

Nonverbal behaviors are a fundamental part of active listening. Practical advice for using nonverbal behaviors in active listening includes the following:

> For example, facing a speaker squarely and maintaining eye contact are behaviors that can communicate the listener's attention and understanding. Nods, facial expressions, and posture can further demonstrate understanding and presence in the conversation. A listener should avoid excessive note taking . . .The nonverbal communication of the speaker also gives the listener important information about the emotions the speaker conveys by body language, eye contact, facial expression, and tone of voice.[373]

Bridget Logstrom Koci, partner at Dorsey & Whitney, suggests a simple exercise to practice active listening skills. She suggests sitting in front of a mirror

---

[371] *See* "Building Relationships Based on Trust through Networking" in section III.

[372] *See* "Changing Markets for Legal Services" in section I.

[373] Hamilton, *supra* note 182, at 158.

while a friend asks you typical interview questions. Answer these questions while looking at the mirror, taking note of such things as eye contact and posture. Also use this exercise to practice giving your thirty-to sixty-second value proposition.[374]

3. Demonstrate Good Listening through Good Listening (Not Just Good Answering)

A very important part of listening is seeking clarification when you do not understand what the other is saying or asking. In particular, if you do not understand the context or reason for the question, you should ask for the other for clarification. At the very least, when asked a complex or ambiguous question, restate the question in your own words to verify whether you understand what the questioner is seeking. In the client–attorney context, it is very important to identify "a client's vaguely or inarticulately stated observations and feelings and . . . [reflect] them back to the client to show understanding or to allow the client to correct a misunderstanding."[375]

"However, active, engaged listening should be distinguished from excessively critiquing the speaker."[376] Don't be too busy forming your next response to the client.[377] Listen carefully and respond slowly. The client wants to know that you are listening to understand, not just listening to respond.

In the same way, an interviewer should not feel that you are only using interview questions as a means to state, over and over again, how impressive you are. Patrick Sinclair, who was hired for the U.S. Attorney's Office in Boston after his 1L year, for the firm Will & Emery after his 2L year, and then again for Will & Emery after graduation, advises:[378]

> I like to chat with people [in an interview] and that was all it was. My suggestion is to let the interviewer talk. As you meet more lawyers, you will find one common trait—they like to talk about themselves. If you let them do that during an interview, they will remember liking the experience and, derivatively, liking you. Trust me, it works.[379]

Likewise, Allan Kassenoff was hired after his 1L year for the New Jersey Attorney General's Office and then offered a full-time position at Kaye, Scholer, Fierman, Hays & Handler after working as a summer associate there after his 2L year.[380] He stresses simply being enjoyable in an interview: "Try to come off

---

[374] *See* the "Overview of the Preliminary Assessments and the Roadmap Template" in section II.

[375] Hamilton, *supra* note 182, at 156.

[376] *Id.*

[377] *Id.*

[378] Miller, *supra* note 369, at 18.

[379] *Id.* at 270–71.

[380] *Id.* at 12.

as a person that the interviewer could tolerate spending seventy-two hours in a row with."[381] Good listening can be even more important than good answering.

Indeed, good listening is essential for good answering. By being a good listener, you will better understand how best to communicate your answers. You will know how to use your tone, posture, and attentiveness to answer well. By demonstrating these skills, you will demonstrate your ability to be a good co-worker and your ability to be attentive to your clients.

4. Listen for the Gap, and Then Respond to Add Value

There is a gap between what your prospective employer has and what your prospective employer wants to have—that is where you need to be. Everyone who gets an interview has fulfilled the threshold requirements for filling that gap: appropriate grades, necessary experiences, and helpful credentials. You do not want to just say that you can add value to the organization. If employers are investing the time in investigating you, they already think that. You want to show them something more.

One way to do this is to observe a gap your employer could respond to in the market. A dean at a recent conference told a story that makes this point. A 3L student really wanted employment at the largest firm in the region but did not have the minimum class rank that the firm was using to screen candidates for its summer program. The student had a strong record of achievement in Division 1 athletics and wanted to propose a business plan to the firm that the student could build a new practice area in sports law. The dean counseled that the odds were very low that this idea would work, but the student went forward with a strong business plan, and the firm's recruitment committee thought the student's effort showed such unusual initiative and drive and understanding of business development that the firm hired the student as an associate.

Assume a student ranks low in the class, but her résumé and cover letter emphasize her volunteer and paid experience at the work the potential employer does, plus she has attached two reference letters to the résumé that make glowing comments about the student's competencies to get the work done with very high quality on time. This student will get substantial interest from employers, and the student will get interviews. Even better, if one of the references makes a phone call and says, "This student is a ball of fire, and you can totally count on her," the employers are going to be even more interested.[382]

Your proposition will need to be tailored according to your prospective employer's individual needs and according to what you have to offer. Thus, the better understanding you have of your employer's business practices, geographic region, office culture, and clientele, the more you can understand the specific ways in which you can add value to the employer.

---

[381] *Id.* at 269.

[382] WALTON, *supra* note 312, at 3.

Not every job applicant will have a new business proposition for a potential employer like the student discussed previously. However, your strong value proposition is a unique plan that will set you apart from your peers. A good value proposition will exist in "the gap" and will create a new one, by demonstrating knowledge of the employer's needs and by showing how you can *uniquely* fulfill those needs. Such a proposition will demonstrate both your ability to think outside of the typical confines of the application process and a developed understanding of yourself and of the prospective employer. You will not just be a particularly special or appropriate applicant; you will be a *different kind* of applicant. You might present a prospective employer with something it did not even know it wanted.

The ability to create and implement such a proposition will be especially necessary in the new legal economy, where competencies not traditionally associated with lawyering will be needed.[383] As the legal economy continues to change with the broader economy, employers will need lawyers who can understand the challenges of the new legal economy and who have an entrepreneurial mindset (as explored in section I), adapt to new situations, and create new plans for changing client needs. Creativity will be especially important in this economy,[384] and your ability to create a unique proposition for a prospective employer will demonstrate your creativity.

This practice, however, should not just be an interview practice. A successful lawyer will constantly seek to add value to his or her clients. You will want to establish a distinctive legal practice that demonstrates a strong commitment to the success of the client and will increase client loyalty. Indeed, this is a good practice for all of your relationships. As you demonstrate a unique value and commitment to all of your relationships, you can build and solidify your legal practice through long-term relationships and varied sources of referrals. You can persuade others of your value by demonstrating your commitment to them.

5. The Importance of a Clear Value Proposition to Create a Lasting Impression

When an interviewer sees a number of potential hires in a day of interviewing, the individual candidates may get lost in a pile of credentials. Likewise, in the litigation context, juries can get lost in the piles of legal jargon and factual issues. To remedy this, attorney Dan Shulman recommends something similar to a value proposition: "As an experienced litigator with juries, I know that I have

---

[383] *See* "Foundational Realities for Every Law Student to Understand" and "Help Wanted: Legal Employers Seek New Lawyers with Professional Competencies" in section I.

[384] *See* "Foundational Realities for Every Law Student to Understand" and "Help Wanted: Legal Employers Seek New Lawyers with Professional Competencies" in section I.

to be able to state my case in one or two straightforward sentences the jury can understand and remember." This is true also in screening interviews.

Bridget Logstrom Koci, the Dorsey & Whitney partner, agrees that this is important, adding that, in an interview, "two main points about your value proposition are an appropriate goal." These are the two strongest competencies you stated in your Roadmap template.

Even when you lack the requisite grades or credentials for a position, you can still demonstrate your value to a potential employer in other ways. When Carolyn Koegler Miller was interviewing for the firm Sulloway & Hollis,[385] the interviewer asked her, "Well, I can see from your grades that you're no legal eagle, so why should I hire you?" Although the question made Carolyn mad, she remembers sort of laughing and telling the interviewer that

> While I got off to a somewhat average start in law school, my grades were steadily improving, and I was confident that they would continue to improve. I also drew his attention to my writing sample as an indication that I write well, and to my résumé as an indication that when I commit to something, I get the job done, and done well.

Reflecting on the experience, she writes, "I don't think the interviewer really cared about my grades that much. I think he was testing me to see how I would react to his question because he offered me a callback, and the firm made me an offer."[386]

Although Carolyn's grades could not compete with those of other job candidates, she set herself apart by fielding a tough question and highlighting her trustworthiness and project management skills. When Avis car rentals was ranked "second best" for client services, advertising experts created one of the most successful campaigns in advertising history. Their slogan was, "We're number two, so we try harder."[387] This brief value proposition leaves a lasting impression and suggests that, in reality, their client services may surpass the services of the number-one-ranking company. Likewise, your value proposition can set you apart from other candidates by leaving a lasting impression about your unique value as an employee.

Make sure that the interviewer knows of your unique value. For example, remember that when an interviewer starts an interview with a question like "Tell me about yourself," the question is actually "Tell me two things about yourself that will help us be successful." Here is your chance to talk about your two strongest competencies that will help this employer be more successful. Just before you leave, consider simply stating, "Before I go, I just wanted to highlight

---

[385] MILLER, *supra* note 369, at 15.

[386] *Id.* at 272.

[387] PAUL LISNEK, THE ART OF LAWYERING: ESSENTIAL KNOWLEDGE FOR BECOMING A GREAT ATTORNEY 38–39 (1st ed. 2010).

(or highlight one more time) two things about myself . . . " Make it something that will stick with the employer, show your dedication to others, and make the interviewer want to be your coworker.[388]

6. A Unified Process

The creation of a value proposition, whether for a potential employer, a supervisor, or a client, should be an ongoing process. As you come to better understand those you are serving, through experienced listening, you will continue to tailor your value proposition according to their needs. As you present your value proposition, take note of their responses, and adjust your proposition accordingly. Thus, the persuasive value of your proposition will depend upon your ability to continue to listen, even after you have convinced others of your value.

Keep in mind that listening and persuasive communication are part of a unified process and that they mutually reinforce each other. Persuasive communication requires that you listen to the other and become more aware of the ways in which *that specific person* can be persuaded that you can help him or her be more successful. At the same time, the ability to listen depends on your ability to persuade the other that you are trustworthy and that he or she can and ought to be open and frank with you. The ability to listen depends on the ability to persuade, and the ability to persuade depends on the ability to listen.

Continue to develop these skills in your time at law school. Seek opportunities and experiences to practice and evidence these competencies. As you continue developing your Roadmap, seek to better understand your potential employers and tailor your value proposition accordingly. Find the gap, and make it known that you can fill it. Make sure your résumé, cover letter, interview strategy, and references are all "on message" in terms of the specific strongest competencies you have that will make an employer more successful.

Now that you have read "Listen to Persuade: How Attentiveness Leads to Value," complete the Reflection Dashboard at **http://ambar.org/roadmap** to develop a better understanding of what developmental stage you are at and what steps you will take to grow to the next stage.

---

[388] Daniel Pink suggests answering three questions in forming a "pitch": "1. What do you want them to *know*? 2. What do you want them to *feel*? 3. What do you want them to *do*?" Daniel H. Pink, To Sell Is Human: The Surprising Truth about Moving Others 179 (1st ed. 2012). Your last words to interviewers should inform them of your unique value, make them like you and want you as a coworker, and encourage them to hire you.

AVAILABLE RESOURCES TO NAVIGATE YOUR ROADMAP

A. Introduction[1]

It is true that taking proactive ownership of your professional development at the beginning of your professional career falls on your shoulders, but during your time in law school, you have many resources at your disposal. The Roadmap process encourages you to seek feedback and input from mentors and coaches on your initial drafts of the Roadmap template and your written networking plan and at each transition point throughout law school.

"Ideas on How to Make Effective Use of the 2L and 3L Curriculum," "Creating Portfolios for Two or Three of Your Strongest Competencies," and "Building Long-Term Relationships Based on Trust through Networking" encouraged you to be very strategic about developing relationships with experienced lawyers, judges, and professors who have good evidence of your strongest competencies. They can also give you feedback on your Roadmap plan.

B. Visit Your School's Office Dedicated to Career and Professional Development

Connecting the dots among your newly created Roadmap plan, your networking plan, and the rest of your law school's available resources is vital. Once you have completed your plan, it is very important to sit down with a representative from your school's office for career and professional development to discuss your plans

---

[1] Authored by Neil W. Hamilton, Shana Tomenes, and Carl J. L. Numrich.

and get his or her feedback on the plans. Representatives also can help you so that your persuasive communication package, which includes your résumé, your cover letter, your interview strategy, and your references, is effective with your target audience of potential employers. For example, they can help you with mock interviews. You should visit your school's office for career and professional development each semester and develop a strong relationship with its representatives.

C. How to Navigate Resources for Researching Potential Employers[2]

1. Introduction

a. Research by Type of Employer

Students who want to research potential employers by type of legal employer (e.g., large firm, small firm, county attorney, etc.) can begin researching their most promising employment options by accessing the University of St. Thomas School of Law research guide on career and professional development resources available at http://libguides.stthomas.edu/law_student_career_resources.

In addition, the other resources listed in sections IV.C.2 and IV.C.3 are intended to give students more resources to start conducting research into their most promising employment areas to further discern whether a practice area is compatible with their competencies. The resources listed here are not exhaustive but intended to assist the student in getting the ball rolling.

b. Research by Practice Area

Students who want to research their most promising employment options by practice area should start by going to the University of St. Thomas School of Law page at http://libguides.stthomas.edu/law_student_career_resources. The site provides both general information and resources on a variety of common legal practice areas, as well as resources on alternative career options and resources related to opening your own solo practice.

c. Employment and Volunteer Opportunities while in Law School

Students can then use the resources listed in parts 2 and 3, which follow, to begin seeking out employment and volunteer opportunities to gain experience at their most promising employment choices to further test whether their options are the best fit for them. Additionally, students should use their networking plans[3] to start building long-term relationships with these employers and conduct informational interviews with attorneys to further refine their most promising employment options. Note that students do not need to

---

[2] Authored by Neil W. Hamilton, Shana Tomenes, and Robert Maloney.

[3] For more information on networking plans, *see* section III's "Building Relationships Based on Trust through Networking."

find an explicit job posting. Students should also seek out an area of employment that interests them and make a connection with that employer—unpaid positions are not always posted or advertised. Students should make themselves available to gain experience by taking initiative and offering to help employers in creative ways.

2. Finding Out More Information about Your Most Promising Employment Options

Large-firm Research	• Martindale-Hubbell Law Firm Practice (http://www.martindale.com/law-firms.htm) • Yale Law School Guide: Law Firm Practice (http://www.law.yale.edu/studentlife/cdoguides.htm) • NALP Directory of Legal Employers (https://www.nalpdirectory.com/) • Why Should I Become an Associate at a Large Law Firm? And if I Do, Then What Should I Expect and How Do I Survive (http://papers.ssrn.com/sol3/papers.cfm?abstract_id=2338275) • Making Partner: It Takes More Than Hard Work and Talent (http://www.americanbar.org/content/newsletter/publications/law_practice_today_home/lpt-archives/may13/making-partner-it-takes-more-than-hard-work-and-talent.html)
Solo or small-firm research	• Yale Law School Guide: Law Firm Practice (http://www.law.yale.edu/studentlife/cdoguides.htm) • ABA Solo or Small Firm Resource Center (http://www.americanbar.org/portals/solo_home.html)
County attorney and public defense research	• Yale Law School Guide: Criminal Prosecution (http://www.law.yale.edu/studentlife/cdoguides.htm) • Yale Law School Guide: Public Defender (http://www.law.yale.edu/studentlife/cdoguides.htm) • From PSJD: Criminal Law: PSJD Guide (http://www.psjd.org/Criminal_Law)
Attorney general research	• Yale Law School Guide: Public Interest Careers (http://www.law.yale.edu/studentlife/cdoguides.htm)
Alternative legal employment options research	• Lawyers in Business: Yale Law School Guide (http://www.law.yale.edu/studentlife/cdoguides.htm) • Jonathan C. Lipson, Beth Engel, Jami Crespo, *Foreword: Who's in the House? The Changing Nature and Role of In-House and General Counsel*, 2012 Wis. L. Rev. 237 (2012). (http://papers.ssrn.com/sol3/papers.cfm?abstract_id=2077854)

(continues)

General (all careers) research	• NALP Career Resources for Law Students/Graduates (http://www.nalp.org/lawstudentsgraduates) • ABA Career Resources (http://www.americanbar.org/careercenter/career_resources.html) • From Georgetown Law Library: Job Searching Research Guide (http://www.law.georgetown.edu/library/research/guides/job_searching.cfm) • From University of San Diego School of Law: Career Resources (http://www.sandiego.edu/law/careers/students/job-search-prep/career-resources.php)

3. Gaining Experience in Your Most Promising Employment Options while You Are in Law School

General (all careers) experience	**ABA: Sponsored Offerings** (http://www.americanbar.org/groups/law_students/resources/intern.html#sponifc) **Law Jobs** (http://www.lawjobs.com) • Job search by location, practice area, and category **BCG Attorney Search** (http://www.bcgsearch.com) • Job search by location, primary area of practice, and firm type **HG Legal Resources** (http://www.hg.org/employment.html) • Job search by position, state, and city **Association of Corporate Counsel** (http://jobline.acc.com/jobs) • Job search by keyword and location **Legal Career Network (http://www.legalstaff.com)** • Job search by location and keyword **Robert Half (http://www.roberthalf.com)** • Job search by keyword and location **Additional Resources:** • http://www.indeed.com • http://www.glassdoor.com • http://www.simplyhired.com • http://www.quintcareers.com
Social justice experience	**Advocates for Human Rights: International Justice Project** • Research international law, including human rights and humanitarian law, international criminal law, international standards and best practices, etc. • Apply at http://www.theadvocatesforhumanrights.org/International_Justice_Internships **Advocates for Human Rights: Human Rights in the U.S. Internship** • Conduct research on issues related to human rights issues in the United States, including immigrant rights, economic and cultural rights, women's rights, human rights education, and others

	• Assist with developing educational and advocacy materials on U.S. human rights issues • Apply at http://www.theadvocatesforhumanrights.org/human_rights_education_program_internships.html **Advocates for Human Rights: Refugee and Immigrant Program Internships** • Answering client phone hotline, providing referrals, conducting phone intakes for potential asylum clients, and communicating with current clients • Writing case summaries • Legal and human rights conditions research • Apply at http://www.theadvocatesforhumanrights.org/refugee_immigrant_program_internships.html **Advocates for Human Rights: Woman's Human Rights Program Internship** • Research international human rights instruments and country laws on violence against women • Apply at http://www.theadvocatesforhumanrights.org/Women_s_Human_Rights_Program_Internships **ACLU Legal Internship (https://www.aclu.org/careers)**
Local and state government experience	**PSJD: State and Local Government Career Resources** • http://www.psjd.org/State_&_Local_Government_Career_Resources • https://www.psjd.org/State_&_Local_Government_Career_Resources_-_State-by-State_List
Federal government experience	**PSJD: Careers in Federal Government** (http://www.psjd.org/Careers_in_Federal_Government) **America Jobs (http://www.americajobs.com)** • Search federal jobs by profession and location **U.S. Department of Justice: Volunteer Legal Internships** (http://www.justice.gov/legal-careers/volunteer-legal-internships) • Every year over 1,800 volunteer legal interns serve in Department of Justice components and U.S. Attorneys' Offices throughout the country. Approximately eight hundred legal interns volunteer during the academic year, and roughly one 3thousand volunteer during the summer. **U.S. Department of Justice: Summer Law Intern Program** (http://www.justice.gov/legal-careers/summer-law-intern-program) **U.S. Department of Justice: Attorney General's Honors Program (Entry-Level Post-Graduate Positions)** (https://www.justice.gov/legal-careers/entry-level-attorneys) USA Jobs (https://www.usajobs.gov/StudentsAndGrads) • Internships and recent graduate jobs

(continues)

Nonprofit experience	**Center for Constitutional Rights (CCR): Jobs and Internships** (http://ccrjustice.org/home/get-involved/jobs) • CCR is a nonprofit legal and educational organization committed to the creative use of law as a positive force for social change • Designed for first- or second-year law students who will assist CCR attorneys with their caseloads while taking part in educational seminars **Homeline: Tenant Advocacy Internships** (https://homelinemn.org/i-want-to-volunteer/volunteer-as-a-student-enrolled-in-lawparalegal-program/) • Extensive training on Minnesota tenant–landlord law from expert attorneys • Training for taking calls to provide legal advice to tenants • Meet with policy makers **Immigrant Law Center of Minnesota: Volunteer Opportunities** (https://www.ilcm.org/get-involved/volunteer/) **National Legal Aid & Defender Association: Job Opportunities** (http://www.nlada.org/Jobs) **Volunteer Match: General Legal Volunteer Opportunities** (http://www.volunteermatch.org) **ACLU of Minnesota: Volunteer Opportunities** (https://www.aclu.org/affiliate/minnesota)

APPENDIX A

OTHER EMPIRICAL EVIDENCE ON THE COMPETENCIES IMPORTANT IN THE HIRING DECISION[1]

There are several recent studies of either the competencies legal employers expect new lawyers to have or the competencies new lawyers report are most significant in their work.[2] The competencies emphasized in these studies are similar to those in table 4 in section I, and the convergence of these data sets tends to affirm the validity of findings within table 4.[3] However, we need more research to test these findings.

For example, one recent study by Susan Wawrose—a law professor at the University of Dayton School of Law—focused on what employers expect of

---

[1] This chapter borrows from Neil W. Hamilton, *Changing Markets Create Opportunities: Emphasizing the Competencies Legal Employers Use in Hiring New Lawyers (Including Professional Formation/Professionalism)*, 65 S.C. L. Rev. 547, 565–72 (2014). *See also* Neil W. Hamilton, *Empirical Research on the Core Competencies Needed to Practice Law: What Do Clients, New Lawyers, and Legal Employers Tell Us?* 83 Bar Examiner (No. 3, 2014), at 6.

[2] *See generally* Steven S. Nettles & James Hellrung, A Study of the Newly Licensed Lawyer 1 (2012) ("The study involved developing lists of job-related tasks, knowledge domains, skills, and abilities."); Susan C. Wawrose, *What Do Legal Employers Want to See in New Graduates? Using Focus Groups to Find Out*, 39 Ohio N.U. L. Rev. 505 (2013) (describing the findings of focus group studies examining what legal employers expect of recent graduates).

[3] *Compare* Wawrose, *supra* note 2, at 522 (listing the skills employers value in attorneys), *and* Nettles & Hellrung, *supra* note 2, at 285 (listing various competencies, including "Tasks, Knowledge Domains, and Skills/Abilities in Survey Order"), *with* table 6 (listing the competencies considered when hiring a new lawyer).

a new attorney.[4] The study used focus groups—with nineteen Dayton, Ohio, attorneys from a variety of practice backgrounds—and explored the questions of "[h]ow . . . [these employers] describe the ideal recent law school graduate" and "[w]hat . . . [these employers] expect a recent law graduate to be able to do."[5] The comments of the legal employers fell into two main categories:

> First and predominant was an employer preference for attorneys who have well-developed professional . . . skills[,] such as strong work ethic, willingness to take initiative, the ability to collaborate well with colleagues and clients, and the ability to adapt to the demands of supervisors. Second, employers wanted new hires with strong fundamental practice skills, i.e., legal research, written and verbal communication, and analysis.[6]

Professor Wawrose stated that "[t]he most surprising outcome of [her] research was the primary importance employers placed on the intra- and interpersonal . . . [skills] needed for workplace success."[7]

In 2011 and 2012, the National Conference of Bar Examiners (NCBE) conducted a web-based survey—with 1,669 usable responses from 19,872 people surveyed—of new lawyers who were one to three years out of law school and practicing in a variety of practice settings and areas.[8] The survey asked what skills, abilities, and knowledge domains are significant to the newly licensed lawyer.[9] On a scale of 1, as "[m]inimally [s]ignificant," to 4, as "[e]xtremely [s]ignificant,"[10] the new lawyers rated twenty-five of the skills and abilities as having an average importance greater than the highest-rated knowledge domains—which were, from first to third, the rules of civil procedure, other court rules of procedure, and the rules of evidence.[11] Table 33 shows the average importance of the top-ranked skills and abilities for new lawyers.

The three highest-rated knowledge domains had an average significance of 3.08, 3.06, and 3.01, respectively.[12]

The NCBE New Lawyer Survey used somewhat different terms than the surveys in tables 1–6 (section I) and table 7, but table 34 synthesizes the NCBE skills and abilities with the table 4 (section I) competencies.[13]

---

[4] See Wawrose, *supra* note 2, at 507.

[5] *Id.* at 515, 518.

[6] *Id.* at 522 (footnotes omitted).

[7] *Id.*

[8] NETTLES & HELLRUNG, *supra* note 2, at 1, 9, 175.

[9] See *id.* at 1.

[10] *Id.* at 7.

[11] *Id.* at 282–85.

[12] *Id.* at 282–83.

[13] *Compare id.* at 285 (listing the NCBE competency terms), *with* tables 1–7 (establishing the author's competency terms) *and* table 34 (synthesizing the NCBE and the author's competency terms).

Table 33 National Conference of Bar Examiners Survey of New Lawyers on
the Most Significant Skills and Abilities

Skills and Abilities for New Lawyers	Average Significance
Written communication	3.77
Paying attention to details	3.67
Listening	3.60
Oral communication	3.58
Professionalism	3.58
Using office technologies (e.g., e-mail and word processing)	3.56
Critical reading and comprehension	3.55
Synthesizing facts and law	3.55
Legal reasoning	3.54
Knowing when to go back and ask questions	3.46
Organizational skills	3.46
Working within established time constraints	3.44
Interpersonal skills	3.44
Issue spotting	3.43
Decisiveness	3.31
Answering questions succinctly	3.30
Judgment	3.29
Computer skills	3.28
Electronic researching	3.26
Diligence	3.26
Advocacy	3.24
Fact-gathering/evaluation	3.22
Consciousness of personal and professional limitations	3.15
Information integrating	3.10
Working collaboratively	2.98

The NCBE New Lawyer Survey emphasizes six of the top eight competencies
from table 6, with the exception of "initiative/ambition/drive/strong work ethic"
and "commitment to the firm/department/office."[14] Note that the NCBE Survey

---

[14] *See* Nettles & Hellrung, *supra* note 2, at 285.

Table 34 Synthesizing the NCBE New-Lawyer Skills and Abilities with the
Table 4 Competencies

---

1. Effective written/oral communication skills (including the NCBE skills and abilities of written communication, listening, oral communication, using office technologies in things like e-mail, answering questions succinctly, and advocacy)

2. Project management: high quality, efficiency, and timeliness (including the NCBE skills and abilities of paying attention to details, using office technologies, knowing when to go back and ask questions, organizational skills, working within established time constraints, and diligence)

3. Integrity/honesty/trustworthiness (including professionalism)

4. Analytical skills: identifying legal issues from facts, applying the law, and drawing conclusions (including critical reading and comprehension, synthesizing facts and law, legal reasoning, issue spotting, and information integrating)

5. Client and team relationship skills (including interpersonal skills, diligence, and working collaboratively)

6. Good judgment/common sense/problem solving (including judgment and decisiveness)

7. Research skills (including computer skills, electronic researching, and fact gathering/evaluation)

8. Seeks feedback/responsive to feedback (including consciousness of personal and professional limitations)

---

ranks project management skills and abilities highly at second (whereas project management is ninth in table 6), and it ranks research skills at seventh (whereas research skills are fourteenth in table 6).[15] As with the data set forth in tables 1–6, the NCBE New Lawyer Survey also rates a substantial number of competencies as more valuable for the new lawyer or candidate for employment than doctrinal law knowledge domains;[16] however, the typical required and elective curriculum at law schools heavily emphasizes doctrinal knowledge in specialized areas of law.[17]

In 2012, the Federation of Law Societies of Canada also conducted a survey of new lawyers recently admitted to practice from 2007 to 2012 to rate both the frequency with which each lawyer performed or used a competency and

---

[15] *Id.*

[16] *See Id.*; *supra* tables 1–6. Of the eighty-six knowledge domains, only three had an average significance score above 3.0. *Id.* at 282–84. Additionally, twenty-five out of the thirty-six skills and abilities included in the survey had average significance scores above 3.0. *Id.* at 285.

[17] *See, e.g.*, Roy Stuckey et al., Best Practices for Legal Education: A Vision and a Road Map 30 (2007), *available at* http://www.cleaweb.org/Resources/Documents/best_practices-full. pdf. ("[W]e mostly teach basic principles of substantive law and a much too limited range of analytical skills and other competencies, such as legal research and writing.").

the lawyer's perception of the severity of the consequences if the lawyer did not possess each competency; the surveyors obtained 1,187 completed responses out of 6,911 people surveyed.[18] This survey reported those competencies with the highest ratings as a group but did not rank them (table 35).[19]

Table 35 Canadian Survey of New Lawyers' Most Important Competencies[20]

Ethics and professional skills
Oral and written communication skills (including eliciting information from clients, obtaining instructions, and negotiating)
Analytical skills (including analyzing possible course of action and the range of possible outcomes and the appropriateness of alternatives)
Research skills (factual and legal)
Client-relationship skills
Practice management skills (including project management skills)

The Federation of Law Societies of Canada study included in *analytical skills* many of the elements of the good judgment/common sense/problem-solving competency.[21] The study's category of *ethics and professionalism* included honesty/integrity/trustworthiness.[22] The Canadian study thus emphasizes five of the top six competencies in table 6, except initiative/ambition/drive/strong work ethic.[23] The study also emphasized practice management skills as one of the most important competencies.[24] Practice management skills overlap with project management, a competency ranked ninth in table 6.[25]

A 2007 study by clinicians at U.S. law schools regarding the competencies needed for effective practice reported similar results, with reasonably close agreement on nine of the ten competencies in table 6.[26] A top-ten competency in table 6 that the clinicians did not include was commitment to the firm/department/office, its goals, and its values.[27]

---

[18] FED'N OF LAW SOC'YS OF CAN., NATIONAL ADMISSIONS STANDARDS PROJECT: NATIONAL ENTRY TO PRACTICE COMPETENCY PROFILE VALIDATION REPORT 1–2 (Sept. 2012).

[19] *Id.* at 4.

[20] *Id.* at 9–11.

[21] *See id.* at 10.

[22] *See* FED'N OF LAW SOC'YS OF CAN., *supra* note 18, at 9; *supra* table 6.

[23] *See* FED'N OF LAW SOC'YS OF CAN., *supra* note 18, at 9–11; *supra* table 6.

[24] *See* FED'N OF LAW SOC'YS OF CAN., *supra* note 18, at 11.

[25] *See id.*; *supra* table 5.

[26] *See* STUCKEY ET AL., *supra* note 17, at 39–40 (citation omitted).

[27] *See id.*; *supra* table 5.

A 2013 Harvard Law School Survey of 124 attorneys at large law firms first asked which business method courses students should take and then asked which knowledge bases and skills—from a list provided to the attorneys—were most important for associates (table 36).[28] According to the study, 83 percent of respondents—including a high percentage of litigators—advised students to take "Accounting and Financial Reporting," and 68 percent advised taking "Corporate Finance."[29] This would fit with the competencies of both good judgment/common sense/problem solving and effective written/oral communication skills—by promoting understanding of the business context of a client's problem—and dedication to client service/responsiveness to clients by promoting understanding of the client's context.[30] Respondents also rated the importance of a list of seven knowledge bases and skills for associates—with 1 being "not at all useful" and 5 being "extremely useful."[31]

Table 36 2013 Harvard Law School Survey of Lawyers at Large Firms on the Best Business Method Courses for Law Students to Take[32]

Business Method Courses	Score
Accounting and financial statement analysis	4.30
Teamwork	4.28
Financial market/products	4.00
Negotiations	3.85
Business strategy/industry analysis	3.68

Again, the knowledge bases that are most important on this list connect to the same competencies listed in the tables.[33] Teamwork is rated an important competency here, as it is in table 6.[34]

Finally, while surprisingly few of the empirical studies analyze the competencies that clients want, Marjorie Shultz and Sheldon Zedeck—in a rigorous survey published in 2011—identified and defined measurable dimensions of "lawyer effectiveness" by asking more than two thousand alumni of the University of California, Berkeley, School of Law who were practicing lawyers the following questions: "If you were looking for a lawyer for an important matter

---

[28] John Coates et al., *What Courses Should Law Students Take? Harvard's Largest Employers Weigh In* 1–2 (Harvard Law Sch. Program on the Legal Profession, Paper No. 2014–12), *available at* http://papers.ssrn.com/sol3/papers.cfm?abstract_id=2397317.

[29] *Id.* at 3.

[30] See *supra* table 6.

[31] Coates et al., *supra* note 28, at 2, 6.

[32] *Id.* at 10.

[33] See *supra* tables 6, 9.

[34] See *supra* tables 6.

for yourself, whom would you identify, and why? What qualities and behavior would cause you to choose that attorney?"[35] The Shultz and Zedeck survey did not rank which effectiveness factors were the most important, but nine of the top-ten competencies listed in table 6—except commitment to the firm/department/office—are included as important effectiveness factors in the Shultz and Zedeck data.[36] Of the next nine competencies (11–19) listed in table 6, the Schultz and Zedeck data include six as effectiveness factors—all except inspires confidence, seeks feedback/responsive to feedback, and leadership.[37]

---

[35] Marjorie M. Shultz & Sheldon Zedeck, *Predicting Lawyer Effectiveness: Broadening the Basis for Law School Admission Decisions*, 36 Law & Soc. Inquiry 620, 629–30 (2011). *See* Table 1.

[36] *See id.* at 630; *supra* table 6.

[37] *See* Schultz & Zedeck, *supra* note 35, at 630; *supra* table 6.

DATA ON THE IMPORTANCE OF SPECIFIC COMPETENCIES IN THE DECISION TO HIRE FOR FOUR TYPES OF LEGAL EMPLOYERS

There are some differences among the four types of legal employers on the importance of some of the competencies in the decision to hire. Students interested in a particular type of employment should take these differences into account in differentiating themselves.

1. The Competencies That Regional Legal Aid Offices Look at in the Hiring Decision

In the period of January to February 2014, a survey of the executive directors of each of the six regional legal aid offices in Minnesota asked each director to indicate the relative importance of the competencies listed in table 37 in the decision to hire a new lawyer—and to add competencies if the director thought one was missing. All six directors responded to the survey.

Table 37 The Relative Importance of Different Competencies in the Decision to Hire a New Lawyer for the Regional Legal Aid Offices in Minnesota[1]

Competencies Considered Very Important to Critically Important	
1.	Good judgment/common sense/problem solving	5
2.	Dedication to client service/responsiveness to client	4.8
3.	Analytical skills: identify legal issues from facts, apply the law, and draw conclusions	4.8
4.	Integrity/honesty/trustworthiness	4.8
5.	Effective written/oral communication skills	4.6
6.	Legal competency/expertise/knowledge	4.6
7.	Commitment to office, its goals, and its values	4.6
8.	Initiates and maintains strong work and team relationships	4.4
9.	Project management including high quality, efficiency, and timeliness	4.4
10.	Initiative/ambition/drive/strong work ethic	4.2
11.	Commitment to professional development toward excellence	4.17
12.	Pro bono/community/bar association involvement (especially for the disadvantaged)[2]	4
13.	Strategic/creative thinking	4
Competencies Considered Important to Very Important	
14.	Seeks feedback/responsive to feedback	3.8
15.	Research skills	3.6
16.	Stress/crisis management	3.6

(continues)

---

[1] Neil W. Hamilton, *Changing Markets Create Opportunities: Emphasizing the Competencies Legal Employers Use in Hiring New Lawyers (Including Professional Formation/Professionalism)*, SOUTH CAROLINA L. REV. 65 (2014), available at http://papers.ssrn.com/sol3/papers.cfm?abstract_id=2412324.

[2] One legal aid director also indicated that "[d]emonstrated commitment and/or experience in working with low-income communities either through volunteerism, paid experience, or clerking" was a factor considered when hiring and provided a rating of 4. Another legal aid director also indicated that "[e]xperience with low-income populations, diverse populations, and disadvantaged persons" was a factor considered when hiring and provided a rating of 4. A third director commented that deep respect for clients and coworkers, regardless of background, and the ability to explain complex concepts to others of different backgrounds clearly was a critically important factor considered in hiring.

Table 37 Continued

Competencies Considered Important to Very Important	
17. Inspires confidence	3.5
18. Ability to work independently	3.4
19. Negotiation skills	3.4
20. Leadership	3
Competencies Considered Somewhat Important to Important	
21. Delegation, supervision, mentoring	2.4
Competencies Slightly Important to Somewhat Important	
22. Candidate's class rank	1.8
Competencies Not Considered to Slightly Important	
23. Rank of candidate's law school	1

2. The Competencies That County Attorneys Offices Look at in the Hiring Decision

In the period of July to August 2013, I created both a list of the county attorneys in the seven Twin Cities metro counties and a list of the eighty remaining county attorneys. All seven metro Twin Cities county attorneys and a random sample of thirty nonmetro county attorneys were included in the survey. I asked each county attorney to indicate the relative importance of each competency listed in table 38 in the decision to hire a new lawyer—and to add competencies if the county attorney thought any were missing. Of the thirty-seven total county attorneys surveyed, eighteen county attorneys—including those from four of the seven metro counties—responded.

Table 38 The Relative Importance of Different Competencies in the Decision to Hire a New Lawyer for Eighteen County Attorneys in Minnesota[3]

Competencies Considered Very Important to Critically Important	
1. Integrity/honesty/trustworthiness	4.83
2. Good judgment/common sense/problem solving	4.56
3. Initiative/ambition/drive/strong work ethic	4.33
4. Initiates and maintains strong work and team relationships	4.33
5. Commitment to development, goals, and values	4.17

(continues)

---

[3] Hamilton, *supra* note 1.

Table 38 Continued

6.	Analytical skills: identify legal issues from facts, apply the law, and draw conclusions	4.00
7.	Ability to work independently	4.00

Competencies Considered Important to Very Important		
8.	Effective written/oral communication skills	3.83
9.	Legal competency/expertise/knowledge	3.72
10.	Stress/crisis management	3.67
11.	Seeks feedback/responsive to feedback	3.56
12.	Project management including high quality, efficiency, and timeliness	3.39
13.	Inspires confidence	3.33
14.	Strategic/creative thinking	3.33
15.	Leadership	3.33
16.	Research skills	3.28
17.	Dedication to client service/responsive to client on civil matters	3.28
18.	Commitment to professional development toward excellence	3.22
19.	Negotiation skills	3.00

Competencies Considered Somewhat Important to Important		
20.	Delegation, supervision, mentoring	2.06

Competencies Slightly Important to Somewhat Important		
21.	Pro bono, community, bar association involvement	1.94

Competencies Not Considered to Slightly Important		
22.	Candidate's class rank	0.89
23.	Rank of candidate's law school	0.67

3. The Competencies That Small Law Firms Look at in the Hiring Decision

In the period of May to July 2013, I created both a list of the 116 total law firms containing two to nine lawyers—including partners, associates, and of counsel lawyers—in the seven Twin Cities metro counties and a list of the 37 total firms of the same size in the rest of Minnesota. A random sample of 50 of the 116 metro law firms and all 37 of the other firms were included in the survey. I asked a partner at each firm to indicate the relative importance of each competency listed in table 39 in the decision to hire a new associate—and to add competencies if the partner thought one was missing. Of the 87 total firms surveyed, 23 firms responded to the survey.[4]

Table 39 The Relative Importance of Different Competencies in the Decision to Hire a New Associate for Twenty-Three Small Minnesota Firms from Two to Nine Lawyers[5]

Competencies Considered **Very Important to Critically Important**	
1. Good judgment/common sense/problem solving	4.61
2. Integrity/honesty/trustworthiness	4.5
3. Dedication to client service/responsiveness to client	4.3
4. Initiative/ambition/drive/strong worth ethic	4.3
5. Effective written/oral communication skills	4.1
6. Ability to work independently	4.1
7. Analytical skills: identify legal issues from facts, apply the law, and draw conclusions	4.0
8. Commitment to firm, its goals, and its values	4.0
9. Project management including high quality, efficiency, and timeliness	4.0
Competencies Considered **Important to Very Important**	
10. Initiates and maintains strong work and team relationships	3.8
1. Legal competency/expertise/knowledge	3.6 9
12. Seeks feedback/responsive to feedback	3.6
13. Commitment to professional development toward excellence	3.4
14. Business development/marketing/client retention	3.4 3
15. Research skills	3.3
16. Strategic/creative thinking	3.3
17. Inspires confidence	3.2 6

(continues)

---

[4] Note that because of an error, the survey form for the small-firm study did not include the candidate's class rank or the rank of the candidate's law school as factors in the hiring decision.

[5] Hamilton, *supra* note 1.

Table 39 Continued

18.	Stress/crisis management	3.0

Competencies Considered Somewhat Important to Important		
19.	Understanding the business of small-firm practice	2.8
20.	Negotiation skills	2.8
21.	Leadership	2.6
22.	Demonstrates interest in business and financial arrangements with clients	2.5
23.	Delegation, supervision, mentoring	2.3
24.	Pro bono, community, bar association involvement	2.1

4. The Competencies That Large Law Firms Look at in the Hiring Decision

In the period of January to March 2013, I asked the ethics partner or general counsel of each of the fourteen largest law firms in Minnesota to indicate the relative importance of the different competencies the firm uses in its evaluation of associates in the firm's decision to hire an associate.[6] The ethics partner or general counsel from all fourteen firms responded; table 40 sets forth the average responses of the fourteen firms on the relative importance of the different competencies for the decision to hire an associate. Note: I did not ask whether the firm used top 10 or top 20 percent in terms of class rank to screen résumés initially, but my understanding is that the large firms all use this type of initial screen. There will still be hundreds of résumés that make the initial screen, and a student's differentiating competencies will be determining factors then.

Table 40 The Relative Importance of Different Competencies in the Decision to Hire a New Associate for the Fourteen Largest Minnesota Law Firms[7]

Competencies Considered Very Important to Critically Important		
1.	Integrity/honesty/trustworthiness	4.8
2.	Effective written/oral communication skills	4.67
3.	Analytical skills: identify legal issues from facts, apply the law, and draw conclusions	4.6
4.	Initiative/ambition/drive/strong work ethic	4.53

(continues)

---

[6] The firms ranged in size from 67 to 740 total lawyers, including lawyers outside of Minnesota.

[7] Hamilton, *supra* note 1.

Table 40 Continued

5.	Good judgment/common sense/problem solving	4.53
6.	Dedication to client service/responsiveness to client	4.47
7.	Commitment to firm, its goals, and its values	4.27
8.	Inspires confidence	4.2
9.	Research skills	4.13
10.	Commitment to professional development toward excellence	4.07
11.	Initiates and maintains strong work and team relationships	4.07
Competencies Considered Important to Very Important		
12.	Project management, including high quality, efficiency, and timeliness	3.93
13.	Strategic/creative thinking	3.8
14.	Legal competency/expertise/knowledge	3.73
15.	Business development/marketing/client retention	3.67
16.	Ability to work independently	3.67
17.	Leadership	3.47
18.	Stress/crisis management	3.4
19.	Candidate's class rank	3.33
20.	Seeks feedback/responsive to feedback	3.13
21.	Negotiation skills	3.07
Competencies Considered Somewhat Important to Important		
22.	Rank of candidate's law school	2.93
23.	Understanding the business of large-firm practice	2.93
24.	Delegation, supervision, mentoring	2.73
25.	Demonstrates interest in business and financial arrangements with clients	2.73
26.	Pro bono, community, bar association involvement	2.53

DATA ON THE IMPORTANCE OF SPECIFIC COMPETENCIES IN THE ASSESSMENT AND HIRING OF NEW BUSINESS MANAGERS

In 1983, Kim S. Cameron and David A. Whetten proposed a variety of competencies necessary to be a successful manager as shown in Table 41.[1]

Mitchell Langbert—through two separate surveys, one in 1992 and one in 1998—discovered that human resource management places its highest value on interpersonal skills and strategic competencies; the results of Langbert's study show that "both groups see interpersonal and strategic competencies as more important than technical competencies."[2]

In 1998, a survey by Lanny Karns and Manuel Mena resulted in the following groups of primary competencies that translated across industries shown in Table 42:[3]

In 2001, A *Journal of Management* study sought to expand the results from the Karns–Mena study in table 42 by examining the extent to which the identified

---

[1] Cameron and Whetten's research included a study of over 400 managers at various hierarchical levels of public and private organizations. Each manager was asked to identify skills that they used regularly. *Id.* K. S. CAMERON AND D. A. WHETTEN, ORGANIZATIONAL EFFECTIVENESS (1982).
[2] *Id.* at 70.
[3] L. A. KARNS & M. A. MENA, SHARPENING THE PERFORMANCE MANAGEMENT FOCUS USING CORE COMPETENCIES: A PILOT STUDY (Academy of Business and Administrative Science, 1998).

Table 41 Characteristics of Effective Managers: Management Skill Topics

Skill	Characteristic
Self-awareness	Personality, values, needs, cognitive style
Managing personal stress	Time management, goals, activity balance
Creative problem solving	Divergent thinking, conceptual blocks, redefining problems
Establishing supportive communication	Listening, empathy, counseling
Improving employee performance/ motivating others	Needs/expectations, rewards, timing
Effective delegation and joint decision making	Assigning tasks, evaluating performance, autonomous versus joint decision making
Gaining power and influence	Sources of power, converting power to influence, beneficial use (not abuse) of power
Managing conflict	Sources of conflict, assertiveness and sensitivity, handling criticism
Improving group decision making	Leading meetings, avoiding pitfalls of bad meetings, making effective presentations

Table 42 Examples of Primary Competencies

Competency	Examples
Process orientation	Energy and initiative, responsibility, job skills, professionalism, relationship management, problem-solving abilities, analytical decision-making skills, quality of work
Communication	Interpersonal effectiveness, oral/written communication, information/communications management, oral/written expression, effectiveness of communication, interpersonal communications
Business acumen	Strategic thinking, business focus, work-flow enhancement, industry/business knowledge, organization interaction, job orientation, business "sense"
Results orientation	Results driven, problem analysis, accountability, professionalism, resource management, judgment, work habits, decision making, dependability, initiative

(continues)

Table 42 Continued

Technical/functional proficiency	Business technical expertise, professional/technical knowledge, job performance, job knowledge
Teamwork	Cross-organizational teamwork, team skills, team effectiveness, culture management
Managing/ developing others	Employee management and development, human resource development, management development and evaluation, administrative skills, supervisory skills

competencies were used by organizations nationwide.[4] This study also sought to develop a list of core competencies that organizations believed were most critical to managers' success.[5] These results are displayed in table 43.

Table 43 Managerial Competencies as Performance Appraisal Criteria

Competency	Assessment[6] (%)
Results oriented	78.3
Leadership skills	76.9
Problem solver	72.9
Customer focus	71.5
Communication skills	69.3
Quality focused	69.3
Interpersonal skills	64.3
Team worker	63.9
Technical expertise	63.5
Dependable	53.1
Business expertise	49.8
Safety conscious	49.8
Staff developer	47.7

(continues)

---

[4] Steve E. Abraham et al., *Managerial Competencies and the Managerial Performance Appraisal Process*, 20 J. MGMT. DEV. 842, 844 (2001) (the study was also conducted by the State University of New York at Oswego).

[5] *Id.*

[6] Percentage of respondents indicating that the competency was actually used in assessing a manager's performance.

Table 43 Continued

Flexible/adaptable	47.4
Hard worker	41.2
Time manager	34.7
Imaginative	21.7
Risk-taker	19.3
Purposeful	19.1
Professional dress	14.4
Uncompromising	5.1
Proficiency in foreign language	2.2
Previous foreign experience	1.9

More recently, Bloomberg surveyed 1,251 employers to determine what competencies employers of MBA graduates were seeking and what competencies of these they felt applicants were lacking.[7] The survey found the skills employers valued more and had the hardest time finding in applicants were strategic thinking, creative problem solving, leadership skills, and communication skills.[8]

Additionally, a 2017 study by the Graduate Management Admissions Council (GMAC) reviewed, among other things, which factors recruiters deemed critical when selecting candidates to interview.[9] The 759 employers interviewed[10] indicated the most critical competencies were a proven ability to perform, strong oral communication skills, and strong technical or quantitative skills.[11] Notably, 38 percent more employers indicated strong oral communication skills were critical than did strong academic success.[12] Table 44 shows the competencies the employers considered most critical when selecting candidates for an interview.

[7] Francesca Levy and Johnathan Rodkin, The Bloomberg Job Skills Report 2016: What Recruiters Want (Bloomberg Business 2016), *available at* https://www.bloomberg.com/graphics/2016-job-skills-report/

[8] *Id.*

[9] Graduate Management Admission Council, Corporate Recruiters survey: 2017 Survey report (Graduate Management Admission Council [GMAC] 2017), *available at* http://www.gmac.com/market-intelligence-and-research/research-library/employment-outlook/2017-corporate-recruiters-survey-report.aspx.

[10] *Id.* at 4.

[11] *Id.* at 26.

[12] *Id.*

Table 44 Critical Factors Considered by Employers in Determining Which (MBA) Candidates to Interview

Competency	% of Respondents[13]
Proven ability to perform	92
Strong oral communication skills	89
Strong technical and/or quantitative skills	84
History of increased job responsibility	62
Strong writing skills	56
Industry of prior work experience	52
Strong academic success	51
Occupation in prior work experience	50
Years of work experience	49
Relevant language skills	48
History of leading teams	46
Reputation of business school	43
Company of prior work experience	41
Internships	38
Professional or employee recommendation	33
Managing people in a formal reporting role	32
Previous leadership recognition/awards	32
Specialization/concentration	31
Managing people in an informal role	29
Global experience	26
Professional certifications/licenses	21
Positive social media presence	7
Verified training certifications from massive open online courses (MOOCs)	3

---

[13] "% of Respondents" refers to the percentage of respondents who indicated that the competency was a critical attribute of potential new hires. Respondents were given the opportunity to select multiple attributes.

In 2015, the Hart Research Associates for the Association of American Colleges and Universities interviewed four hundred employers[14] to determine which competencies and learning outcomes would increase college graduates' potential for success (the "Hart Study").[15] Overall, the study determined employers believed that colleges and universities should be placing more emphasis on specific learning outcomes to increase graduates' success.[16] The most critical competencies and learning outcomes identified by the interviewed employers were written and oral communication, critical thinking and analytical reasoning, application of knowledge and skills in real-world settings, complex problem solving and analysis, ethical decision making, teamwork skills, innovation and creativity, and knowledge of concepts and developments in science and technology.[17] Table 45 shows the percentage of employers identifying these competencies and learning outcomes as critical to graduates' success.[18]

Table 45 Employer-Identified Competencies and Learning Outcomes That Colleges Should Emphasize More

Learning Outcome	% of Respondents
The ability to effectively communicate orally	85
The ability to work effectively in teams	83
The ability to effectively communicate in writing	82
Critical thinking and analytical reasoning skills	81
Ethical judgment and decision making	81
The ability to apply knowledge and skills to real-world settings	80
The ability to analyze and solve complex problems	70
The ability to locate, organize, and evaluate information from multiple sources	68
The ability to innovate and be creative	65
Staying current on changing technologies and their applications to the workplace	60

(continues)

[14] Respondents were executives at private-sector and nonprofit organizations, including owners, chief executive officers, presidents, and vice presidents, at organizations with at least twenty-five employees and report that 25 percent or more of their new hires hold either an associate degree from a two-year college or a bachelor's degree from a four-year college.

[15] HART RESEARCH ASSOCS., FALLING SHORT? COLLEGE LEARNING AND CAREER SUCCESS 8 (Ass'n of Am. Colls. & Univs. Jan. 20, 2015), https://www.aacu.org/leap/public-opinion-research/2015-survey-results.

[16] *Id.*

[17] *Id.*

[18] *Id.*

Table 45 Continued

The ability to analyze and solve problems with people from different backgrounds and cultures	56
The ability to work with numbers and understand statistics	56
Awareness of and experience with diverse cultures and communities within the United States	37
Knowledge about the role of the United States in the world	35
Knowledge about democratic institutions and values	27
Staying current on developments in science	26
Staying current on global developments and trends	25
Proficiency in a language other than English	23
Awareness of and experience with cultures and societies outside of the United States	23

Another example is the 2015 National Association of Colleges and Employers (NACE) *Job Outlook* survey.[19] The NACE determined that employers consider the competencies in table 46 to be the most important when hiring new college graduates.[20]

Table 46 Attributes Employers Consider When Hiring New College Graduates (NACE 2015 Survey)

Attribute	% of Respondents
Ability to work on a team	77.8
Leadership	77.8
Communication skills (written)	73.4
Problem-solving skills	70.9
Strong work ethic	70.4
Analytical/quantitative skills	68.0
Technical skills	67.5
Communication skills (verbal)	67.0
Initiative	66.5
Computer skills	62.6

(continues)

---

[19] *See generally* JOB OUTLOOK: THE CANDIDATE SKILLS/QUALITIES EMPLOYERS WANT, THE INFLUENCE OF ATTRIBUTES (Nov. 12, 2014).
[18] *Id.*

Table 46 Continued

Flexibility/adaptability	62.1
Interpersonal skills (relates well to others)	60.6
Detail oriented	57.6
Organizational ability	42.4
Strategic planning	35.0
Friendly/outgoing personality	29.1
Entrepreneurial skill/risk-taker	25.1
Tactfulness	23.2

Supporting evidence of these business competencies can also be found through products from the Hay Group, a global-management consulting firm. One such product, the Competency Behavior Inventory, is an instrument used to help measure business competencies of individuals in four distinct categories:

1. Individual excellence—meeting others' needs with confidence and drive
2. Solving problems—making the most out of critical information
3. Leading others—managing, developing, and directing others with integrity
4. Working with others—interacting with others with tact, empathy, and impact[21]

---

[20] *Competency Behavior Inventory*, HAY GROUP, http://www.haygroup.com/leadershipondemand/ourproducts (last visited May 30, 2013).

INDEX

From the Solo, Small Firm and General Practice Division

ABA GPSOLO
Solo, Small Firm and General Practice Division
YOUR SUCCESS, OUR MISSION™

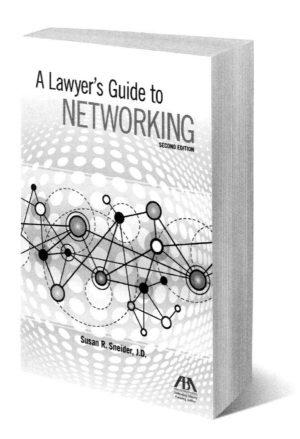

A Lawyer's Guide to Networking
Second Edition
Susan R. Sneider, J.D.

To order 🌐 visit **www.ShopABA.org**
or call 📞 **(800) 285-2221.**

AMERICAN BAR ASSOCIATION
ABA Publishing

From the Solo, Small Firm and General Practice Division

ÆA GPSOLO
Solo, Small Firm and General Practice Division
YOUR SUCCESS, OUR MISSION™

From Law School to Lawyer
Jonathan D. McDowell

To order 🌐 visit **www.ShopABA.org**
or call 📞 **(800) 285-2221.**

From the Center For Professional Responsibility

Center for Professional Responsibility
AMERICAN BAR ASSOCIATION

Legal Ethics and Social Media
A Practitioner's Handbook
Jan L. Jacobowitz and John G. Browning

To order 🌐 visit **www.ShopABA.org**
or call 📞 **(800) 285-2221.**

AMERICAN BAR ASSOCIATION
ABA Publishing